GETTING
TO
JOY

*A Western Householder's Spiritual
Journey with Mata Amritanandamayi*

KARUNA POOLE

SHĀNTINĪ CENTER
Seattle, Washington

GETTING TO JOY
A Western Householder's Spiritual
Journey with Mata Amritanandamayi

PUBLISHED BY:
Shantini Center
3212 - 25th Avenue South
Seattle, Washington 98144

Cover Design by Alfred Rordame iv

ISBN 0-9643629-2-9

DEDICATION

I dedicate this book to the service
of Mata Amritanandamayi, my spiritual
teacher over lifetimes.

All royalties from this book will be donated to
Mata Amritanandamayi for use in her charitable service projects.

ACKNOWLEDGEMENTS

I acknowledge and thank Jean, Elaine, Lee, Pam, and Sandy who taught and guided me during the early years of my healing journey.

I acknowledge and thank Lee, Joan, Emile, Vince, Gillian and Shobana whose support I counted on during the period of time covered in Book 1.

I acknowledge and thank Shobana, Madhuri, Joan, Vince, Rick, Dave and all of the members of my satsang group who were my sources of support during the period covered in Book 2.

I acknowledge and thank Tom and Rand who edited Book 1, and Joe, Maheswari and Oceana who edited Book 2. I also send appreciation to the many friends and satsang members who read and gave feedback on the various drafts. Thanks also to Alfred who did all of the layout and typography on both editions of the book.

I acknowledge and thank my children, Chaitanya and Sreejit, who have shared this journey with me and whose journey with Mother has been as remarkable as my own.

Most of all, I give thanks to my beloved teacher, Mata Amritanandamayi, who made this story possible.

TABLE OF CONTENTS

BOOK 1

BOOK 2

INTRODUCTION

Children, Jesus was crucified, Sri Krishna was killed by an arrow. Only by their Will did these things happen. Without their Will nobody could go near them. They could burn to ashes those who opposed them. They assumed a body to set an example for the world. They came to show us what sacrifice is.[1]

One day, in June of 1993, while waiting for the beginning of a program being led by Mata Amritanandamayi[2], whom I will most frequently call Ammachi[3] or simply Mother, I heard a voice deep within me say, "Write the story of your last four years, the story of your spiritual journey with Mother." I thought for a few moments and then responded, "Why not!" Immediately, memories of the previous four years started pouring into my head, often coming in the form of whole paragraphs. I started writing down the words, soon having scraps of paper everywhere. This process continued over the next several weeks. When I later organized all the scraps of paper, I discovered I had compiled a very complete representation of my journey.

I spent the next month editing the material and then circulated it among friends for evaluation and feedback. Next, I asked an editor for suggestions for improvement. Once the manuscript was complete, I made it available to anyone interested in reading it.

As I wrote my story, I stayed open to discovering the purpose behind the project. I found it rewarding and enlightening to view my experiences in this way. I discovered patterns I had not noticed before, and thus learned even more about the process of receiving and working through lessons. As my clients read the manuscript, they were better able to understand why I choose to spend so much of my life with Ammachi. Those clients were better able to maintain their sense of connection with me during the months I was in India.

---

[1] Mata Amritanandamayi, *Amritanandam*, 36/37, November/December 1989, back cover.
[2] Mata Amritanandamayi - Mother of Immortal Bliss.
[3] Ammachi - Respected Mother.

As the manuscript continued to circulate by word of mouth, I started receiving phone calls. Some were from individuals who had had similar occurrences during their lives and were excited to see an experience like theirs in writing. Some were from devotees[4] of Ammachi who loved reading new Mother stories and being reminded of their own. Still others were from people who wanted to know how they could meet Mother. One devotee gave the manuscript to her father in hopes that he would better understand her pull to Ammachi. Once reading my manuscript, he was eager to hear his daughter's stories.

The original manuscript was written in 1993, more than three years ago. When I decided to prepare it for publication, I considered enlarging it to include the period between 1993 and 1996. After pondering the question for some time, I decided it best to follow the original direction, that is, to write the story of my first four years with Mother. Perhaps someday there will be a sequel! While I have re-edited the book, I have taken care to keep the content essentially the same as that which emerged from all of those pieces of scrap paper in the summer of 1993.

April 1997

❀ ❀ ❀

In the spring of 1993, I attended a workshop that combined Native American spiritual processes and psychotherapeutic processes. At one point during that program, each participant was asked to choose a card from a deck of Medicine[5] cards. On each of the cards was a picture of an animal. Native Americans believe that each animal has its own type of medicine and if we are willing to learn, the spirit of the animal will teach us how to live in unity with one another. Depicted on the card I drew was a moose. The workshop participants were asked to look at the picture on their card and determine in what ways they were like that animal. I knew almost nothing about the Native American tradition and even less about moose, so was unable to make any associations. Later, I learned that the Moose card depicts one who tells their story to the world with a deep sense of joyfulness, coming not from the seeking of approval or attention, but rather from the spontaneous joy that erupts from the core of one's

---

[4] Devotee - one who is strongly dedicated to someone or something.
[5] Medicine, in the Native American tradition, is defined as anything which improves one's connection to God and to life.

being when the story is told. Much of the joy comes from the hope that sharing one's story will help others in walking their own paths. [6] It is from that place in me that this book emerges.

My journey with Mother has been packed with challenges and adventures. There are a seemingly endless number of stories I could share. I am amused to remember that in 1984, I could write every memory of the first eighteen years of my life on a single sheet of paper. I probably could have listed the memories of the next eighteen years on another sheet. In contrast, it is likely I could fill several books with stories from my first four years with Ammachi.

My conscious healing journey actually began in 1984 when I decided to enter a psychotherapeutic process. During this period, I deemed it important to avoid reading about anything related to psychotherapy, wanting to have my own experiences and make my own interpretations rather than have them contaminated by others' thoughts. I have carried this attitude into my spiritual journey as well. Since I have read almost nothing about spiritual processes, most interpretations I make are mine alone. Therefore, some of my conclusions are likely to be incorrect. And, of course, my conclusions change moment to moment as I grow in my own understanding of how the universe works.

Over the years of my journey, there were a few times I started to keep a daily journal but my endeavor never lasted more than a few days. While I could talk for hours, days, or weeks about everything that has happened since I met Ammachi, the fact that the stories are not from a written diary may mean that some of the dates are in error.

Before I share my story, it is important that I note several things. First of all, my understanding of events, of my sense of being internally directed, and even my accounting of things Ammachi said to me, are mine and not necessarily as intended by Ammachi. I am all too aware that projection of personal beliefs and biases can be immediate. Sometimes I have been unable to remember her exact words even minutes after the translation was made. I learned to minimize this problem by writing down her answer as soon as possible. Also, Ammachi gives direction and lessons to each person on an individual basis. Therefore, something she said to me, or suggested I do, may not fit for someone else.

---

[6] Jamie Sams and David Carson, *Medicine Cards*, Santa Fe: Bear and Co., 1988, pp 81-83.

My path has led me through spiritual communities in both the east and the west. It seems to me that what the east calls Divine Mother, the west calls Holy Ghost or Holy Spirit. From the beginning, it has seemed obvious to me that the roots of the eastern path and the western path are the same. As the similarities become more and more apparent, the different paths merge in my mind. I will relate the lessons I have learned, no matter where they originated. As a result, the vocabulary I use may switch between eastern and western from moment-to-moment. When I use a new word from eastern tradition, I will define it in a footnote. In addition, I will place it in the glossary located at the back of the book.

It is impossible for me to describe fully what my experience with Ammachi has been like, words often being far too limiting. After reading the original manuscript, my friend Dean sent me a story he had received at a workshop. The story was about a three-year-old who was overheard saying urgently and passionately to her infant sister, "Baby, Baby, tell me about God. I'm forgetting!"

Dean enclosed a note along with the story. Dean's note:

> A story about remembering God
> Is for everyone, about everyone.
> How many people do you want to touch?
> The memories are for you.
> The specifics of the ashram are for all devotees.
> But the story of you remembering God is for all.
> Everyone wants to know.
> Everyone wants to remember.

I don't often think of my journey being for the purpose of remembering God, but I know he was right. My hope is that this book will aid others in their search to remember.

❀ ❀ ❀

Mata Amritanandamayi, who was originally named Sudhamani, was born on September 27, 1953, in a small fishing village in southern India. Her birth was unusual because of its silence and its peacefulness. As the new mother gazed down on her quiet, newly born child, the baby rewarded her with a beaming smile. The family was disturbed, however, by the blue/black color of Sudhamani's skin. Her skin tone, being much darker than other members of the family, was considered an abnormality.

Sudhamani's growth and development was unusual in a variety of ways. Normally infants proceed through the developmental stages of rolling over, sitting, crawling, walking and then running. Sudhamani, bypassing these stages, started walking at six months of age and began running shortly thereafter. She started speaking Malayalam, the language of her people, at the same time she began to walk.

At two, Sudhamani started spontaneously saying prayers in praise of Krishna, a Divine Incarnation[7] who lived in India five thousand years ago. By five, she was composing songs of deep spiritual significance. She played to Krishna night and day, carrying a picture of him everywhere.

From a very early age, Sudhamani participated in the household chores. Once she started school, she completed her chores before and after classes. She spent any spare time praying and meditating.

The family was very disturbed by Sudhamani's unusual behavior, that is, her constant devotional singing and prayers, and by her skin color. They treated her like a servant. By age nine, she spent so much time doing chores that she was rarely able to go to school. Her chores included beating the coconut husks, tidying the house and the yard, walking to the village tap some distance away to get water, cooking the meals and cleaning up the dishes. She was also expected to prepare the younger children for school, take care of them when they returned home, wash the family clothes, and to collect vegetable scraps and gruel from the neighbors to feed the cows. When visiting neighbors' houses she was expected to complete any unfinished chores. Her chores lasted from 3 am to 11 p.m. each day. If Sudhamani did not wake up on time or fell asleep during the day, her mother would pour a bucket of water over her. If she made any mistakes, she would be physically punished.

---

[7] Divine Incarnation - God taking a human birth to re-establish the ways of righteousness, religion, duty, responsibility, virtue, justice, goodness and truth.

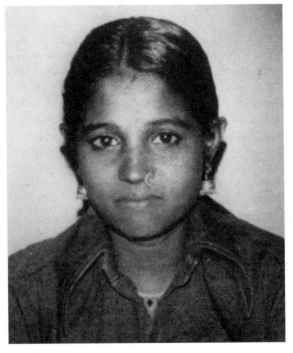

Sudhamani accepted everything that happened as a gift from God. No matter how much work she was given, she maintained a selfless attitude, always chanting the name of Krishna. This is not to imply that Sudhamani was mild-mannered at all times. While she did the expected chores, she was occasionally very impertinent to her mother. Once when her mother was complaining about Sudhamani to her father, Sudhamani shouted, "I am not your daughter! I must be your daughter-in-law!" implying that no mother would treat a daughter the way her mother treated her.

At the end of the fourth grade, Sudhamani left school entirely. When she was thirteen, she was sent to be the servant in the homes of her relatives. This meant that she had to walk the long distances to and from the relatives' houses in addition to doing the chores that were demanded of her at home.

From a very young age, Sudhamani displayed compassion for the poor. She constantly gave away food and money, despite her family's disapproval of the behavior. She would give away her family's milk and then dilute the remaining milk with water. She would be punished anytime she was caught. Once, when there was no food to offer, she donated some of her mother's jewelry. Even though she was severely beaten for this action, Sudhamani continued sharing her family's belongings.

Each year Sudhamani experienced deeper and longer altered states of consciousness. She often lost all sense of time and place, sometimes completely losing her external consciousness and falling to the sand. Not surprisingly, her family and many village members considered her to be crazy.

One day, when she was twenty-one, Sudhamani passed a home where the *Srimad Bhagavatam*, a book about the incarnations of Lord Vishnu, especially Krishna, was being read. As the people began to sing, she entered a state of extreme bliss. Overwhelmed by the bliss, she took on the appearance and identity of her Lord, Sri Krishna. The people present believed Krishna himself had come to them. A crowd began to gather.

Skeptics taunted her saying that if she indeed was Krishna, she must perform a miracle. She responded:

> *Miracles are illusionary. That is not the essential principle*
> *behind spirituality. Not only that, once a miracle is shown*
> *you will desire and demand to see it again and again. I am*
> *not here to create desire, but to remove it.*[8]

The skeptics and doubters persisted and eventually Sudhamani relented. She said in order to build faith she would agree to perform one miracle, adding they were not to ask again. She told any who doubted to come to the next reading of the *Bhagavatam*.

Almost a thousand people came to see what would happen. Two men were asked to bring pots of water. The first dipped his hand into one of the pots only to discover the contents had turned to milk. The milk was given to those present. The other man put his finger into the second pot and found the water had become panchamritam, a sweet pudding made of bananas, sugar, honey, rock sugar and butter. The pudding was

---

[8] Brahmachari Amritatma Chaitanya, *Mata Amritanandamayi: Life and Experiences of Devotees*, Vallickavu: Mata Amritanandamayi Mission Trust, 1988, p. 76.

distributed to everyone. The pot remained full to the brim even after each person had been fed. The smell of the pudding stayed for days on the hands of the astonished people.

One day Sudhamani had a vision of the Divine Mother. Afterwards, she dedicated her every moment to praising and calling for the Divine Mother with the same passion she had directed towards Krishna. Her altered states became even longer, lasting hours at a time. Her family would shake or pour water over her to bring her back to normal consciousness. She was less and less able to perform her family responsibilities. Eventually, her family forced her to leave the household.

For months, Sudhamani lived outside, meditating throughout the day and night. She was surrounded by animals (that is, dogs, cats, cows, snakes, goats, squirrels, pigeons, parrots, and eagles) who fed her, kept her warm, and protected her. A cow came each day, waited for her to come out of the altered state and then offered her its udder. A dog brought food, kept her warm at night, and barked at any sign of danger. The animals were more successful than humans at bringing her back to external consciousness. On many occasions, an eagle would circle overhead and drop a fish into her lap. During this time, Sudhamani could not tolerate food cooked by humans, but was able to eat anything that the animals brought her.

After many months, the Divine Mother appeared before Sudhamani, "dazzling like a million suns." The Mother smiled and then merged into her. Sudhamani hid from everyone, enjoying the bliss of God-Realization. Soon after this time she heard the following directive:

> My child, I dwell in the heart of all beings and have no fixed abode. Your birth is not for merely enjoying the unalloyed Bliss of the Self, but for comforting suffering humanity. Henceforth, worship me in the hearts of all beings and relieve them of the sufferings of worldly existence.[9]

Since that day, Sudhamani, who became known as Amma[10], Ammachi, or Mother, has dedicated her every moment to giving solace

---

[9] Brahmachari Amritatma Chaitanya, *Mata Amritanandamayi: Life and Experiences of Devotees*, Vallickavu: Mata Amritanandamayi Mission Trust, 1988, p. 128.

[10] Amma - mother.

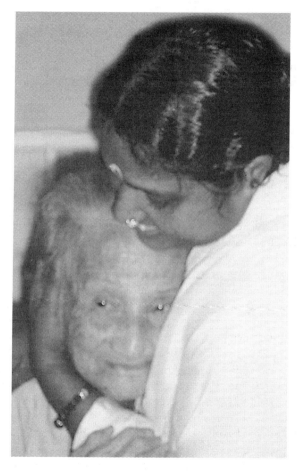

and help to the world. She comforts all who come to her and answers questions, both worldly and spiritual.

There were many doubters who wished to stop Ammachi's actions. They formed an organization called the "Committee to Remove Blind Beliefs." These people tried to kill her through poisoning her food, spreading poisoned darts on the ground where she would dance, hiring sorcerers to perform black magic, and stabbing her. One man jumped up, pressing a knife against her chest. As he pulled it back to stab her, he experienced an excruciating pain in the same location as where he had pressed the knife onto her skin. Another person who had been hired to kill her, dropped the knife and fell to his knees at the sight of her.

At one point, Ammachi's father became so distressed by the taunts of the doubters and by his inability to arrange a marriage for his daughter, that he demanded that Devi, the Divine Mother, give his daughter back to him. No one could reason with him. After some time Ammachi's body fell to the ground, all signs of life ceased.

The crowd erupted with grief at their loss. They were furious with her father. When he realized what he had done, he fell to the ground unconscious. Candles surrounded Ammachi's body and the people mourned and prayed. When her father came back to consciousness, eight hours after her death, he begged God for forgiveness. Within minutes, life started coming back into Ammachi's body.

Many experienced or witnessed miracles simply by being in Mother's presence. Many who were sick became well. Numerous people related that Ammachi had appeared in distant places when they needed help. Mother was able to consistently answer the questions of religious scholars even though she had left school after the fourth grade.

While the stories concerning Ammachi seem endless, I will share a few of them that show both her spiritual power and her sense of compassion. One day, a young girl died as the result of severe breathing problems. Her grandmother brought her body to the shrine where Ammachi received visitors and placed her on Mother's seat. Mother, who was singing at a nearby house, felt restless and rushed to the shrine. When Mother saw the grandmother grieving over the child's body, she sat down on the floor, took the child in her arms and held her. After some time, the child opened her eyes and life returned to her body.

A man with an advanced case of leprosy came to the ashram, his whole body covered with infected, pus-draining wounds. His hair was gone and he had only two small slits for eyes. A putrid smell rose up from him. He said he had not heard a compassionate word for years. Typically, passersby would hold their noses as they walked past, some spitting on him. When he entered the ashram grounds, Ammachi walked up to him, treating him as she would anyone else. Thereafter, each time she saw him, she would wash his wounds, suck out the pus, lick the wounds and spread sacred ash over them. In time, his eyes opened, his hair returned and most of the wounds healed.

One day, while preparing for a puja[11], Ammachi's brother, one of her most vicious critics, broke all of the oil lamps needed for the ceremony. Ammachi told the crowds not to worry and requested they bring her shells filled with water. She placed a wick in each shell and lit it. The wicks burned all night long, with water as their only fuel.

I have heard Mother say that the reason we must eat is because we believe eating to be necessary. There have been periods in which Ammachi lived for months without food or sleep. Even now, she eats and sleeps minimally, often taking nourishment or rest only at the insistence of her devotees. Years ago, after being pestered by Swami Paramatmananda (then called Brahmachari[12] Nealu), Ammachi agreed to eat. When she had consumed the food the brahmachari had served her, she demanded more and when she had finished that, asked for more. Soon she had eaten all of the food in the ashram[13] and from a nearby chai[14] shop, far more than humanly possible. The young brahmachari eventually recognized the lesson and vowed to not pester her to eat again.

Ammachi generally spends five to fifteen hours a day, six or seven days a week offering comfort to those who come to her. When in India, it is not uncommon to have crowds of 10,000 to 15,000 devotees. While she spends some time in her ashram in Amritapuri, India, during much of the year she conducts programs throughout other parts of India and the rest of the world. Mother's world tours take her to the United States, Australia, Japan, Singapore, Belgium, England, France, Germany, Sweden, Italy, Switzerland and Reunion Island. After being in Mother's presence, many begin ongoing spiritual practices.

In addition to Ammachi's main ashram in Amritapuri, India, there are branch ashrams throughout India and in the United States, Reunion Island and France. Mother's charitable service projects multiply at a phenomenal rate. At the time of this writing she operates many schools and medical clinics for the poor, an orphanage for 500 children, a computer learning center, a vocational training center, an engineering college, a hospice, a rehabilitation center for women and numerous temples. After years of building homes for widows, she has recently begun a massive project to build houses for India's poor. Other projects include an Herb

---

[11] Puja - worship rite.

[12] Brahmachari - celibate student under the training of a Guru.

[13] Ashram - residence and teaching center of a saint.

[14] Chai - tea.

Conservation park, an Ayurvedic Research Center and an 800-bed tertiary care hospital near Cochin.

Ammachi has been recognized by the larger world community in
several ways. In 1993, she was named "Hindu of the Year" by the journal
Hinduism Today. Later that same year, she was elected one of the three
presidents of Hinduism by the Parliament of the World's Religions. In
1995, she was among the religious leaders invited to speak during the
United Nation's 50th Anniversary celebrations.

No matter how much Mother does, she continues to exemplify humility in its purest form. If you ask her who she is, she will likely respond,
"I'm just a crazy village girl." She is the very model of all of the qualities
which earmark a holy life, that is, compassion for everyone, humility of
spirit, sacrifice of self for the good of others, purity of body and mind,
simplicity of action, innocence, equal treatment of all, detachment from
worldly things, and the ability to see the good in all things.

❁ ❁ ❁

Many paths lead to God. Within Hinduism itself are numerous recognized paths. Among them are hatha yoga (path of physical and
mental exercises), jnana yoga (path of knowledge and wisdom), karma
yoga (path of selfless service), bhakti yoga (path of devotion), kundalini
yoga (path of meditation, breathing, and purification) and raga yoga (restraint, observance, exercise, breath control, withdrawal, concentration,
meditation and samadhi[15]). The goal of each path is to achieve self-realization, that state where there is direct knowing of the Self, God. This
has been described as the state that is attained when "the mystic kundalini
force pierces through the chakra at the crown of the head... bringing the
realization or 'non experience' of That which exists beyond the mind,
beyond time, form and space."[16]

Whichever path is chosen, spiritual evolution takes individuals to
realms and energies they have no knowledge of and no skills to handle.
In the same way that it would be difficult and risky to proceed without a
map or a guide through territory that is unknown and potentially danger-

---

[15] Samadhi - state of absorption in the Self.
[16] Satguru Sivaya Subramuniyaswami, *Dancing with Shiva*, India, USA: Himalayan Academy, 1993, p. 813.

ous, it is important that individuals entering one of the yogic paths find a guru. The guru serves as teacher, disciplinarian and role model, pushing students to their limits, intervening only when the test is too much for the student to handle.

The word guru means "dispeller of darkness." We have many gurus during our life. Our first gurus are our parents. During our school years, our teachers are our gurus. Those of us who are looking for someone to take us to God, need a Satguru, a teacher of the Supreme Truth. When speaking of the characteristics of a Satguru, Swami Paramatmananda stated:

> *All Realized people have the identical inner experiences of Reality. They radiate the beatific peace of Brahman.*[17] *What is the experience we get in their presence? Exceptional peace of mind, a blossoming of the heart and a feeling of awe and respect. One may also feel that they know the innermost thoughts in one's heart. One may feel they cannot live without their company. A unique happiness is experienced in association with them. However they may appear or act, one cannot deny the intensity of feeling that one experiences near them. Ultimately one's heart convinces one of their spiritual greatness.*[18]

Teachers operate in many ways. Kornfield stated:

> *Some teachers are rascals and coyotes who trick and surprise their students; some are harsh task-masters trying to whittle down ego and pride; others teach more through honoring and encouragement, nurturing the best in the student; some teachers lecture like a professor; others can melt us open with their love and compassion.*[19]

---

[17] Brahman - the Absolute, the Whole.

[18] Swami Paramatmananda, "For my Children: talks by Br. Nealu based on Mother's FOR MY CHILDREN," *Amritanandam*, First Quarter, 1994, p. 14.

[19] Jack Kornfield, *A Path with Heart*, New York: Bantam Books, 1993, p. 228.

Ammachi has said that, due to our lack of self-discipline, the yogic path of devotion is best suited for those from the west. Embarking on the devotional path, however, presents a number of immediate challenges. First, devotees will need to learn to live from their hearts instead of their minds, not an easy task for someone from the west! Another major obstacle is that westerners are taught from birth to be self-reliant and individualistic. Seeking help is often seen as a weakness to be avoided. The western devotee can expect that, in addition to dealing with their own sense of skepticism and uncertainty, they are likely to be criticized for giving up their power to another human being, for being dependent, and for being less spiritually sophisticated than those who go without a teacher, or who go from teacher to teacher.

Ammachi has said that those who choose to follow her will experience three main phases in their spiritual development. During the first phase, devotees fall in love with her. Ammachi has described herself as a "plain-clothes" detective who sets out to "capture" people's hearts. When Mother looks at an individual, they often feel as if she can see down to their most core parts. God's love pours through her. Many people, experiencing her love and the sense of being known, burst into heart-felt tears.

When devotees are fully bonded, the second phase, the stage of being "cooked," begins. In this stage, Mother helps devotees see their weaknesses and negative tendencies. It is then the job of the individual to do the work necessary to eliminate those behaviors. A Christian missionary, Jean Nell Maxie, in describing her conception of this stage of spiritual development, said that at this point God "arrests" us, in effect saying, "Enough is enough." Spiritual aspirants begin to experience "conscience attacks" any time they engage in destructive behaviors.

During the "cooking" stage an important aspect of the devotees' work is to learn to stay calm no matter the circumstance. If each event in their life is accepted as a potential lesson, devotees are more likely to quickly learn what they need to learn, with a minimum of discomfort. Pain usually comes from resistance. Being willing to accept and go through the lessons is an essential part of moving along the spiritual path. I have heard Ammachi say, "You ask me to clean you up, but then you won't hold still for the bath!"

Mother actively resists feeding minds, particularly the minds of westerners. She has said that westerners are ninety-five percent intellect when they are meant to be five percent. During the "cooking" stage, many of the lessons she "sends" require devotees to let go of intellect and operate from intuition and heart. When asked for information, Ammachi will frequently respond, "Don't worry," "Everything's fine," or some other non-intellectual response. She will give information only when it will benefit a devotee's process. Mother has said one can learn everything one needs to learn simply by watching her.

At some point during the "cooking" stage, devotees will experience being weaned from dependence on Ammachi's form. In the same way that the Gopis[20] could not achieve self-realization until Krishna left them, devotees cannot reach the last phase of spiritual development until they have cultivated an internal relationship with Mother. At some point, she may actually send them away. Their job then is to remember how much they are loved and to accept each lesson with the attitude, "This is for my own good." During the third and last stage of the spiritual process, devotees merge with Amma in the same way that the Divine Mother merged into Sudhamani.

While some spiritual seekers may choose the full renunciate life style of an ashram, many will choose the path of the householder, one who seeks God while fulfilling the responsibilities of the world. The Hindu scriptures identify four stages in the life of a householder, each spanning as many as twenty-five years. While spiritual development is a thread that runs throughout all of the stages, the degree of focus differs from one stage to another.

During the first stage of life, the focus of the householder is on skill and character building; during the second, family and community life and moderate enjoyment of pleasures. When in the third stage, householders withdraw from many worldly duties but remain available for consultation. In the last stage seekers, having no social obligations, are free to pursue their spiritual path without restriction. The challenge for the householder is to learn to be *in* the world but not of the world.

At times throughout my journey with Mother, I have longed to move into an ashram, but at the same time I have been exceedingly clear that is not my path, at least not at this point in my life. Perhaps, during the fourth stage, living in an ashram will seem appropriate. For now, I am where I need to be and, for the most part, where I want to be.

---

[20] Gopis - Cowherd girls known for their devotion to Sri Krishna.

Many believe Mother to be an Avatar, that is, a Divine Incarnation come to earth to help people return to God. Some talk of her as being a reincarnation of Krishna, Jesus, Mary, Ramakrishna or others. While I find myself more and more convinced that Ammachi is indeed an Avatar, I have not found it particularly useful to spend time and energy focusing on who Ammachi is or whom she might have been in previous lives. What I know is that I love who she is now, that she knows much more than I do, that she overflows with compassion and bliss and that she makes a difference in the lives of everyone with whom she makes contact. She has said she will teach me what she knows and will lead me to God. Who she was in the past seems totally irrelevant to me. If I do not learn all I need to know in this lifetime, I am comforted by her statement that she will take on as many births as necessary to bring all of her children Home.

I also have not concerned myself with my destination. Self-Realization seems to me to be an incomprehensible concept. What I know is that on every step of my journey, I have felt more and more alive. My life during the last eight years has been filled with countless, exhilarating adventures. I feel more and more loved and loving. I frequently experience a level of joy I never knew existed. Every day I become more centered and more intuitive. I love the journey and that is enough. I know that wherever it leads, it will be for my good.

July 1993

PART I

The Sun is constantly shining. It bestows its light equally on everyone, to all the beings in the world. But suppose we sit in our room with all the doors and windows closed. How can we get the light? How can we see the sun? We must open the doors and the windows and let the light come in; only then will it enter.[1]

My First 40 Years

I was born October 28, 1948, in Albuquerque, New Mexico. My mother was an elementary school teacher, my father a career army officer. I was the oldest child, my brothers being born three and five years later. Throughout my childhood, we moved every two to three years (New Mexico to Florida to North Carolina to Germany to Georgia to New Mexico to Hawaii and then back to Florida). There was little warmth and almost no physical contact in our household. My father's attitude towards children was blatantly demonstrated when he stated, "I would have preferred to have had dogs." My mother parented us to the best of her ability. I now realize she lived with an overwhelming terror that my father would leave her. As a result, she was unable to give us much that we needed.

The environment of our household was very competitive. I started baby-sitting my brothers at age nine, thus initiating a constant power struggle between us. Years later, I commented to my mother that I sensed my father had never held me as a child. Her immediate response was a defensive, "Well, he never held me, either." I had discovered the root of our family's competition.

---

[1] Mata Amritanandamayi, *Amritanandam*, 2nd Quarter 1994, p. 6.

Since we were not allowed to express feelings, I learned to be withdrawn, sulky, sneaky and independent. I have been told that I would make only one friend at a time, becoming very depressed when that friend found another. I have essentially no memory of specific friends until my high school years.

Around twelve years of age, I started reading stories of the Catholic nuns and saints. I had an inner sense that I was "supposed" to be a nun. This emerging belief was very confusing to me because I was not Catholic! When I was thirteen, I attended a Billy Graham crusade and became a "born again" Christian. I joined Youth for Christ and became very involved in religious activities. What I remember most about that time was the ecstasy of riding to meetings on a bus, singing spiritual songs. In a way, even though I remember no individuals, this seemed like my first real family.

The next year, my father retired from the army and our family moved to Florida. I became very involved in my mother's church, but never felt at home there. Since it was my desire to become a missionary, as I neared graduation I started looking for a Christian college. I was miserable at home. I remember at one point checking off the days before I could leave home on a three-year calendar. I purposefully picked a college in Seattle, Washington, about as far from Florida as one could go.

The college I chose was religiously conservative, one run by the Free Methodist Church. The United States at that time was in the throes of the civil rights and Vietnam war crises. As I made my way through my four years of study, I became increasingly infuriated with my fellow students and the faculty for their seeming lack of sensitivity and awareness of the world's great challenges. It seemed to me that they were choosing instead to bury their heads in their Bibles. By the time I graduated, I considered myself an atheist.

I graduated with my Bachelor of Science in Nursing degree in June of 1970. I longed to do something other than nursing for the summer, so decided, along with three friends, to work as a migrant farm laborer! We picked fruits and vegetables in Florida, Georgia, South Carolina, Maryland, Pennsylvania and Washington. That summer impacted me tremendously. Seeing and experiencing racism so closely led me to a place where I was so infuriated with the white race, that I vowed never to bring a white child into the world. I thought mixing of the races would be the best way to take care of the problem. A year later, I married a black man who had long been a close friend.

When I married Al in 1971, my father disowned me and has not spoken to me since. My father and I had never been close, so at the time his reaction did not have much of an impact on me. He returned my Christmas presents and letters and did his best to interfere with my relationship with my mother. He hung up on me the few times he answered the phone when I called their home. As the years passed, I craved to have a father who loved and cared for my children and myself.

The next few years I worked as a nurse in labor and delivery or postpartum units, first in California and then back in Washington. I completed my Masters in Nursing degree in 1974, and for five years worked at the University of Washington, first as an instructor, then as an assistant professor. I was considered a good academician. I taught nursing classes, published many articles, taught workshops all over the United States and in Canada and completed numerous research projects. When I tired of that, I became a Maternal Newborn Nurse Clinical Specialist at Swedish Hospital Medical Center in Seattle. In 1980, I was involved in the creation of a satellite baccalaureate program for the hospital's registered nurses. The program was associated with the same school from which I had received my baccalaureate degree. When I left that school in 1970, my classmates, with great amusement, predicted I would come back some day as an instructor, and there I was!

My son, Sreejit[2], was born in 1974 and, three years later, my daughter, Chaitanya[3], was born. My husband and I did not get along well so seven years into our marriage he moved out. He would visit the children occasionally, but was not involved with them in any significant way until 1985. The years I parented alone were difficult and I became very depressed. I saw a social worker for counseling for about a year, and then toward the end of 1984 began more in-depth personal therapy.

I committed the next few years to my psychological healing. As I recovered from my childhood wounds, I was able to develop deep and meaningful friendships. My life blossomed, as did the lives of my children. As I began to feel loved and loving, I was able to provide my children with the love and care they needed.

When I approached completion of my own therapy process, I started assisting in groups and intensives within the therapy community. Soon I found I was enjoying my volunteer work much more than my job! I discov-

---

[2] Sreejit's birth name was Michael. He requested and received a spiritual name from Ammachi in the summer of 1992.

[3] Chaitanya's birth name was Kristy. She requested and received a spiritual name from Ammachi in the summer of 1998.

ered that the coursework I had taken during my Master's and pre-doctoral studies,[4] in conjunction with all of the volunteer work I had performed in the therapy community, qualified me to take the American Nurses Association credentialing exam for Adult Psychiatric and Mental Health Nursing. I passed the exam and began a private psychotherapy practice.

The Dawn Breaks

In the fall of 1988, Lee, one of my mentors, suggested I meet an acquaintance named Diane. Diane and I discovered we had much in common. A striking difference between us, however, was that she was very involved in spiritual process, whereas I actively avoided anything related to spirituality. The same week I met Diane, Elaine, another mentor, introduced me to a spiritual healer named Christananda. My response to him was immediate and powerful. I did not like him and I did not trust him! I was concerned about his increasing involvement with my friends and associates.

I was sure the man was a fake and was determined to prove it. It occurred to me that I knew numerous people involved in spiritual processes, so I began introducing them to him, hoping they would expose him as the charlatan I believed him to be. To my surprise and consternation, I had to admit that he was telling these people things that even I knew were absolutely "right on."

After Diane had met him, she made a quiet aside to me, "Well Carol (my name at that time), with the quality of spiritual people you are surrounding yourself with, you can't resist much longer." My reaction was "Harummph, fat chance!"

In March or April of 1989, Diane informed me that a woman saint from India would be holding public programs in Seattle in June. She had been in the presence of this woman twice before and reported having had intense heart-opening experiences each time. When she asked if I would like to go, I immediately said, "Yes," and then regretted it for months. I could not imagine why in the world I had agreed to do such a "stupid" thing.

That same April, I felt an overwhelming desire to go see *Field of Dreams*, a movie about a son who wished to reconnect with his dad. I wept through most of the movie and when the film arrived at the final

---

[4] I completed two years of pre-doctoral study during the mid-eighties.

scenes, I was thrust into a wave of grief, the likes of which I had never before experienced. It took me twenty minutes to get up from my seat and exit the theater. I then sat outside on the curb crying for another half-hour. The scars from my father-abandonment wounds were torn wide open. I became so physically sick that I was bed-ridden for three weeks. I called Elaine and asked her advice. When she told me to go see Christananda, I replied, "Not a chance." I soon recovered.

The next month, I felt compelled to see *Field of Dreams* again. I was a little suspicious and apprehensive, but had a cocky, "I already know how it ends," attitude as I re-entered the theater. I ended up in bed for another week! I decided to call for an appointment with Christananda.

The session was fascinating. After hearing my recent experiences, he came to two conclusions. He hypothesized that my father's spirit was calling me and suggested I show up unannounced at his doorstep when I traveled to Florida in July. Strangely enough, I believed that on a spiritual level my father's spirit could indeed be calling me, but I had a real problem with the advice to give my father an impromptu visit. When I had written my father several years before, I received a message in return, through my mother, informing me that if I continued to contact *him*, he would divorce *her*! It was crazy, but I believed he would follow through on his threat and therefore gave great weight to the probability of a major blowup were I to show up at his doorstep. Christananda's second conclusion was that I was undergoing a series of spiritual initiations and that meeting the woman saint from India (Ammachi) the next week would be another one. I was interested and intrigued.

The First Meeting

The day of Ammachi's program arrived. I had clients scheduled throughout the day and into the early evening, so was unable to be present when the program began. I walked into a room already packed with people and found a seat against the back wall. Immediately, a very strange thing happened. I have always had mild curvature of the spine and I tend to sit fairly hunchbacked, probably as much from habit as necessity. As I sat down on the floor, cross-legged, my back spontaneously straightened until I was sitting as straight and tall as it was possible for me to sit. Needless to say, I was quite shocked!

When I had recovered sufficiently to look around, I noticed Ammachi in the front of the room speaking to the crowd through a translator. Soon thereafter, she and the brahmacharis began to sing. I immediately slipped into a deep altered state of consciousness. I knew other people were in the room, but lost awareness of them. As my whole being filled with the music, I began to weep uncontrollably. Diane had warned me that it would take time to become accustomed to the different culture. Instead of feeling as if I was in a foreign culture, I had the overwhelming sense that I had come Home. I felt as if I had been starving for a lifetime and that every cell in my body was opening to take in the nourishment offered by the music. I fed and fed and cried and cried.

In a few short minutes, my entire view of the world changed. I had entered that room a non-believer in reincarnation, although so many of my friends and my clients believed in the concept, I had become slightly open to the possibility. I had never had any contact with any eastern religious or philosophical process, yet here in the presence of an Indian guru, I had found Home. It was immediately obvious to me that past lives must exist. What else could explain my experience?

The music program ended with a song I later discovered was called *Arati*. Two women circled a flame in front of Ammachi as the group sang.[5] Weeks afterward I repeatedly heard myself say to friends, "There was this song and this flame," as I cried with the memory.

When the musical program was over, Diane led me closer to the front so I could watch what was happening. Ammachi was placing everyone individually on her lap, rubbing their backs, and then giving them a hug. I kept thinking over and over, "That's what we do... that's what we do." (A significant part of our therapy process is meeting clients needs for touch and nurturing through holding.) I also internally added, "And we do it better because we hold them *much* longer!" Little did I know the powerful results of being held by Ammachi for a single minute!

While waiting in line to be held, I noticed two things. I concluded that waiting was more than a passive waste of time, it was a true test of patience. Also, waiting provided the opportunity to watch and learn from the behavior of those around me. There was a woman within my

---

[6]During the process known as *Arati*, burning camphor is circled in front of a holy person as way of giving them salutations and honor. The burning camphor, which leaves no residue, represents annihilation of the ego.

eyesight who was very angry with people who were cutting into the darshan line. As I was being very judgmental about *her* nasty behavior, it occurred to me I was being given a chance to examine my own judgmental nature. I purposely quieted my mind and simply watched.

Finally it was my turn to be held... and then it was over. Being held was not a big deal. After all, I had been held many times over the years, and *we* did it better! Perhaps my expectations were too high. Besides, as far as I was concerned, it was the *music* that generated the power and energy.

I had kept my calendar for the next evening clear in the unlikely event I wanted to attend another program. I was intrigued enough with my experience that I decided not only to go to the next evening program, but after I met with my morning clients, I would go to the morning program as well. When morning arrived, all of my clients canceled! Clearly, I was supposed to go back, and did.

As I waited in the line to be held, the woman who had been so nasty and rude about people cutting into the line, cut in front of me! I was surprised, but laughed and internally said, "I decided last night I was not going to make judgments about this, you decided to test me again?" As I write this I am a bit surprised at how early I was aware of the process of being given lessons and tests.

I decided to ask Mother about Christananda's advice to go unannounced to my parents' home. After hearing my concerns, she replied that I should not go to his house, but instead should pray for him. That tactic felt very right to me. Later, I puzzled over the fact that after years of feeling disgusted and repulsed whenever I heard religious or spiritual terminology, I now felt comfortable being told to pray for someone. Again, I wondered about what was happening to me.

Throughout the day, I thought about the bracelet Diane wore, one she had purchased at Ammachi's program the previous year. It was called a panchaloha bracelet and was made of five metals, brass, copper, gold, silver and bronze. Although I was not aware of it at the time, each bracelet was inscribed with a mantra.[6] Mantras directed towards the Divine Mother, Christ, Krishna, Shiva and Ammachi were available. Although the bracelets were said to have great healing properties, that thought did not interest me. I had no idea why I wanted one, but I did. Later, I

---

[6] Mantra - a sacred formula, the repetition of which can awaken one's spiritual energies. The repetition of a mantra also helps one in focusing and controlling the mind.

discovered the mantra on my bracelet was *Om Para Shaktyai Namah*, Salutations to the Absolute Supreme Energy, a mantra to the Divine Mother.

When the music started that night, I drifted into a deep meditative state. First, I experienced exhilarating joy, then deep sorrow. My tears poured throughout the night. I was aware of a wide variety of energy surges in my body, some I knew from my therapy process were associated with memories of my father. The one sensation I recall was the sense of danger coming from the right. I believed I was shedding many of the energetic memories stored in my cells.

Ammachi was conducting a retreat in Orcas Island, Washington, starting the following day. I was unwilling to ignore the responsibilities I had in Seattle during the next few days, so decided to attend only the last day of the retreat. That morning I took the ferry to Orcas Island and was met by Ron, a devotee who is now a brahmachari. As we drove to the retreat center, he spoke at length about his life with Ammachi. I was fascinated both by him and his topic. I liked his enthusiasm and I liked him.

I was able to enter the darshan[7] line as soon as I arrived at the retreat center. I was excited, and in a way, relieved to be with her again. Besides, this way of being held was beginning to feel really good.

I was told Ammachi would conduct a program that night called Devi Bhava. Devi Bhava is difficult to explain. The words mean to take on the mood of the Goddess. The explanation I find most helpful is that in order for Ammachi to look like us, she has to put on many "veils" over her true nature. During Devi Bhava, it is as if she takes off one of those "veils" and thus demonstrates qualities that are closer to her true self. During this program, she is dressed the way the Hindu scriptures portray the Goddess, that is in a silk sari, with a crown and jewelry. (Her normal attire is a simple white sari.) I was told Mother would look and behave differently, that her vibrational level would be higher and that she would seem more distant. Her color might even become darker.

I was still in the initial stages of connecting with her and had no desire for her to be any different. In fact, I had a strong desire for her to

---

[7] Darshan - to be in the presence of a great soul. When Ammachi gives darshan she holds or hugs each person, strokes up and down their spine, and then gives them flower petals and a Hershey's kiss! Sometimes she puts sandlewood paste on their third eye, the eye of intuition. While waiting for darshan, everyone sits in line, providing both the opportunity to watch Mother interact with others and the chance for her to make eye contact throughout the crowd.

stay exactly the same. When the program began, I was greatly relieved to discover that Mother looked and acted exactly as she had the rest of the week, she was simply dressed differently. You might imagine my surprise the next day, when I overheard people commenting on the remarkable physical changes that had occurred once Mother entered the Devi Bhava state. What had they seen that I had not? Were they crazy... or was I?

During the evening I was asked if I wanted a mantra. I said yes without knowing why. When the brahmachari asked who was my beloved deity, that is, the focus of my devotion, I said I did not know. I was still very angry with Christ, so I certainly did not want *him*! I had not understood that a mantra directed towards Ammachi was an option so I felt stuck. I remembered that Ammachi as a child had prayed constantly to Krishna and was aware my tears flowed most profusely when we sang Krishna songs, so I responded, "Krishna." I have no conscious memory of what happened when Mother gave me that mantra, but remember afterwards sensing that this had been one of the most significant moments of my life. Later, I learned that at the time Ammachi gives someone a mantra, she takes on permanent responsibility for guiding that person's spiritual development.

Ammachi during Devi Bhava.

The retreat ended with that Devi Bhava program. The next morning, I was invited to join people who were seeing Ammachi off at the Orcas Island airport. When we arrived at the small airport, Mother was standing beside the plane. The pilot himself was scanning the passengers with a metal detector, looking for weapons. The scene of this group of holy people being searched looked pretty absurd. While the brahmacharis were being searched, the metal detector kept sounding for no apparent reason. Ammachi was standing to the side with her back to the scene, laughing. Many people were convinced she was purposefully making the machine trigger. As she prepared to leave, I started crying as if my heart was going to break. I found my behavior extremely bizarre since I barely knew this woman and I judged that our relationship did not warrant this display of emotion.

During the next few days I felt full and happy. I believed that I had been given the bliss of the previous week as preparation for my upcoming visit to family members in North Carolina and Florida. I had learned only a few months earlier that my youngest brother, who lived in North Carolina, was going to die from colon cancer. My mother, who lived in Florida, had been sick for years with inoperable breast cancer. I had not

My brother and mother.

been to Florida for fourteen years. When my father learned I was coming, he ordered me, once again through my mother, to stay away from their house. I realized it would be easier for me to cope with the trip if I could be with Ammachi afterwards, so I made arrangements to attend her New Hampshire retreat in July.

My memories of that family visit are few. Most memorable was the discovery that I *liked* my brother and his wife. We had had only a few brief contacts since I had left home in 1966. Now I recognized that I wanted to spend as much time with him as possible before he died. While I was with my family, I thought endlessly of my experiences with Ammachi and looked forward to my trip to New Hampshire.

The first morning of the New Hampshire retreat, I sat watching Mother as she held each person who came to her. I found myself wishing she would speak to me in English but I believed that was an unreasonable desire as, to my knowledge, she spoke only Malayalam. I began my journey through the darshan line. This time when she held me, she whispered, "My daughter," into my ear, in English! I burst into tears. In hindsight, I believe this was the moment I gave her my heart.

My father was very present in my mind throughout the retreat. I saw many people carrying pictures for Mother to bless and wished I had brought a picture of my father. After lunch, my traveling companion, Christine, asked me a question. I told her I did not know the answer off the top of my head, but knew that there was a book in our room which contained the answer. When I returned to our room and opened the book, I felt a shock go through my body. There in the book was a picture of my father! I stumbled out of the dorm, eager to tell Christine what had happened. As I held the picture during the evening bhajans,[8] I had the sense Mother was blessing him through me. By the time the music was over, I no longer felt any need to take the picture to her.

That night, I experienced a horrific nightmare in which I was being chased by a two-headed dog. What remains most vivid in my memory is the image of my hand and the dog's heads. Every time I freed my hand from one of the dog's mouths, the other mouth would grab it. Finally, in terror and desperation I screamed, "MOTHER!" with my entire being. At that instant everything exploded into light. I woke up feeling the remnants of terror and wonder at what had occurred.

---

[8] Bhajan - devotional song

The next night, another Devi Bhava program was scheduled. As I mentioned earlier, in Seattle I had experienced no difference between her state in Devi Bhava and her normal state. This time she seemed very different in that her energy was massively shifted. The energy was so intense that by the time I was ten feet from her, it was palpable. I was so terrified, I had to force myself forward. After she held me, she told me to sit close, so I sat behind her for a few minutes. I was still frightened. My mind was filled with negative thoughts. "You did not hear her correctly." "This is where people getting mantras are to sit." "You already have a mantra." "You don't belong here." "You don't belong here." "You don't belong here." I left, relieved to be out of the intense energy field.

While at the New Hampshire retreat, I reflected on the events of the last month and how they fit into the larger picture of my life. I began to sense that some part of me had been preparing for this for years. During the previous four years, I had had my friend Lee's voice "in my head" most of the time. I "talked" to him every moment my mind was not being used for something else. While this always seemed rather bizarre, I had assumed at first that it was somehow part of my personal therapy process. I became a little concerned, however, when the internal dialogue continued after I finished my therapy. When I spoke to Lee about this, he passed it off saying he thought it occurred because I had no boyfriend. I found that explanation unconvincing, but as the process seemed harmless, did not think much more about it. During those four years, I also experienced a tremendous degree of love for Lee. While there were plenty of reasons to love him, the intensity of my emotion seemed excessive.

The moment I met Ammachi, the internal conversations with Lee stopped and my mind became focused on her. The intense feeling of love, which I now recognized as devotional energy, shifted from Lee to Ammachi. I realized the ongoing mental conversations had somehow been training for single-minded concentration, and that they had contributed markedly to the rapid spiritual awakening I was now undergoing.

It occurred to me that I had experienced another form of preparation as well. During my therapy process, I had formed intense attachments to Pam Levin, a psychotherapist from California and Jean Illsley Clarke, a parent educator from Minnesota. Whenever I was with them, I experienced tremendous emotional pain knowing that one of us would be leaving soon. The level of my grief seemed very excessive. Over the years, I had to learn many skills to cope with our respective comings and goings. I eventually was able to separate from them with only a minimum of discomfort. I now understood this to have been training for the coming to and going from Ammachi. I could not imagine what leaving would have been like if I had not accumulated so many coping tools.

During the morning of the last day of the retreat, the repetitive message, "Call Jean Clarke ... Call Jean Clarke," rose into my consciousness. I responded internally, "I will be seeing her in Seattle a few days after the retreat." The direction continued. I finally responded, "*Okay, I will call her when I get home!*"

The following morning, Christine and I drove to the airport, hours before my scheduled departure. There was a plane leaving for Seattle shortly. I was told that it was tremendously overbooked and there was no chance of my being able to take the flight. I requested the attendant place me on standby anyway. An hour later, I found myself aboard the plane and, to my further amazement, there were empty seats on both sides of me. Also, due to the seat configuration, I had the best view of the movie screen on the entire plane! I felt like royalty. Once in the air, I discovered this flight had a quick layover in Minneapolis, Minnesota, home of Jean Clarke! Needless to say, I disembarked and phoned her.

A New Life
Summer/Fall 1989

About the time I returned from New Hampshire, I lost any desire to eat beef or pork. I also completely stopped watching television, an amazing feat since I had a lifetime pattern of watching television many hours a day. No one had instructed me to change those behaviors, the desires simply disappeared.

I knew I was changing and was concerned about what my children might say to my ex-husband, so I decided to speak to him myself. I was astonished to find that he was more than casually interested, asking me one question after another. As our conversation ended, I asked if he wanted to borrow one of my bhajan tapes. He said he would indeed like to listen to one.

Three weeks went by as I waited for him to return the tape. I owned only three tapes of Ammachi's music at that time and was very eager to have my tape back. When Al finally returned the tape, he informed me that an astonishing thing had happened. After listening to the tape, he had lost all desire to smoke! My children and I had been pushing him to quit smoking for years. Whenever any of us had broached the subject, he became angry. Now he had listened to a tape of spiritual songs that had absolutely nothing to do with smoking and had quit cold turkey! To this day, he is still a non-smoker.

There were other strange occurrences. I was experiencing nightly nightmares. Each morning I awoke exhausted and frightened with no memory of the dreams. One evening when preparing for bed, I looked for my cats in order to put them in the basement, the only safe place due to their occasional urine spraying. I found our black cat, Blackie, curled up comfortably in a cardboard box. I remember thinking, "Oh, that's cute." I picked up the box and the cat and took them to the basement. Later that night, I heard a scratching noise outside my ground floor window. I went to the window and looked out only to discover Blackie staring back at me. Since I was alone in the house, the entire situation was more than a little unnerving.

The next morning, I searched for the open window I was sure Blackie had used to escape from the basement. I found no opening anywhere. That was more frightening than finding the cat outside. Later when I passed my white cat, Dee Dee, I flashed back into the New Hampshire dream about the two-headed dog. My body filled with terror as I gazed at the cat. That night, I was very aware that my dreams were filled with images of being chased and attacked by animals. In addition, one dream contained important information about one of my clients. I woke up with the sense that the nightmares were happening not only for my own benefit, but in some unknown way were also for the benefit of my clients. The nightmares stopped shortly thereafter.

To this day, I have no idea how Blackie got outside. It is obvious to me, however, that the episode happened at least in part to bring deeply buried dream material into a more conscious space.

Another curious incident occurred about that point in time. I had started listening repeatedly to a tape of English devotional songs to Mother. One day, I carried the tape to work so I could enjoy listening to it between client appointments. "What would I do if I did not have this tape?" I thought. The tape was instrumental in helping me maintain my sense of connection to Ammachi. As I left work that evening, I accidentally dropped the tape on the ground when entering my car. I picked it up and placed it on the seat beside me. When I returned home, I reached for the tape only to discover it was not on the seat! I was astonished. I scoured the area inside the car for some time. The cassette had disappeared into thin air! Even though it was about 11:00 p.m., I took the twenty minute drive back to my office and searched the ground between the car and the office door, no tape.

The next morning, I completely emptied my fully packed car, which was stuffed with supplies for a weekend therapy intensive. I found no tape. I returned to the office to look in the daylight, to no avail. To this day, that cassette has never surfaced.

I had experienced another lost-tape incident a few years before. In that instance, once I had accepted the fact that the tape was gone, it reappeared in a spot I had searched many times. I assumed that, once again, I was being given a lesson in letting-go. Over the next several days, songs from the lost tape started popping into my head, a phrase at a time. Soon I could sing nearly all of the songs on the tape.

At that weekend's therapy intensive, a remarkable thing happened. One of my clients had felt inclined to see Ammachi when she was visiting Seattle, but had not followed through. During the intensive that same client, with the help of my co-therapist, began to set up a piece of therapeutic work. As I watched the process, my eyes started opening wide and wider. The scene she was creating was incredibly similar to my New Hampshire dog nightmare! I approached my co-therapist and whispered in his ear that I thought I knew what was going to happen. Indeed, the piece ended with the client spontaneously screaming "MOTHER!" at which time we, her therapists, intervened in the role of healthy parents. Once again, I was astounded by the process that was occurring within and around me.

Soon after I returned from New Hampshire, my friend, Emile, handed me a tape he thought I would enjoy. The cassette was *Jai Ma Kirtan* (Songs to the Divine Mother), published by Baba Hari Dass' ashram in Santa Cruz, California. A few days later, I put the tape into the recorder as I began some housework. The instant the first song (*Hymn to the Goddess Mother*) started, I was overcome with such a sense of reverence I was incapable of standing. I dropped to my knees and went into a deep meditative state. When that song ended and the next one (*Jai Durga Lakshmi*) began, I experienced an enormous sense of grief, along with a flood of tears. The first notes of the third song

(*Amba Parameshwari*) sent waves of exhilarating joy coursing through my body. When that song ended, I stopped the tape. Enough for one day!

I was meeting with Christananda once or twice a week for help in opening energy blockages. I was frequently experiencing sensations in my body that were similar to those my clients were noting in theirs. If those sensations occurred in a body location in which I had stuck energy of my own, I felt piercing pain. Christananda also helped me learn to cope with the events that were occurring in my life. I brought the *Jai Ma Kirtan* tape to one of our sessions. As I listened to it, I once again experienced the wide range of emotions. For the next month or so prior to a session with Christananda, someone would invariably hand me a tape that profoundly impacted me. Christananda would greet me at the door chuckling, "I know, you have another tape."

For several weeks after the New Hampshire retreat, I had trouble coping with involuntary altered states of consciousness. Driving, in particular, was a problem. Once, when driving to meet a friend for lunch, I started drifting into a meditative state. Fortunately, I was able to stay clear enough to safely arrive at our meeting place.

When I stopped the car, however, the altered state further intensified. I was losing more and more awareness of the outer world. When my friend saw my condition, she helped me out of my car so that I could sit on the ground. I rubbed my hands on the cement trying to bring myself back to normal consciousness. My friend shook me, saying, "I've been trying to do that (that is, leave her body) for years! You come back here and tell me how *you* are doing it!" As my work with Christananda continued, I found it easier to stay grounded in this reality.

One morning, I awoke with an overwhelming desire to obtain a harmonium, an Indian instrument that is a cross between an accordion and a piano. I found one in Seattle but was dismayed to discover that it cost $450, much more than I anticipated. I was not at all sure I was willing to spend that much money, so decided to take some time to mull it over.

The thought of the instrument plagued my mind. Soon, I decided to take the plunge and simply buy it. Almost immediately, I began receiving phone calls from new and existing clients. Within a few hours, I had scheduled enough new appointments to pay for the harmonium. This was my first experience in learning that when you follow God's direction, the resources will be provided.

A New Life

As we had in each of the previous ten years, my children and I prepared for a weeklong camp sponsored by the Unitarian Church at Seabeck, Washington. (Never mind that I had not been to church for years, I still loved their camp!) I had one client session scheduled the day we were to leave for camp. As my client entered the office, she handed me two items Christananda had asked her to deliver, a picture of a man and a package of incense. As I glanced at the picture, I felt an immediate wave of terror wash through me. I breathed deeply to ground myself and then focused on the client.

After the session, I picked up my children and headed towards camp, still feeling the terror the picture had induced. At this particular summer camp, participants volunteer to teach workshops to other participants. A few days into the camp, I was preparing to teach a workshop about stages of psychological development. Just prior to the class, I burned some of the incense Christananda had sent me. Shortly thereafter, I noticed I was beginning to experience symptoms of chronic fatigue syndrome, a disease I had suffered with for about five years. Over the next few hours, I started not only feeling physically miserable, but also depressed over the fact I was spiraling downwards into the disease once again. I decided to call my friend Diane for reassurance. When I told her of the events of the last few days, she responded with anger, angry that Christananda had given me the picture as I was leaving town. I recognized that I was also angry with him, so called and told him so.

When Christananda heard my story, he told me he had felt directed to send me the two items. The picture, he said, was that of a saint. (He certainly did not look like a saint to *me*!) Christananda told me the incense was called Shiva's Garden incense. Shiva is the aspect of God that destroys delusion and other negativities such as disease. Christananda's interpretation was that the incense and the picture had been used to induce a healing crisis. He said that spiritual masters such as Ammachi will often purposely provoke a chronic disease. The Master may then take the disease onto themselves, as they can process it through their body much faster than can the disciple. This process can occur whether or not the disciple is in physical proximity to the teacher. Christananda said I could burn the picture if I wished, but I was not to discard it.

That night, my son and I burned the picture in the camp parking lot. Immediately afterwards, I felt intensely pulled to the evening church services. Never before had I felt the slightest urge to go to the evening service, so that in itself was more than a little strange! As I walked into the chapel, the people started singing the chant, *Om Namah Shivaya*. A Sanskrit chant in a Unitarian church service! And the subject of the chant was *Shiva*! What else could I do? I sat down and quickly went into deep meditation.

Earlier that same day, a fellow camper told me of a tape he wanted me to hear. How familiar that statement had become! When I asked him for the tape the next day, I was flabbergasted to discover it was a ninety-minute chant of *Om Namah Shivaya*. I put the tape on "auto reverse," lay down and went to sleep. When I woke up, all symptoms of the disease were gone. Prior to this instance, it had taken me weeks to months to recover from a flare-up. Since that time, I have had almost no trouble with chronic fatigue syndrome.

The incense, the evening chant and the tape were all Shiva-related. *Om Namah Shivaya* is a mantra that has been used by more people in history than any other. There are many translations of that particular mantra. The interpretation I like best in actuality combines three of those translations. It states, "I bow to the universal God, I bow to the God within me, I bow to the aspect of God that is Shiva." In the years since this incident, my friends, clients and I have repeatedly used this cassette by Robert Gass and the Wings of Song to alleviate headaches and many other forms of emotional and physical distress.

While I was at camp, I discovered a significant attitude change had occurred within me. During some of the classes, participants shared their belief that the miracles in the Bible were metaphors as opposed to reality. They laughed mockingly at what they considered the absurdity of anyone believing that someone would actually cut through a roof to lower a sick person to Jesus. As I listened to them, I realized that after spending only six days with Ammachi, I had no trouble at all believing that the miracles had actually occurred. I also discovered I no longer felt angry with Jesus. My remaining anger was directed towards the Christian church for its perversion of his message.

When I came home from Seabeck, my ex-husband phoned saying, "Do I have a story for you!" My daughter had told him I had become vegetarian. His response had been, "Well, I'm not going to!" He related that a few days later, while sitting in the park, an old man had walked up to him, looked him directly in the eye and said, "If you ate more fruits and vegetables, you would not need that cane." (Al has multiple sclerosis.) Al told me that, even as we spoke, he was cleaning fruits and vegetables, and hating every minute of it!

Upon returning from Seabeck, I decided to start a weekly chanting group. Our group sang Native American, East Indian, Christian, and Jewish chants. Many participants began searching for their own spiritual paths after attending these sessions. One day, a woman woke up with the words, "Mata Amritanandamayi" on her mind. Not knowing that this was the formal name for Ammachi, she started off on a quest to discover the meaning of the words. Her search took her to a bookstore in downtown Seattle. Her attention was drawn to a very small, white book on the top shelf, one that had no words on the spine. She pulled the book down and discovered it to be *For My Children*, by Mata Amritanandamayi (Ammachi)!

At the New Hampshire retreat, devotees had been told they were welcome to visit Ammachi's ashram in San Ramon, California. Soon after returning from my week at Seabeck, I made arrangements for a visit. When I arrived at the ashram, I was taken on a tour of the grounds. As my guide and I stepped inside the meditation hall, I experienced such a huge force of spiritual energy that I was pulled immediately into a deep meditative state. This happened so quickly that I had to lean on the nearest wall to keep from falling down. Soon thereafter, I practically crawled to my room and slept for hours.

My weekend was awesome. Normally, I did not enjoy being in new places with people I did not know. Here, however, I felt completely at home even though I didn't know anyone. I worked in the garden, the office and the kitchen. Each night as we sang bhajans my entire being filled either with unbridled joy or profound grief. The joy once again felt like a melding of coming home and of being nourished. The grief came primarily from my realization that I would have to leave the ashram at the end of the weekend. As I sang new songs and read or heard new information, I had a strong sense I was simply remembering something I had once known.

Returning to Seattle, I was continually assailed by intense grief. I felt as if a part of me was starving. I could not be with Ammachi and I could not move to California. What was I to do? I began attending Sunday services at the Ananda Center in Seattle, run by devotees of

Yogananada. I enjoyed the people but the energy felt too western for me, so I knew that my hunger could not be satiated there.

One day, I listened as one of my clients described a spiritual gathering in which the people sat cross-legged on the floor, chanted Sanskrit songs and bowed to a picture of a woman guru. Naturally, her words grabbed my attention. The place she described was the Siddha Yoga Center, run by devotees of Gurumayi Chidvilasananda. I immediately made arrangements to attend.

The instant the group started to sing, my head spontaneously moved to the floor in the East Indian style of prostration. I burst into tears that continued to flow throughout the entire two-hour program. I felt as if Ammachi was standing behind me, her hand on my shoulder, saying, "You can come here to be fed." I never felt any interest in becoming involved with the people or the programs at the Center, but participation in their music program seemed essential for my survival during that first year after meeting Ammachi.

I was not the only one noticing changes in me. Other people remarked at differences almost from the beginning. I had worn eyeglasses from the time I was ten years old. During that first month after meeting Ammachi, I realized how I hid behind my glasses, using them to feel separate and protected. That feeling of separation became intolerable and soon after Mother left the country, I had myself fitted for contact lenses. In the months that followed, I noticed (as did others) that I was becoming more feminine, softer and more nurturing. It was as if the "Mother" part of *me* was emerging. Even though the grief I experienced so frequently was painful and difficult to endure, I was convinced it was also very healing.

Sometime during the fall, I decided to learn something about Krishna, the deity to whom my mantra was directed. I looked in Joseph Campbell's *Oriental Mythology* and my eyes locked onto a statement about Krishna and the Gopis:

> ...(he) began to move among them freely, playing still upon
> his flute, 'O place thy lotus hands,' they cried, 'upon our
> aching breasts, upon our heads!' And the dance began.[9]

---

[9]Joseph Campbell, *Oriental Mythology: The Masks of God,* New York: Penguin Group, 1962 (1991 reprint), p. 345.

I was horrified! I had had almost no intimate contact with men since I separated from Al twelve years before and the thought of my acting like *that* around *any* man was totally repulsive. My reaction was so intense, I was fully aware my excess energy must be due to "unfinished business" with men. It was obvious that having a mantra to Krishna was no "accident." I decided to trust the process rather than rid myself of the mantra, although I must admit I chose to say it very infrequently. As you might imagine, there will be more to this story later!

As my October birthday approached, I felt directed to prepare a special experience for myself and a few of my closest friends. During the next few days the content of that experience came into my mind, piecemeal. The evening "program" would consist of a mixture of songs, some on tape, and some to be sung by those present. We would also chant 108 names of the Divine Mother. As the content "came," it quickly became obvious that I was not in charge of this process.

I reacted to one piece that arrived in my mind with an immediate internal response, "They would not like that, they would be bored." (In actuality, I thought it was boring.) During the next ten minutes, I bumped my head three times. After the third "whack," I quickly said, "Okay, we will do it!" Over the next few weeks my friends and I rehearsed the songs and prepared for the big evening. None of my friends, at that point, had even met Ammachi. The evening seemed to be an initiation of some kind for me, and I had a sense that it was for all who joined me as well.

One day in November, I felt guided to make an appointment with Puru, the minister of the Ananda Center. I did what I felt directed to do, even though I did not know why I was doing it. The morning of my appointment with Puru, a client handed me a note sent by Christananda. Remembering my previous experience of having received an unexpected "gift" from Christananda, I chose to not look at the note until I had completed my client session. When I read the note, I discovered that Christananda was no longer willing to see me as a client, stating he needed to deal with personal issues of his own. Ordinarily, I would have panicked, since he had become such an important part of my process. It seemed no accident, however, that this happened immediately before my appointment with Puru. I believed I was being shown once again that if I follow God's direction, I would be provided with what I need.

I was also learning the importance of living in the moment. I knew when I made plans and set goals, I must be willing to be flexible and to adjust to plans as necessary. Further, I was discovering that holding on to plans, relationships, opinions, expectations, and so forth, was likely to result in disappointment and pain. If I did not hold on, I was much more capable of staying calm and centered no matter what happened.

I decided to invite my son, Sreejit, to go with me to the California ashram. I was not sure why I was doing so, as he was fifteen and had shown no interest whatsoever in either Ammachi or my spiritual process. As surprising to me as my invitation, was his acceptance. We decided to go for the Thanksgiving weekend.

Sreejit had been raised with the minimum of spiritual activity, so when he sat in the meditation room hour after hour, both the ashram residents and I were dumbfounded. When I asked him if he was meditating, he replied, "No," adding, "I just like being in the room." He particularly loved the music sung during each night's bhajan programs. (I will share more of his story later.)

Sometime during the fall, I started preparing for a trip to India. I do not remember ever making any decision to go. I just knew I was going.

On Christmas day, I attended a party given by one of my co-therapists. His wife, Lynn, also a friend of mine, asked, "What's new?" I laughed as I began to relate the short version of what had been happening, the long version would have taken hours. As I began to share about my upcoming trip, she listened very intently and asked lots of questions. At the end of the conversation, she said, "I'm going with you." I was shocked. After all I had been through during the last nine months, I was used to surprises, but this bit of news truly took me aback. My trip was to occur in less than three weeks. It had taken me months of planning to obtain airline tickets, a passport, visa, and the items I would take with me, yet Lynn was setting out to accomplish all that in less than three weeks! Lynn had never had any contact with nor interest in anything East Indian, the only exception being that the week before she had felt drawn to buy a little wooden elephant, made in India!

PART 2

Listen to the call of my heart... O Mother
Darkness has spread all around
The path is not visible to me
How shall I search for You? O Mother
How shall I see you
Mother listen to me.

This child of Yours is just a toddler.
How can he live alone, without his Mother.
Who will take care of him?
Who will nourish him with love?
O Mother, listen to me.[1]

India!
January 1990

L ynn was easily able to make all of the necessary travel arrangements and on January 16, we were off! As I headed towards India, I reflected once again on the many ways my life had changed during the previous seven months, not the least of which was the fact that this trip was occurring. After a childhood of moving, I had actively avoided traveling. From birth, my children had lived in the same house. Now in the short time since I had met Ammachi, I had flown to Florida, New Hampshire, twice to California and here I was on my way to India!

---

[1] "Sun Le Pukar," *1996 Bhajan Supplement,* San Ramon: Mata Amritanandamayi Center, p. 50.

We traveled all the way without incident. It seemed like any other trip, only longer! That feeling of familiarity disappeared the instant we left the airport. Never mind that it was 1:00 a.m. As we exited the baggage claim area and walked outside into the Madras night, we had to immediately elbow our way through hordes of people. There were family members eagerly awaiting travelers, malformed lepers, undernourished children, mothers carrying flaccid infants and many others begging for money, food or whatever they could get. As we inched our way through the crowd, a young man stepped up to us and asked if we would like a taxi. With relief, we said, "Yes!" He proceeded to guide us about six feet and announced, "Here is the taxi stand." He then demanded a tip. After we arranged for a prepaid taxi, a man, whom we assumed was the driver, said he would take us to our taxi. He then took us about fifty feet, said, "Here is your taxi," and demanded a tip! We knew we had arrived in India!

Among my first vivid memories of India was the experience of riding in a taxi from the airport to the ashram. In that part of the country, the roads, often peppered with potholes, are just barely wide enough for two cars to travel side by side. Cars drive very fast down the middle of the street, in both directions at the same time. Just before impact, both vehicles swerve to their left, often missing each other by inches. There seemed to be a hierarchy on the road, pedestrians having no right of way, then in ascending order, bicycles, rickshaws, buses, cars and taxis. Add to this scene trucks overloaded with hay or other cargo, cows, oxen, dogs, cats and an occasional elephant, and you begin to comprehend the chaos. Everyone honks their horns when they are ready to pass. I felt as though I was on a high-speed roller coaster with a driver who was amazingly skilled and had nerves of steel. He seemed relaxed and confident even under what seemed the most hazardous of circumstances.

I had expected to be overwhelmed by the poverty in India. While the poverty certainly was massive, the conditions in the state of Kerala (southwestern India) were not as dire as I expected to find. As we drove from town to town, something felt very familiar. I realized I was reminded of my experience of living in the migrant farm labor camps, the summer following my college graduation. I was once again thankful for the lessons I have learned throughout my life and noted how well they had prepared me for my present-day experience.

We arrived at the ashram shortly before the beginning of darshan. When I reached the front of the line, I was dismayed to discover that

Ammachi did not seem at all impressed that I had come so far to see her. When I later pondered her behavior, I considered the possibility that she was acting as a mirror, reflecting the part of me that still considered the music to be the source of the extraordinary events in my life.[2]

My first evening at the ashram was very moving. The bhajans were wonderful, as always. Then, we sang *Arati*, the song that had impacted me so profoundly in the United States. This time, the singers were ac-

Karuna in India.

---

[2] Writing this manuscript has helped me to see how many realities were co-exisiting at the same time. On the one hand, I could say, and mean, I had given her my heart and as a result had followed her half way across the world, yet another part of me still considered her to be "excess baggage."

companied by a large bell, a gong and a conch shell, in addition to the harmonium and drums. The instant those sounds began, my entire being exploded into grief. Incapable of standing, I fell to the ground and sobbed. It was as if these sounds took me directly to the core of the grief about being separated from God. I wept for hours. My body strongly reacted to those particular sounds for several nights thereafter. I still cry when I recall that experience.

Learning to live at the ashram was a major endeavor. At that point, there were only a few toilets in the ashram and each morning found long lines of impatient people. Each visit to the toilet stirred up unpleasant memories of traveling cross-country with my father, who was always upset and impatient when we asked for bathroom stops.

There was little running water at the ashram in those days. Each time we used the toilet, we had to pump and carry a bucket of water for flushing. Squatting over the eastern-style commode was not only difficult for me, but was also slightly revolting. We were asked not to use toilet paper, as that would clog the pipes. Needless to say, that was hard for me to get used to.

When we wanted to shower, we had to pump a bucket of water, take it to a small building, and then "shower" ourselves using one cup of water at a time. In those days, only well water, which had a very peculiar and unpleasant odor, was available. I was bothered that I could never escape that odor. There were no hot water heaters, thus no hot water. Fortunately, however, the weather was so hot that one of the highlights of our day was to be able to take a cold shower. When we wanted to wash our clothes, we would take them, along with some pumped water, to some special flat stones. We would then attempt to scrub and beat the clothes on the stones until they were clean. The Indian women were able to get their clothes spotless in this manner. Not surprisingly, *we* were less successful!

All of these tasks took time and energy to complete. During our first week, we spent most of our time doing what would normally be minor activities of daily living in the United States.

Ashram life was fascinating for many reasons, not the least of which was that both Lynn and I were experiencing our thoughts and desires almost immediately becoming reality. For example, Lynn was responsible for sweeping one floor of the temple. Most of the brooms in India are very short, about a half the size of the ones we use in the United States. As Lynn is very tall, sweeping in this manner was very uncomfortable for

Indian and Western devotees at washing stones.

her. One day, she wished she had a taller broom. Within minutes some-one brought her one. The next day, she wished she had some help. Mo-ments later, two people offered to help.

Another example occurred the day Lynn and I explored the village closest to the ashram. As we walked, I wondered out loud if Mother would ever let us live in the village instead of the ashram. Within twenty-four hours, we were moved out of our cheery, clean, bright room in the guesthouse into a dark, filthy, bug-ridden building which had recently been deserted by villagers and purchased by the ashram. A few days later, we were delighted to be moved again, into a room in the temple. Mother must have decided we had learned what we needed to learn from that experience!

I recognize that to say Ammachi decided we had learned what we needed to learn implies that I believe she was consciously orchestrating this whole process. In actuality, I have no idea how the process works. What I do know is that when we are around her, lessons are sent and learned and desires met at a rate that is much faster than in the course of "normal" living.

During our stay, we accompanied Mother on two bus trips. At one point, our group of voyagers started singing, bringing back memories of the bliss I had experienced in high school when traveling on the church bus singing spiritual songs to my heart's content. Soon, I found myself teaching and leading the songs we sang in my chanting group in Seattle. Later, someone introduced a song that was new to me, *Gopala, Gopala, Devakinandana, Gopala*. Three of us sang that song for more than two hours straight! Later, we attempted to sing *Aiye Guru Maharani*. I tried to lead it, but could not without my harmonium. We asked Ammachi to help but she ignored us. Years later, I realized that particular song is directed towards her, asking her to give us protection and refuge. Therefore, it would have been improper for her to be the person to lead it. When I think back to that time, I am struck by the fact that I could lead songs in her presence and never think twice about it. That experience, more than any other I can remember, symbolizes my innocence at that time.

From my first day in India, I experienced immense grief knowing that soon I would have to leave. I was so saddened that I began to wonder if I was stuck in a pattern of unnecessary and useless suffering. After pondering that possibility, I decided that staying in touch with the reality of my eventual leaving was a necessity if I was going to be able to tear myself away when the time to leave actually came.

One morning, I woke up with a song (*Jai Saraswati*) playing in my mind as if on a radio. Later, during the morning program, Ammachi sang that very song. For the rest of my days in India, whenever I began to experience grief from the inevitability of my leaving, that song would start playing in my head. With it came a sense of peace at knowing she was with me.

Whenever we traveled to and from the ashram, we crossed the backwaters in a canoe. Each time as I witnessed the beauty above, under, in front and behind me I wondered why any of us live anywhere else. The endless palm trees, water, blue sky, brilliant sunrises and sunsets were very different from my preconceptions of India. To me, this was truly paradise.

Ammachi has said that those of us who are drawn to her have been with her in other lifetimes. As I learned more about Mother's teachings, I was struck by how many of my attitudes were already in harmony with hers. An example that came to my attention on this trip concerned disclosure of past life information. For years, I had been disturbed by my friends' pursuit of information about their past lives. It seemed to me that

if the information was important for one to have, it would come to consciousness on its own. If the information was not important, then I saw no value in knowing it. I discovered that Ammachi was usually unwilling to discuss either her own past lives or anyone else's. She said if a person found out they had done bad things, then they would be depressed. If, on other hand, they discovered they had done good things or had been very important, then it would build ego, which in most religious traditions is considered an impediment to spiritual growth. I totally resonated with this point of view.

I had anticipated, due to the extreme grief I experienced each time I left the California ashram, that it was going to be even harder to leave India. Before I left the United States, I had asked several friends to give me letters saying whatever they thought would help bring me home. I opened those letters about seventy-two hours before I was to leave the ashram. I read the following:

> *You have left the womb of your mother,*
> *Teary eyed and serene, flying the metalic wings of the skybird.*
> *"Now what?" you ask*
> *"Where from here does my longing go?"*
>
> *...Even before I crossed your threshold, dear Mother out*
> *into the world, I longed for your loving eyes.*
>
> *You are with me, I know*
> *Your love is with me, I know*

Your eyes are with me, I know
Your breath is with me, <u>I know</u>

Mother! Great spirit that I am

I will call on you in my sleep
I will close my eyes and see your face looking back
I will breathe, and into my depth ... <u>feel you</u>
                    ...vibrating
                    ...glowing.

Dazed by the longing and love—
loved

                                        Emile

You have a mission
It is solitary.
It is joined with others.
The two are the same.
To leave India
To return to your mission in Seattle,
To reenter <u>your connections</u>
          your life
          your mission
Is to remain in India.
Thus to embrace your life, is to embrace Ammachi

                    Love   Lee, friend, Spirit

When it is time to come home, come home.
You have so many this-life years ahead!
You don't have to do it all now.

When my poet friend Julia Stein was near death, she went down the long tunnel to the light. She stood at the bank of the river, enveloped in the light and the love. She said she

*was tired and wanted to cross, to be in the light always.
The light-love said, "Go back. You are not finished. Your
children need you. You have other things to do." She went
back, but she was changed, stronger, more centered, more
peaceful.*

*You can choose to come home now.
Later there will be a time and a place for the rest of your
dreams, for your other homes.*

Love, Jean

I become teary even now as I read these letters and re-experience
the love and wisdom of the people in my life. At that point, none of
these people had even met Ammachi, yet they understood.

My grief about leaving was so intense, I wondered if I was going to be
able to walk out of the ashram gate. A Devi Bhava program was scheduled
on our last night in India. When I sat near Mother, I went into a meditative state so profound that it lifted only a few short times over a three-hour
span, just long enough for me to notice the time. When I came out of that
altered state, I felt calm and peaceful, even when I thought about leaving.

That sense of acceptance and peace lasted until we approached the
United States coastline. At that point, my grief returned with the overwhelming thought, "I do NOT want to come back to THIS home." When
I walked off the plane in Seattle, I threw my arms around the people who
came to meet me and sobbed.

A Glimpse of the Future
Winter/Spring 1990

It took me many months to adjust to being back in the United States. I
thought of the bright eyed Indian children who had so little materially,
but so much spiritually. I was angry at the petty things with which we in
this country concerned ourselves when there was so much we could do to
help the world. I detested the materialism that pervaded everywhere. I
longed to go back to India.

When I first returned to the United States, I shared my experience with people who were interested. One of these people, Shelley, went home after our talk and wrote a poem, one she felt she was "given."

The Courage to Believe,
for Carol Poole

The pot looked empty. It was a clay pot, orange and cracked from the rain. On Mondays people came to fill it and the water, somewhat yellowed, seeped out the bottom.

At first I wondered why they didn't patch it. But looking closely, I saw their need to bend slightly to the right. Some called it agility, but really they were trying to keep their hands on the hole.

Now you choose a jug, and songs arise from its clay. And the rhythms of drums from inside, the moon-roundness of it takes on the form of a woman with the courage to believe.

The jug is round and smooth, and the water is always full.

Shelley Tucker

When I first saw the poem I was struck by several things. The music and the drums were a significant part of my current spiritual process. Also, during my therapy process, I had often stated that I felt like a bucket with a hole in the bottom. No matter how much I was given, it seemed like I still felt empty. The point at which the hole first sealed and the bucket started to fill was etched in my memory. As I reread the poem in preparing this manuscript, I realized how accurate a metaphor it was for my spiritual process as well. For the first three years, I felt as if I once again was a jug with a hole in the bottom. Now the jug is sealed and while I don't always feel full, I certainly do not feel anywhere near empty. I also have become much more rounded and smooth in the process!

When I returned from India, I expected I would experience a strong desire to meditate. Not only did I have no strong desire… I had *no* desire to meditate. I felt instead as if I were being directed to put my energy into yoga, an activity I had started a few weeks before my trip to India, and to learn to play the tabla[3] I had purchased while in India.

For the most part, the "paranormal" events I had experienced when I first met Ammachi ceased. I had a sense that I had been shown a new world, a world in which it was possible for me to live, but now I had to do the work to return to it. I believed I could go no further with this process until I prepared my body and mind through the discipline of yoga and the tabla. I set about in earnest to learn both.

I still occasionally received calls from clients and friends concerning Ammachi. One client called to say she had seen a book about Mother at the bookstore. She described the book in detail and then stopped talking, almost mid-sentence. After a few moments she quietly said, "I haven't been to a bookstore recently."

Another woman attended a workshop I conducted, one which met three times at monthly intervals. At one point, this woman revealed that an Indian woman had "come" to her in dreams or guided imagery experiences three different times since the beginning of the workshop. When I showed her a picture of Ammachi, she said, "Yes, that is her." I have always been amazed at how many people have such experiences and then feel no draw to meet Mother.

That April, I had what seemed to me to be a very significant elevator dream. Throughout my childhood and adult life, I had had recurrent nightmares of being in an elevator that starts ascending, builds up speed and bursts through the roof into the sky. The last time I had had that dream was in 1984. This dream was different. While I was standing in the elevator, I pushed the button for the 10th floor, the top floor. When the door opened, I saw a world consisting entirely of gray clouds. It appeared peaceful and inviting but I knew that if I stepped out, I would die, as I had no skills to live in that world. I shut the door and looked at my options. I was drawn to the button marked 3/4[4], so I pushed that button and waited as the elevator descended. When the door opened again, I stepped out into a surreal world made up of huge red, orange and yellow objects. The objects were of many geometric shapes- squares, circles and triangles. I knew that it was my job to learn to live in *this* world. Even though I did not know how to live there, it was at least possible. I found

---

[3] Tabla - drums.
[4] as if it were a combination of the third and the fourth floors.

I was basically on my own but every so often a woman would stroll nearby me. She did not interact with me but I sensed it was her job to see that I was safe and was learning what I needed to learn. I believed if I was in danger, she would have helped me.

When I woke up, I saw how clearly this dream reflected my spiritual journey with Ammachi. I would occasionally be given glimpses of the spiritual worlds of my future, but would not be able to stay there. My evolutionary journey would be one step at a time. I would be asked to stretch, but would not be expected to do what was impossible. Ammachi would be available should I need help, but would mostly guide my process from afar.

Learning to Let Go!
1990 Summer Tour

As spring arrived, I started anticipating Ammachi's summer tour. I decided to go to retreats in San Ramon, California and Seattle as well as to public programs in Vancouver, Canada and New York. One morning I found myself being continually drawn to the calendar, looking at one particular weekend. I kept thinking, "Why aren't you with Mother on that weekend?" Finally, I responded, "I don't know, I'm certainly free!" and went to look at the tour schedule. Ammachi was going to be in Dallas, so I decided to add that city to my itinerary. Within a few hours of making the decision, new and existing clients started calling for appointments. Once again, I received more than enough money to meet my expenses.

That year, Ammachi's tour started in California. I had an important question I intended to ask. In April, I had been invited to attend a workshop given by a channeled guru. Although I had always had many biases against channeling, I discovered that when I was in his presence I felt many of the same sensations I experienced when I was with Mother. I concluded that Ammachi had sent me to him and that I was to spend time with both of them. That way I would receive both father and mother energy. I believed it was important for me to check my thinking with Mother, however, so I came to the California retreat with that as my primary agenda. I wanted very much to spend time with the other guru, so I feared asking a question to which the answer could be "No." Nevertheless, I prepared my question very carefully so that I was being very straight and in no way manipulative.

The process of going through the darshan and question lines was amazing. As I waited in line, I began to have the sensation of layers of fear washing off of me. First, I recognized I had a great deal of emotional attachment to whatever her answer would be. As that layer of thought and fear fell away, the next came. I was afraid my question would be offensive. Layers of fear continued to fall away. By the time I arrived at the head of the line, I did not care in the slightest what her answer would be. As the translator began to read my question, Mother started shaking her head "No," not stopping until the translation ended.

Ammachi told me it was fine for me to learn from the other guru, but that I should not bond with him. She said if we follow two paths our energy would inevitably be split between them. This was advice I consistently give my clients in relation to their therapy process, but I had rationalized that my situation was different! She also told me the channel had not done her own work and could not take me where I needed to go.

As I let go of my remaining attachment to being with the other guru, I felt a powerful rush of devotional energy towards my path with Mother. I was abundantly aware how right her answer was for me.

As I prepared to leave California and return home, I plummeted into my now familiar separation grief. I was aghast to realize that I had planned my summer in such a way that I was going to experience leaving *five* different times! How was I going to survive the emotional roller coaster?

During my last night in California, I woke up with a song blasting through my head, as if a radio was inside with the volume turned all the way up. The song, *Vedambike*, was one I recognized, but did not know. That song "played" night and day (luckily at a lower volume!), for the next ten days. The process was immensely valuable in helping me feel connected to Mother when I was not with her. When I looked up the translation weeks later, I discovered the phrases going through my head meant *"O Mother of the Vedas, O Mother of Sound, I bow to Thee...bestowing love, bestowing the radiance of the lotus, O Lover of music take me across this ocean of misery."*[5] I felt known, seen and cared for and was exceedingly grateful.

---

[5] "Vedambike," *Bhajanamritam: Devotional Songs,* Vallickavu: Mata Amritanandamayi Mission Trust, 1987 (1990 reprint) p. I-63.

That year my son Sreejit, my ex-husband and many of my friends and clients met Mother during the Seattle programs. Sreejit, in particular, seemed entranced by her. After he went for darshan, I mentioned to Leela, one of the California ashram residents that my son had just been with Mother. She said, "*That* was your son? I looked at the way he looked at her and the way she looked at him and said to myself, 'He is going to be a brahmachari'." I did not tell Sreejit of Leela's comment until years later. I was aware soon thereafter, however, that her statement was in all likelihood prophetic.

My ex-husband, whom you might remember has multiple sclerosis, did not go for darshan, but remarked how strongly he felt Ammachi's energy when she walked past him. He left the program soon after darshan began and walked home. The next morning, he called, bursting with enthusiasm, exclaiming that after being near Ammachi, he had felt so physically well he had beat the bus home!

When the Seattle retreat began, I mentally said to Mother, "Since you don't want me to work with the other guru, I want you to push me the way he pushes his people." I thought no more about that request. By the end of the second day of the retreat, I noticed I was feeling extremely agitated and upset and had no idea why. During the evening talk, my legs hurt and I was feeling restless. I finally thought, "Let's get on with the music, I'm tired of all this talk." Mother immediately said, "That's enough talk, we will sing now." She hesitated a moment and then said, "You all need to stretch, stand up!" (I have never seen that happen, before or since.) When we sat down, my legs still felt cramped and sore. She looked directly at me and said, "Stretch your legs out in front of you." This was a position I had been told one is never to take, that is, feet stretched out towards a guru, as the position is considered disrespectful. Nevertheless, I followed her direction thinking, "Okay, I get it. You see me. You hear me. You know me. *Please* no more attention for now. That is *enough*!"

When I looked back over that entire day, I realized my connection with Mother had been blocked one time after another. The day had started out with my placing a pillow to mark my space at the front of the room. I felt a bit proud and cocky that I knew the system well enough to sit where I wanted to sit. Just as I was getting ready to settle into my seat, she changed the meeting site. I soon found myself sitting in the back of the new room.

At lunch, she had served each participant his or her meal, touching and giving eye contact to every person she served, in effect giving each another darshan. When I approached her, however, she handed me my plate without so much as a glance.

Later on, she announced the group meditation would be moved from 5:30 p.m. to 6:00 p.m., so I had busied myself doing something else. When I arrived at the meditation site, I discovered Ammachi had shown up at 5:30! Once again, I found myself sitting in the back of the crowd, and to make matters worse, my view was totally blocked by someone sitting on a high pillow.

I concluded all this had happened because I had asked to be pushed. At that moment, I resolved I would never again challenge Mother to push me. I would trust whatever pace she chose for me. I have maintained that attitude to this day.

During this retreat, I discovered something else. People were consistently coming up to me and remarking, "Your face, look at what is happening to your face!" Devotees had made similar remarks to me in India. When in Ammachi's presence, I found it almost impossible to tear my eyes away from her, watching hour after hour. As I sat there, totally absorbed in her presence, it was as if my actual body chemistry was changing. Every day, I was looking younger and younger.

I decided to ask Mother for a spiritual name. I had watched that process the previous year and was aware she gave names to some people immediately, others she told to wait. I decided I would ask in Vancouver if she would name me in Seattle. I liked the idea of being named in my hometown and thought, by giving her warning, I could minimize my chances of being told to wait! I looked forward to the moving moment of connection we would have when I asked my question. Wrong! What I received instead was another lesson in "Don't have expectations." When Swami Amritaswarupananda (most often called Swamiji) translated my question, she responded "Yes" without even looking at me!

I had two goals for the subsequent Seattle retreat, I wanted my spiritual name and I wanted to be a line monitor.[6] By Sunday, the last day of the retreat, I had accomplished neither. I had not even been able to find out how one becomes a line monitor. No one seemed able to answer that question. As darshan began Sunday morning, I glanced to the front of the line and was surprised to discover there was no line monitor present. I thought, "Here's my opportunity," and moved into that position.

---

[6] Line monitor - one of the people assigned to help the darshan line run efficiently.

As the morning progressed, I realized my chances of receiving a spiritual name that day were becoming slimmer. The question line was very long and it was obvious Mother wanted to end the program soon. I finally leaned over to Swamiji and told him I wanted a spiritual name. I asked if it would be better for me to wait until Dallas. He breathed what seemed to be a sigh of relief and said, "Yes."

Swamiji.

I traveled to Dallas, determined to be named. On the first night, however, the line monitor job was open so I took it. The second morning, the position was open again so I settled in. That day I was determined to get my name as well. At one point, I noticed the question line was very short, so I arranged for someone to relieve me for a "few minutes" and scooted over to the question line. I told Swamiji what I wanted. He said, "Wait," and then proceeded to ignore me. After about an hour of sitting and waiting, I began to worry that I had done something inappropriate. Normally, one does not go through the question line until they have gone through the darshan line. I worried about that for a while and then leaned over and asked Swamiji if I should go through the darshan line first. He immediately said, "Yes," so I spent the next hour or so going through the darshan line. By the time I was through that line, the question line was very long. As I inched my way through that line, I started worrying that I had again done something inappropriate. I should have waited where I had been told to wait in the first place, that is, I should never have left Swamiji's side. When I finally arrived at the front of the line, I reminded him of my request. He said, "Wait over there," indicating that I should sit up on the steps behind him.

Suddenly, I realized what had been happening to me. I had been given a battery of tests and lessons over the last few weeks and it was time to *let go!* Laughing, I realized it would not be at all surprising if I left the day's program without a spiritual name. At the end of the program, Swamiji told me to come directly to the front of the line the next day and he would ask Mother to name me. He said I would not have to wait in any more lines!

The next morning, with single-minded attention, anticipation and eagerness, I went directly for the name. The moment of connection, the one I had so eagerly expected in Vancouver and wanted here, had finally arrived. Her eyes met mine, she smiled and said simply, "Karuna" (Compassion). I went back to my seat, crying in gratitude.

My son, Sreejit, had not been interested in going to the Seattle retreat, but decided he did want to go to the New York programs, provided he could go sightseeing. We departed for New York with that agreement in place. When we arrived, we took a taxi to our destination. As we arrived at our apartment, he looked at me and said, "I've seen all of New York I want to see. I just want to be with Ammachi." He then spent day after day sitting in her presence.

High on my agenda for this trip was for Mother to know that Sreejit was my son. I was nearly certain that she knew everything already, but I wanted to be sure! The first evening program was very busy so I felt it inappropriate to go for darshan when so many had not yet seen her that year. Since I wanted to be sure Mother saw us together in the hall, however, I positioned us in a place I knew she would pass as she exited. You'd think by now I would have learned to quit trying to control the situation, but not so! As she prepared to leave, she headed in a completely different direction than I had predicted, weaving her way around the room in a random manner. I recognized, with a chuckle, that this was yet another lesson in letting go and did so. She immediately walked up to Sreejit and me and hugged us together! I wept. No desire or lesson is too small for *this* mother!

One Step at a Time
Summer/Fall 1990

Soon after the summer tour, I took my twelve-year-old daughter, Chaitanya, and a friend of hers on a trip to the southwest. We stopped at Bryce Canyon, Utah. As we walked down into the canyon, I started drifting into a deep meditative state. I sensed I had walked into the land of my elevator dream. After a few minutes, Chaitanya started pulling on my arm, obviously bored and wanting to go. I intuited, "This is the right place, the wrong time, the wrong company." I committed to return the following year.

A new phase in my journey was about to begin. My tabla teacher, Joe, had the vision of bringing spiritual messages to people through the music of his rock band, Tribal Therapy. When I told him I wanted to hear his band, he replied he did not think I would like the music, but I was welcome to come.

What occurred inside of me the first time I heard the band's music shocked me to my core. I felt an immediate heart opening and was infused with love and peace. My body started dancing easily to the music, a behavior that was very foreign to me as I generally have "two left feet" when it comes to dancing. I began to attend the band's performances as often as possible. Once again, I was quite astonished by my process. In 1989, Carol Poole became the follower of an Indian guru and in 1990, she becomes a rock band groupie. Unbelievable! What could possibly be next?

As you might recall when I returned from India earlier in the year, I had felt directed to put my energy into learning yoga. That fall my yoga teacher, Aadil, decided he would no longer teach beginning yoga classes. As being near him helped me maintain my sense of connection to India, I felt devastated. I had been participating in his classes, but as I had much less than optimal enthusiasm and dedication, I was certainly not ready for level two. His new policy gave me the "kick" I needed. I found another teacher and began attending three classes a week, with the goal of returning to Aadil's class as soon as possible.

One autumn day, I started feeling agitated. I sensed I was supposed to know the answer to a particular question but could not even determine the question. The question that finally entered my mind was, "If Ammachi asked you to move to India, would you? What is your level of commitment to this process?" While I believed she would never ask such a thing of me, I knew it was important for me to know both my level of commitment and my willingness to be obedient. I felt completely comfortable with my answer, "No, I would not move to India."

Part 3

The Lord is my shepherd, I shall not want; he maketh me to lie down in green pastures. He leadeth me beside the still waters; he restoreth my soul.

He leadeth me in the paths of righteousness for his name's sake. Yea, though I walk through the valley of the shadow of death, I will fear no evil, for thou art with me; thy rod and thy staff they comfort me.

Thou preparest a table before me in the presence of my enemies; thou anointest my head with oil, my cup runneth over. Surely goodness and mercy shall follow me all the days of my life; and I will dwell in the house of the Lord for ever.[1]

Lessons in Many Forms
December 1990- January 1991 India trip

My primary goal for my second trip to India was to reach the point where the primitive physical conditions of the ashram did not bother me. Little did I know what method would be used to help me attain my goal.

My companion that year was Christine, the woman who had accompanied me to the New Hampshire retreat in 1989. We arrived at the Seattle-Tacoma airport early on the morning of our departure, only to

---

[1] *Psalm 23, Holy Bible*, King James Version, 1611.

discover that the plane had mechanical difficulties. We would have to wait while they fixed the problem. Minutes turned into hours. Finally, one of the airline agents told us that the problem was not repairable and we would have to come back the following day. If we followed those instructions, we would not only have to delay our departure but would also miss all of our connecting flights! Going back home was totally unacceptable, so we began looking for another airline to take us to our destination. Ultimately, we discovered we could go to India journeying not west, but east. The airline staff took great care to assure us we would be staying far away from the Persian Gulf, where the war raged. Imagine our surprise and dismay when we landed for fuel in Saudi Arabia!

Once we arrived in Madras, India, we settled in for a good night's sleep, spent the next morning being tourists, and then leisurely headed to the airport, arriving an hour and a half before our plane to Trivandrum was to leave. Upon arrival at the airport, we discovered the flight schedule had been changed and our plane had already departed! Furious and harried, we found a helpful official who offered to phone the appropriate office to determine the departure time of the next flight. He phoned repeatedly without making a connection. After about an hour of attempts, he declared that *this* was not working. He said he would have to walk to the other office to find out the answer. We soon discovered he had spent an hour trying to call an office in the same building, one that was just two doors down the hall. India! When he returned, he informed us that there would be no flight to Trivandrum for two days, and at that time there was only one available seat. He suggested we take the train.

For westerners who have never witnessed an Indian train station, it should be pointed out that it was nearly indescribable in its chaos, noise and odor. Every open area was filled to the rafters with humans and animals. It was literally a sea of humanity, full of travelers carrying baggage and poultry on their heads and beggars asking for money and food. Only the passing of bodies moved the moist, fetid air.

This was a festival time, so the station was even more teeming with travelers than normal. Thousands of people were arriving daily, mostly men dressed in black.[2] We stood in one line after another attempting to buy a train ticket. Each time we reached the front of the line, we were told we had been standing in the wrong line. Finally, we found the foreigners' office where, after waiting for hours, we were informed we were

---

[2] Devotees of Swami Ayyappo.

crazy to expect to purchase a ticket for travel on that same day! The next available time was two days hence and then there was only one seat available. This was becoming a familiar statement!

We sat down in a state of frustration and despair. A man who had been watching us said, "Get in *that* line NOW." I obeyed. I soon discovered that at 5:00 p.m. the tickets for third class accommodations went on sale. I bought two tickets, ecstatic that we had finally found a way to Trivandrum. When our train arrived at the station, a mass of people clamored to get on. I jumped on the train, trying like every one else to push my way in. I felt a hand on my shoulder. I turned around to discover that the hand belonged to a young Malaysian student. "You are NOT going on this train," he said. "Get off NOW." He spoke with such authority, I disembarked immediately. I soon learned that Christine had never even attempted to board the train. She informed me she had decided that if I left on that train, she would go back home.

Once I was off the train, the Malaysian boy told us there was no way we could have survived that experience. He said we would have been standing for eighteen hours, that there were no restroom facilities and that someone would undoubtedly have stolen our luggage. I agreed, I was not ready for *that*! He directed us to travel via bus. He then stood in line for us and attempted, unsuccessfully, to obtain refunds for our train tickets. He accompanied us to the bus station, showed us how to fill out the appropriate forms and indicated in which line we were to stand. He insisted on staying with us until we were actually on the bus. Since our arrival in India, beggars had inundated us. This boy would not even let us reimburse him for expenses he incurred because of us. We felt very graced and very thankful.

While waiting for the bus to arrive, Christine decided to use the public restroom. She came back looking very green. She said that there had been waste products filled with maggots and worms lying all over the restroom. I decided I did not and would not have any need to use that facility.[3]

When the bus came, we were delighted. The seats were very comfortable, not all that different from a Greyhound bus in the United States, although there was no restroom on board. Women were given VIP seats in the front. We believed we "had it made."

---

[3] The condition of the public restrooms in India has improved markedly since that time!

The feeling of having it made lasted only until the bus departed, then I remembered what it was like to travel in India. The bus drove all night at top speed. The streets were filled with holes and the vehicle was constantly dodging people, bicycles, cars, and taxis. The driver blew the horn nonstop. There were only four ten-minute stops during the eighteen-hour trip. We never knew how long the stop would be. When the driver stepped onto the bus, the bus left. Much of the time, we could not even find a restroom. When we did, it often consisted only of an open trench that ran along the side of a large room.

At one point in the trip, when the bus made a fuel stop, I was forced to demand the driver allow me to relieve myself. The driver blew his horn continuously until I got back on the bus. By the time we arrived in Trivandrum, we were tired, miserable and totally incapable of enduring the three-hour taxi ride to the ashram that night. We rented a hotel room and collapsed onto our beds.

The next day, we eagerly hired a taxi and three hours later were at the ashram. We quickly discovered we would be the first people to use the newly completed western toilets and western showers. I was in Heaven! My primary goal had already been met. There was no way I would complain about accommodations at the ashram after our recent experiences. The joy of having western toilets was indescribable!

While in Trivandrum, the thought "I wish Ammachi would ask me about my children," ran through my mind. I wanted her to ask me about all of my children, my biological daughter and my therapy sons and daughters[4], not just Sreejit, who was the son she had met. I did not consider this desire reasonable, as it would require her to be aware of specific details about my life, so I quickly dismissed it.

As I moved through the darshan line that first day, Ammachi seemed very excited to see me. She talked to someone nearby and pointed out that I had arrived. I felt very seen and acknowledged by her, such a difference from the previous year. When she held me she asked me, in English, "Are your children happy?" Once again I was filled with wonder and gratitude. I appreciated the reminder that the best chance of manifesting a desire is to let go of it, especially when near Ammachi!

Repeatedly throughout this visit to the ashram, I experienced being drawn into a state of sleep. Frequently when I sat near Mother, I

---

[4] Clients have the option of making parenting contracts with me as part of their healing process.

would start to feel unbearably drowsy. Before long, I could do nothing other than go to bed. Immediately, I would fall into a deep sleep and have an intense dream. When I woke up, the whole process would start again. I thought perhaps I needed to process thoughts and feelings that my conscious mind was not yet capable of handling. Sleeping would allow my unconscious mind to do whatever work was needed.

I found I had much more energy than the previous year and wished to participate in seva activities.[5] The form of seva that meant the most to me was brick seva. In those days, when bricks were needed for a building project, they were first brought by truck to Vallickavu, the village closest to the ashram. They were then stacked one by one at the side of the road. Next, they were loaded into canoes and taken across the backwaters. Once deposited on the shore of the ashram grounds, the bricks were transferred one at a time to a handcart. When the handcart reached its destination, the bricks were moved via a human chain to their final location, in this case, to the top of the six-story temple. What I liked most about this experience was knowing that every brick I touched during the process had some of my energy in it. Participating gave me both the experience of contributing and the pleasure of knowing that when I left India, a part of me would be able to stay. I realized how much we have lost in the west because we surround ourselves with material things we have had no hand in creating.

When doing the seva, I also experienced great satisfaction at being physically healthy enough to be able to participate. I felt sad that our culture has changed in a way that little physical exertion is demanded of most of us. We have to actually *create* exercise opportunities for ourselves if we want to prevent the deterioration of our bodies.

Ammachi teaches that in order to experience bliss, we must be able to quiet our minds. Repetitive activities such as carrying bricks, scrubbing laundry on rocks, and folding paper at the presses create altered states of consciousness that naturally quiet the mind.

Stephen Gilligan, an Ericksonian hypnotherapist, teaches that our bodies must have trance (i.e., altered state) experiences and that if we do not get that trance in a healthy way, we will create it through unhealthy behaviors such as obsessive thinking, compulsions, and addictions. I realized that, through the seva activity, Ammachi had created a mecha-

---

[5] Seva - service given without thought of reward or personal gain.

nism whereby minds will easily quiet down. I felt sad at how our western life styles and technologies have robbed us of so many of the opportunities to create healthy trance states.

Each year as I review the lessons I am moving through, I see themes emerging. As I examined my lessons that year, the common denominator seemed to be insights into self-indulgence. I thought about the many ways we in the west are self-indulgent in both thought and behavior. I believe we are self-indulgent when we expect immediate gratification, presuming our desires will be realized without any effort on our part. I recalled a woman I had encountered in a New York City program the previous year, who had informed me that she would achieve self-realization soon. I thought that a rather strange pronouncement, so asked what she was doing to make that happen. She said "Nothing." I was shocked!

When we do not receive what we want, we often become angry and self-righteous. That often leads to a pattern of obsessive thinking which in turn may lead to non-productive suffering.

It seemed to me that we in the west are also self-indulgent when we accumulate and hoard material possessions and forget what "enough" is. We are self-indulgent when we knowingly use a disproportionate share of the world's food supply and the world's natural resources such as oil, water, and timber. We are self-indulgent when we overuse natural resources without acknowledging the effect on the environment. We are self-indulgent when we are content to have so much wealth when so much of the world lives in poverty. As I continued to ponder this subject, I recognized that food, sex, alcohol, work, drugs, spending, and gambling addictions each have a self-indulgent component to them.

After musing about the ways I saw our culture being self-indulgent, I looked at my own self-indulgent behaviors of eating when I was not hungry, eating more than I needed, misusing electricity and water, not consistently recycling, and creating more trash than necessary. I resolved to focus on changing these behaviors. I was excited about my insights and looked forward to teaching the material to my clients when I returned to Seattle.

That year I stayed in the women's dorm. One woman in the dorm complained bitterly about how mean Ammachi was being to her. I could not imagine Ammachi being mean to anyone, but heard her complaints and gave them some thought. In the days that followed, I observed how she refused to keep the few "rules" that existed in the ashram. We were expected to attend the morning chanting of the 1000 names of the Divine Mother, the evening bhajan program, and to complete one hour of seva. She did none of that. I asked how long she had been with Ammachi, expecting her to say this was her first year. Instead, she answered, "three years." I recalled Ammachi saying that at first she does whatever it takes to grab our hearts. After we are bonded to her, she starts giving structure and discipline. It seemed to me that refusing to do required activities after three years would certainly have some consequences. When I shared this insight with the woman, she angrily responded, "I come here for nurturing. If I wanted discipline I could stay home." I quickly backed off.

I still could not imagine Ammachi being mean to her, so I began watching their interactions. I could not discern any treatment by Mother that was in any way mean. On the contrary, she seemed to treat the woman in exactly the same way she treated everyone else. This discrepancy bothered me, so I asked the woman what she meant, exactly, by being treated meanly. She replied, "Because she talks to other people while she holds *me*!" Suddenly, everything made sense. I was seeing a clear example of how we create scarcity and misery for ourselves through our attitudes. In this instance, focusing on the fact that Mother was talking to someone else robbed the woman of the pleasure of being held, not to mention the fact that her focus totally obliterated the reality that she

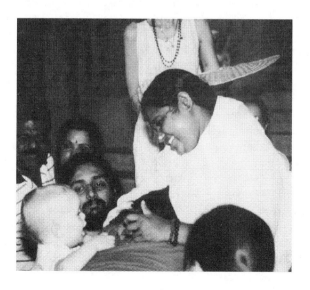

was probably being held two or three times longer than she would have been if Mother was not doing two things at once. She could instead have created abundance for herself by taking the attitude, "Mother, it's fine with me if you forget I'm on your lap. Talk to anyone you like, forever!"

I reflected on ways I make *myself* miserable. I scare myself unnecessarily by worrying about what other people think about me. I do things no one has asked me to do and then get upset when my actions are not appreciated. I do not make effort to spend time with friends, and then feel resentful when I am not included in their plans. So much of the pain we suffer is not externally caused but is simply the consequence of our attitudes and behaviors. I recalled a cartoon I had been given years before which stated, "Lord, help me meet this self-imposed and totally unnecessary challenge!"

Sometime in 1990, I had stopped using the Krishna mantra entirely. In the fall of 1990, I decided to confront my avoidance by starting to say the mantra again, trusting I would be able to learn from whatever came up. There was one small problem, I was not sure what words were in the mantra. I started saying it to the best of my memory. Not much later, on a trip to the California ashram, I told Swami Paramatmananda the mantra as I was repeating it. His eyes grew very big. "Do NOT say that!" he exclaimed. He instructed me to consult with Swami Ramakrishnananda as soon as I arrived in India so I could find out what my mantra was *supposed* to be. To this day, I have no idea what I had been saying, but took refuge in Ammachi's stories that what is most important is a spirit of innocence! When I arrived in India, I talked to Swami Ramakrishnananda and found out how to say the mantra correctly.

As I write about the preceding incident, I am reminded of a story that I heard years later. A friend of mine was recalling a time when he walked by the hut where Mother was giving darshan and found a group of brahmacharis outside laughing, practically to the point of hysteria. He asked what was happening and was told that inside a western devotee was singing a song in Malayalam with great passion and devotion. The devotee thought he was saying, *Come, Mother, Come* when in reality he was singing, *Go, Donkey, Go*. Mother, of course was responding only to the devotion. I was amused to think of what else she must hear us unwittingly say. I marveled at her ability to keep a straight face!

When in the presence of Ammachi, or other enlightened beings, one is often inundated by a deluge of critical thoughts. Some people wait until the thoughts subside before they come to her. Mother says this is like waiting until you are well before you go to the doctor. The emergence of the critical thoughts is part of a purification process. When the thoughts bubble up, we have the opportunity for insight into the personal issues we need to address.

One year, a woman I met at the ashram in India shared an experience that had happened to a friend of hers the previous year at a Dallas program. This friend was from one of the states in the South. While absorbed in meditation, the thought "I can't believe I'm bowing to a *nigger!*" came into his mind. He was horrified. He looked at Mother, only to discover her looking back at him, laughing. Recalling this story helps me to remember two important facts: 1) The critical thoughts are part of a normal and healthy process and, 2) the nonsense that flows through our mind does not hurt Mother in any way.

Swami Paramatmananda once shared an incident that has also been of value to me. In his early years at the ashram, he was often critical of the behavior of the other brahmacharis. One day Mother looked at him sternly, saying "Let my children be where they are!" This story reminds me that we are all on a journey, struggling to find our way. For the most part, we do not intentionally cause harm or do disrespectful things.

While I had generally been able to watch my critical thoughts with a minimum of discomfort, this year was an exception. A very distasteful and upsetting form of thinking emerged from within me. Whenever I looked at Mother during Devi Bhava, I found myself thinking, "That is a cheap-looking, probably fake silver crown you are wearing." "You are fat." and "You are ugly." Those three thoughts came into my mind again and again. I was truly distressed because I knew she could read my mind if she wanted to. I was very relieved that she did not acknowledge them. I tried everything I could imagine to stop the thoughts, but nothing worked.

I decided I was being given an opportunity to learn to eliminate distracting or negative thoughts through the use of my mantra. Therefore, as soon as the thoughts arose, I acknowledged them and started repeating my mantra. I learned that my mind could work on two or three "tracks" at the same time. I found that if I sped up the mantra until the other thoughts were drowned out, my focus would soon be solely on the mantra. Although it took about a year for those particular thoughts to disappear completely, it did not take nearly that long to learn to convert the negative energy I had towards them.

Several times since 1987, in guided imagery experiences or in dreams, I had, in one form or another, received the gift of blue-white light. Each experience had so profoundly moved me that I decided to ask Ammachi what the light represented. She informed me that blue-white light is the color that occurs when the soul merges with God. She added as an afterthought, "That is good." Good... what an understatement!

During this visit I accompanied Ammachi and other ashram residents on a three-day trip to a town near Cochin. Prior to the trip, a woman told me about an incident that had occurred when a friend of hers visited the ashram of Sai Baba, a guru from another part of India. She described her friend's husband as an adamant skeptic. On the last day of their visit, he told his wife he would not believe in Sai Baba unless "that character" created a rainbow for him. That same day as Sai Baba was strolling through the crowd that had gathered for a glimpse of him, he passed this man. After a moment, the guru turned and came back to him. Sai Baba said "Hello, character!" and then pointed to the sky. There in front of him was a rainbow, one which went straight up and down! The man was mightily impressed!

The day of my trip with Ammachi arrived. As we drove throughout the countryside, I took in the beautiful scenery. It was a glorious day. The sky was very blue, not a cloud was to be seen. At one point as I gazed at the sky, I found a bright rainbow in my line of vision. It was only half-formed, starting in the middle of the sky and descending to the ground. How could a rainbow be formed when there were neither clouds nor haze? How could it start in the middle of the sky when there was nothing there to hide the other half? I was filled with wonder. My inner skeptic was impressed.

As we approached our destination, we noticed crowds forming everywhere. There were literally tens of thousands of people lining the streets and the rooftops. There were elephants and dancers. What an awesome sight it was! As we disembarked, the crowd swarmed toward Ammachi. Men formed human chains around her to protect her and to guide her through the streets. This was my first experience at seeing how people would do anything to be near her, even if their fervor put her at risk of being trampled. Mother gave individual darshan to about 7,000 people that night and again the next morning, once again evidencing her seemingly endless compassion.

For most of this trip to India, I had an unwarranted sense that I was going to have to leave the ashram earlier than scheduled. As in the previous year, I experienced almost continual grief at knowing I would eventually have to return to my United States home. The thought of the emotional trauma of an abrupt departure was almost too much to bear. I decided to be prepared to leave early, even though there was no reasonable explanation for my dread.

Seventy-two hours before my international flight was to leave Madras, I traveled to Oachira, a nearby village, to confirm my flights. That was not as simple as it might sound. After taking a motorized rickshaw to Oachira, I discovered the only public telephone sat on a desk in the middle of an alley. Any phone call attracted a small but curious crowd of onlookers. A man sat at the desk, dialing requested numbers. After many attempts to get through to the airline, a connection was finally made. The woman on the other end of the line directed me to come to Trivandrum, three hours away, to confirm the flight. She then hung up on me. I had the telephone man redial the number. Luckily, someone who was willing to confirm my reservation over the phone answered the call. Moments later, however, I was informed that my name was not on the reservation list. My reservation, according to the agent, was worthless as long as my name was not on his list. He instructed me to call back in twenty minutes. At that time he told me to call back in an hour. An hour later he said, "Call back in four hours." I headed back to Amritapuri, feeling frustrated and defeated.

On the drive back, I realized if I returned to Oachira in four hours I would miss my last opportunity to hear Mother sing. I felt devastated. In tears, I told Swami Amritatmananda (then Br. Rao) of my dilemma. He told me not to worry, *he* would handle the problem.

At 10:00 p.m., I checked in with Swami Amritatmananda and discovered he had been able to place me on a standby list. I would, however, have to leave the ashram at five o'clock the next morning. I felt immensely grateful that I had been "warned" for days of an early departure, and as a result I was emotionally and physically prepared.

I made standby and left Trivandrum for Madras the next day. That meant I arrived in Madras two nights before my international flight was scheduled to depart. Fortunately, the ashram had made arrangements for me to stay with people who took very good care of me. A major problem existed, however. I was not alone. Sharing my room was an army of red ants that left me covered with hundreds of bites, the remnants of which lasted for weeks following my return to the United States.

The next morning, I said goodbye to my hosts and hustled off to find other, less painful, accommodations. I was unwilling to go to the $120 per night hotel my travel agent had booked. (It seemed immoral to me to live that luxuriously in India.) I decided to ask someone at the airport for the name of a moderately priced hotel. It did not occur to me that what they would consider to be "moderately" priced and what I would consider moderate would be vastly different.

The good news was that the room cost only six dollars a night. The problem was that I got what I paid for! The bed had no sheets and there were no towels. Both the bathroom and the main door had multiple six-inch bolts attached. I wondered if I should be concerned for my safety. It was, however, clean and ant-free! I was exhausted, emotionally and physically, so I decided to stay.

I assumed that this was not the kind of place where one could reliably ask for a "wake-up call", and that presented me with another problem. My international flight departed very early the next morning and my travel companion had returned to the United States the previous week, taking the alarm clock with her.

My dilemma reminded me of a story Swamiji had shared only days before. He had described an incident which had occurred early in his relationship with Ammachi. Mother had instructed him to start some task at 2:00 a.m., saying she would awaken him at the appropriate time. Since she would be giving darshan to the devotees who had come for Devi Bhava at that time, Swamiji doubted Mother would actually wake him up. As a result, he set an alarm clock, just in case! A minute before the alarm was to sound, a picture of Mother fell off its mount on the wall and hit him on the head. The following day, Mother told him that if he had trusted her, she would have come to awaken him. Since he had chosen not to trust, he had been given a much less gentle, and less desirable, wake-up call!

I recognized the situation in which I now found myself had some remarkable similarities to Swamiji's story. Swamiji had taught us that if we ask Mother to do something for us, she will do it. I wondered if I was being "tested." This was certainly an opportunity to let go and trust. I rationalized, however, that she had not told *me* she would awaken me, and that I was not as close to her as Swamiji. In addition, the stakes were much too high. I was not about to experiment with trust and then miss my flight! As a result, I spent most of the night looking at my watch. At one point, I noticed there were two more hours before I had to get up. I thought I stayed awake from that point, but when I looked at my watch, shortly thereafter, I discovered the entire two hours had passed. With wonder, I realized I had been "awakened" at the exact time I needed to arise, even though I had chosen not let go and trust that she would take care of me. I was extremely relieved that my consequence for not trusting was fatigue, as opposed to a delay in my departure from India!

I'm Changing!
Winter/Spring 1991

My transition back into life in the United States went much smoother than the previous year. I had arranged ahead of time to receive some hypnotherapy, focused on integrating the two parts of my life, upon my return. I still experienced grief about not living at the ashram and frustration over the materialism and what I believed to be misplaced priorities of the American lifestyle.

I noted more changes in my attitudes and ways of being in the world. I was continuing to soften and become more feminine and nurturing. My attitude towards money was changing. I sensed that a portion of my money should be considered God's, not mine. If I felt "directed" to use money for a particular project, I would do so. I also noticed a change in my attitude about my children. I now felt that they were God's children, not "mine." I had been given the gift of facilitating their growth into adulthood.

Claiming and Being Claimed
1991 Summer Tour

I decided to attend all four of the summer retreats, (one in Washington, two in California and one in Rhode Island) plus spend time with Mother during some of the public programs in Seattle, Vancouver, San Ramon, New York and Boston. During the first few programs in Vancouver, I experienced anger and grief at not being in India. I wanted to be in the temple in India, hearing Ammachi singing with fifty brahmacharis not six!

I continued experiencing grief so immense that I was beginning to feel crazy. There was no rational, here and now explanation for my level of emotion. I missed India but I did not really want to live there. I knew some of my emotion was separation grief, but even so my level of energy seemed excessive.

Generally, Mother will not answer questions about past-life experiences, but I decided to present her with my theory anyway. I told her I believed I had lived with her in an ashram before and that I grieved to return to that familiar "home." I added that I thought my "job" in this lifetime was to be in service in the world and to learn to feel connected to her when I was not with her. It seemed to me that it was fine for me to come to the ashram every year, but that I should not live there. When my comments were translated, Ammachi responded, "I recognize you." I looked at the translator, puzzled. "She is telling you, you are right," he said. My eyes filled with tears. She had said she knew *me*! I experienced the joy of being known and the relief of having my reasoning validated. I was not crazy. There was a logical, albeit unusual, explanation for my overwhelming grief. I was thankful she had been willing to set aside her normal practice of withholding past-life information.

By now, I was aware that I experienced different forms of grief. I grieved being separated from Ammachi and my home in India. In addition, my soul grieved being separated from God, that is, the original separation. Some times I was clear about which form of grief I was experiencing. At other times, I had no idea which was present.

I have a hard time finding words to describe what happens to me during bhajans. It is as if every cell in my body comes alive. Tremendous surges of joy flow through me. At times I sense that a part of me is somewhere else, at a party to which I, in my conscious state, have not been invited. I used to resent not being "invited to my own party." Then it occurred to me that my grief would be even more intense if I knew what I was leaving. I decided this was yet another demonstration of Mother taking care of me and was thankful that I had someone to guide my process.

Throughout the first portion of the summer tour, numerous people told me they had asked Mother for permission to come to India. It had never even occurred to me to ask for permission to come to the ashram. I began to worry that I had acted presumptuously. During the California retreat, I decided I needed to address the issue. I told Mother, through the translator, that I recognized I may have acted inappropriately and if so, I was sorry. I asked for permission to come to India that year. I feared asking the question, because the thought of hearing "No" was almost more than I could bear. As the question was translated, I watched Ammachi's affect and anxiously awaited her answer. She looked concerned and then said, "I am your Mother. You do not have to ask *anyone's* permission to come home. You just come home." The impact of hearing that simple sentiment was overwhelming after having been told for twenty years that I was not welcome in my parents' home. Like so many times before, I knelt and wept in gratitude. Even as I write this, my tears flow.

After two years of trying to make peace with the Krishna mantra, I felt I had accomplished that task. I still did not feel connected to Krishna, however, so I decided to ask for help. I told Mother I did not feel connected, and asked her to help me love him. She looked at me and said, "If you do not feel connected to Krishna, change your mantra." I could not believe what I heard! After criticizing myself briefly for not having talked with her years before, I realized I had not wasted time and energy. I had learned much from this leela.[6] I calmed myself, and at the first opportunity, changed my mantra! This time I made Mother the focus of my devotional energy.

An interesting event occurred during the Seattle retreat. A Jewish friend, who had come from Florida to attend the retreat, was disturbed to see people bow to Ammachi. She refused to do so herself. She was aware that her resistance stemmed from her religious background. Exodus 20: 3-5 states:

> *Thou shalt have no other gods before me. Thou shalt not make unto thee any graven image, or any likeness of any thing that is in heaven above, or that is in the water under the earth. Thou shalt not bow down thyself to them, nor serve them, for I the Lord thy God am a jealous God.*[7]

As bowing is totally a matter of personal choice, her decision not to prostrate more than acceptable. During the Devi Bhava program, I watched my friend inch her way through the darshan line. Minutes before her turn to be held, I watched with amazement as my friend's head descended to the floor in the typical Eastern style of prostration. I could not believe it! I was intrigued and eager to hear her story. Later, she told me as she had approached Mother, her body had spontaneously moved into that position. In that instant, she "blacked out," waking moments later in Ammachi's arms. I was reminded of another scripture, Phillipians 2: 10-11 that states:

> *That at the name of Jesus every knee should bow, of things in heaven, and things in earth, and things under the earth. And that every tongue should confess that Jesus Christ is Lord, to the glory of God the Father.*[8]

---

[6] Leela - God's play
[7] *Exodus 20: 3-5, Holy Bible*, King James Version, 1611.
[8] *Phillipians 2:10-11, Holy Bible*, King James Version, 1611.

Perhaps her higher self could see and respond to the presence of Divine Energy even though her conscious self would not.

Swamiji teaches classes during each of the retreats. He often lectures about the importance of being obedient to the guru. The spiritual path can be dangerous and it is important to have a guide. My yoga teacher, Aadil, once wrote, "Only when we are willing to sacrifice egoistic independence and thought-bound logic for the teacher's whim, are we on the way to discovering freedom."[9] That obedience, however, is not to come from blind faith. Ammachi has said that there are many false gurus and it is extremely important that we pick our teachers very carefully. We must scrutinize their life and their actions to be sure they are a model of what they teach, that is, do they "walk their talk." She also suggests we look at the fruit of the guru's work, especially observing the people around them. Do their disciples have qualities we wish to develop?

Even if the teacher is worthy of devotion, it is important that obedience not be without discrimination. Mother tells the story of a guru and a disciple who traveled in an oxcart. While the guru slept, the walking stick he carried fell from the cart. The disciple ignored it and continued on. When the guru awoke, he noticed the walking stick was missing and asked where it was. The disciple told him the stick had fallen from

Mother and Swamiji.

[9] Aadil Palkhivala, *Yoga Centers Newsletter*, Bellevue: Yoga Centers, 3(1): 1, January-August 1992.

the cart. The guru was very angry and told the disciple that in the future he was to pick up anything that fell from the cart. As they continued on the journey, the ox dropped a load of dung, which the disciple obediently picked up and threw into the cart, right onto the face of the guru! The guru was enraged. He then made a list of everything of value in the cart and told the disciple that if anything fell out, he was to consult the list. If the item was on the list, he was to stop the cart and pick it up. They drove on and the guru fell asleep. The cart hit a pothole and the guru fell out of the cart. The disciple dutifully consulted the list, found the guru was not on it, and drove on. The obvious moral, "Obedience is never to be without discrimination!" We were given a mind and we are expected to use it.

Obedience is something that must be learned. Swamiji suggested we say we will surrender to Ammachi's will even though we know we do not mean it completely. Having the intention to surrender is the first step. Once we discover the rewards that come with surrender, it will develop naturally.

I find myself struggling with the frustration of not being able to find words to adequately describe what it is like to be with Mother. What words can describe what happens when one looks into the eyes of, or for that matter is looked at by, a woman who can see parts of me that I don't even know exist, whose eyes radiate compassion and love, who loves me with all the love of God yet no more nor no less than any other being on earth. What words can I use to describe what it feels like to sink into the embrace of one whose every cell is filled with the love of God, who somehow is able to take away my sicknesses and my sorrows. How can I describe watching her hour after hour, day after day, year after year, seeing how her every expression engenders feelings within me and others. Her laughter starts laughter rippling through the crowd. When she reflects the sadness or concern of those who bring their pain to her, tears well up in the eyes of those around her. How can I find the words to describe the overwhelming sense of love I feel as I gaze at her, my heart sometimes feeling as if it will explode? Love for her who knows me, who guides me, who is there when I need her, one who is the mother for whom my soul has hungered for lifetimes.

How can I describe the Devi Bhava nights, where the music flows hour after hour, singing till my heart is totally content, until I finally have the experience of being fully satiated, of having experienced "enough?"

How can I fully describe what it is like to be the recipient of the flower petals she showers on the crowd at the end of each Devi Bhava, of receiving them as if they were petals descending from the heavens? How can I fully describe the sensations that flow within me as she stands gazing at the crowd she has so recently showered with flowers, appearing more Goddess than human. Watching, with tears pouring down my face, pondering, "Does she really know how much I love her?" "Does she really know how much difference she is making in my life?" As she looks at us, is she feeling satisfied at seeing the results of her work? As she looks at us, is she feeling that she has accomplished what she has come here to do?

How do I find the words to describe the profound peace that comes as she steps backwards, the curtains close, and the final prayers begin?

As I struggled with the impossible task of fully sharing these experiences, I found myself repeatedly compelled to listen to a tape of English devotional songs. Eventually, laughing at how long it took me to get the "message," I realized I could use the lyrics from some of the songs on that tape as a way of sharing others' experience of Mother.

Mother, please come to me, your love is my all.
Mother, please bless my soul, your gaze is my call.
Divine Mother, help me to believe.
That this sweet love you have, I can receive.

Mother, I bloom in your light, your love is so pure.
Mother, you nourish my light, my flower's for you.
O Divine Mother, help me to believe
That this sweet love you have, I can receive.

Mother, your eyes so clear, they sing to my soul.
Mother those you hold near, their hearts become whole.
O Divine Mother, help me to believe
That this sweet love you have, I can receive.

Mother, I feel your love, in your radiant smile.
Mother, you know this child, stay with me awhile.
O Divine Mother, help me to believe
That this sweet love you have, I can receive.[10]

O Divine Mother,
My heart belongs to Thee;
And flowers of devotion,
I offer at Thy blue lotus feet.
O Divine Mother, you are deeper than the sky;

---

[10] "Mother, Please Come To Me," *Jaya: Songs to Ammachi*, Madison: Blackburnian Records, 1989.

More golden than the shimmering sun
As it sets behind the mountains at night.
My heart at rest in your warm bosom
As I dream of the bliss to come.
When every soul ever born,
Realizes your love.[11]

Mother, as you stand here now in your blissful form
Your flowers, they shower me and I feel reborn
I love you; I love you; I love you.[12]

Going Where the Spirit Says Go
Summer/Fall 1991

One morning in early August, I decided to walk to the service station near my home, inexplicably taking a different route from the one I would normally use. As I passed an open field, I noticed a sign that read, "Tent Revival- Starting August 28." I felt a huge "YES!" arise throughout my whole being. I was a bit shocked by my reaction, as I was still quite angry at the Christian church, particularly the fundamentalist portion of it.

I awaited the revival with great anticipation. When that night finally arrived, my friend Joan and I attended the opening program. The revival was sponsored by the Church of God in Christ (COGIC), a black Pentecostal denomination. As I entered the tent, a woman, whom I later discovered to be a minister's wife, took my arm and ushered us to seats directly in front of hers. I soon discovered that Joan and I were the only white people in the tent. Although I felt very conspicuous and uneasy, that feeling shifted quickly into ecstatic joy once the music began. I breathed in whiffs of Ammachi's fragrance numerous times during the evening. I took that to indicate her presence and support of my being at the program.[13]

---

[11] "O Divine Mother," *Jaya: Songs to Ammachi*, Madison: Blackburnian Records, 1989.

[12] "Mother As You Stand Here Now," *Jaya: Songs to Ammachi*, Madison: Blackburnian Records, 1989.

[13] Ammachi will occasionally "check up" on devotees, coming in her subtle body. When this happens devotees often experience her fragrance filling their nostrils.

The night was wondrous. When the people filled with Spirit energy, they began spontaneous and uncontrollable dancing. The congregation would flow with the process in a way that seemed similar to our group therapy process. They would surround the person dancing, protecting them from bumping into chairs and hurting themselves. Nothing else would happen, that is, sermon, offering, or choir selections as long as someone was showing this spontaneous manifestation of God's presence. My inner voice said, "You can learn to be fully in your body here."

I attended almost every night of the revival's fourteen-day run. I discovered that some of the church's teachings were very similar to Ammachi's, others I needed only to reframe in order to accept. The gospel music affected me in much the same way as the bhajans. Of particular delight was the church's focus on gratitude, that is, praising God and thanking Him for what He has done for us. One way the congregation praised God was by clapping while chanting the mantra, *Thank you Jesus, Thank you Jesus, Thank you Jesus.* Praising God in this way created sensations of immeasurable joy within me. One of the ministers taught that worry is an insult to God. They suggested we ask for what we want and then start praising and thanking God as if the desire had already manifested.

Almost every night, the ministers performed some kind of "laying on of hands." The parishioners usually formed a line and were quickly touched on the forehead by the minister. One night, there was a minister who gave much more individual attention to those attending. I could not decide whether or not to get in the line. I wanted to, but being one of only two white faces in an all black crowd, I did not want to feel any more visible than I did already. Joan, who also felt Mother's presence, closed her eyes and internally asked if she should go through the line. She experienced Mother laughing and saying "Sure, go ahead." Watching Joan go through the line did not help in my decision making process, I was still torn. Then a thought drifted to the surface of my mind, "You keep saying you are fully committed to this process. If you are, then GET IN LINE!" I joined the line!

I soon found myself at the head of the line facing the preacher, his hand reaching for me. When he touched my forehead, I went into an immediate and pronounced altered state of consciousness. I stumbled back to Joan. As I leaned against her, my body began to shake and the tears started pouring. I heard two people say, "Just go through it, you are okay." Since my eyes were closed at the time, I could only guess that the two people talking were the minister whose church was coordinating the revival and his wife.

I focused on my breathing and let the process evolve. When the altered state lifted slightly, about twenty minutes later, I discovered the person supporting me was the very preacher who had touched me at the front of the congregation. I had resisted going through the line in an effort to not be singled-out and now I found that I had been, for some twenty minutes, the single focus of the cleric himself! I laughed and shook my head at the leela.

When Joan and I walked out into the night air, I quickly discovered that unless I was walking or talking with some of the others present, I went quickly back into the altered state. Since I was totally incapable of driving a car, Joan and I walked the long way home, and then talked for a while. When Joan left, I called another friend and chatted for an hour. Then I went to bed, assuming I would be able to sleep quite easily. The moment I lay down, my arms began spontaneously thrashing around. This seizure-like agitation happened every forty-five seconds or so, each episode lasting around five seconds. The process lasted about an hour. Early on, I had a strong sense that what I was experiencing was kundalini[14] energy release. I believed there was no reason to fear what was occurring. I *knew* I needed simply to breathe and let the process evolve naturally.

The next day when I told friends about my experience, I kept describing the minister as a huge man in a white robe, a man well over six feet tall! When I later discovered he was actually about 5' 8", I had immediate evidence that I had been in an altered state of consciousness!

I was not ready for the revival to end. I learned that the revival's sponsor, Power House Church of God in Christ, was only three blocks from my house. I wanted to attend the church but knowing that many of their beliefs were *very* different from mine, I did not want to go under false pretenses. (They believe the only path to God is through Jesus and that the only infallible word of God is the Bible.) Consequently, I made an appointment to talk with the minister, Pastor Jenkins.

I knew the slight opening I had to Christianity was largely due to an incident that had occurred the previous year. A young woman had been referred to me by a therapist she had called via the Yellow Pages. I was quite surprised, as I did not think I knew anyone who advertised in the Yellow Pages. I was concerned when the woman said she was Pente-

---

[14] Kundalini - spiritual energy depicted as the serpent power coiled at the root of the spine which rises to the head by spiritual practices, leading one to Liberation.

costal. The language sometimes used by group members during "anger work" had been offensive to previous fundamentalist Christian clients. I also thought their therapy process had been hampered by their belief that everything that happened to them was God's will. In my mind, this attitude interfered with their taking a proactive approach to solving problems. When I shared my concerns, the woman assured me these issues would not be a problem

She then related something that had occurred during one of her recent meditations. Jesus had come, chanting "*Shanti, shanti, shanti,*" the Sanskrit word for peace. The thought of Jesus speaking to her in Sanskrit astonished me. I then told her my therapy center was named the Shantini Center, *shantini* being the feminine derivative of the word *shanti*. From that moment on we both *knew* we were to work together.

When I met with Pastor Jenkins, I spoke of Ammachi and of many of my spiritual beliefs. I informed him that I wanted to start attending his church services but needed to hear that he would not spend any energy trying to "save" me, now that he knew more about me. His response amazed me. He told me that if Ammachi was doing the kind of healings I described and if she was capable of launching me onto such an intense spiritual path, she must be doing something right. He said he believed in preaching what God told him to preach. Therefore, he was likely to say things in church that I did not like. He suggested, in those instances, that I assume he was being given guidance for someone other than me. He said his approach was to follow the direction God gives to him and then get out of the way and let God do His own work! His openness was wonderful and astounding, certainly challenging my stereotypes of fundamental Christianity. I had a similar, though less detailed, conversation with his wife, who also welcomed my participation.

The day following the revival's end, I started feeling the panicky grief that arises when I leave India. I became so overwhelmed with emotion, I called Pastor Jenkins and asked for his help. We sat on the church stairs and talked for about an hour. I told him how much I missed being with my teacher in India. I likened my feelings to what it would be like for him to in the presence of Jesus and then have to leave. He had tears in his eyes as he told me about his yearly trip to Memphis, where 40,000 people come together to worship and praise God. He said it was always hard for him to leave Memphis, but at the same time knew that it was important for him to be available to his church family. I felt heard and understood.

The Pastor had built Power House church from the ground up. I could see he put all of his time and energy into doing God's work and that he had the same level of passion for his path as I had for mine. I told him how much I enjoyed the physical labor that occurs at Ammachi's ashram in India and asked if I could help him in similar work at Power House. He told me about his projects and suggested ways I could help.

I also shared my difficulty in disciplining myself to meditate daily. I asked if he would allow me to meditate and pray in the church each morning. To my amazement, he said, "Yes." A fundamentalist Christian minister was opening his church to someone of an entirely different faith! All of my stereotypes were being challenged and consequently were falling away. That hour of sharing was a very important experience for me, and I suspect for him as well.

I started praying at the church each weekday morning. One day, someone entered the back of the church while I was chanting a Sanskrit chant. I assumed it was Pastor Jenkins, so I continued. As I left the church, one of the deacons came up to me, demanding to know who I was and what I was doing. I answered him to the best of my ability. Shortly thereafter, I called Pastor Jenkins and related the story of the confrontation. I was concerned that my actions would get him "in trouble" with the church members. He told me not to worry and assured me he would handle the situation. When I saw the deacon the following Sunday, he was very friendly and open. I was astounded and more than a little curious about how Pastor Jenkins had managed to help him convert his energy so entirely.

Thus, the unusual ways that Ammachi had given me to stay connected with her and with God continued. In 1989, I became the devotee of a guru. In 1990 I became a band groupie. Now in 1991, I was attending a black Pentecostal church! After spending years disgusted with Christianity, I found that incredible. I continue to be an active participant in that church to this day. The church and its congregation have come to mean more to me than words can express.

I soon learned that the denomination had many churches near my home and that one or the other of them was almost always having a revival. What I had been given was the opportunity to be surrounded in the energy of devotional music as often as I desired. It was becoming easier and easier for me to learn from their sermons, reframing what needed to be reframed. I knew I was growing spiritually. My ability to live in the present, as opposed to focusing on the past or future, was enhanced by being able to feel so much joy on a day-to-day or week-to-week basis rather than yearning for what I would feel during the summer tour or on my yearly trip to India. I realized I was receiving many of the benefits of ashram life while still living in the world.

I experienced a major jolt the day I first heard Pastor Jenkins express strong condemnation and mocking of homosexuality. I was frantic! I believed staying and listening was a betrayal to my own values as well as a betrayal of my homosexual clients, yet being at the church brought me so much joy I could not imagine leaving. I was in a quandary. I could not leave and I could not stay.

It finally occurred to me that I could ask for support and advice from someone at the California ashram. After describing my experiences to Br. Ron, he responded incredulously, "I don't get it. You say that you feel close to Mother there, your entire meditation pattern has changed (that is, I was meditating!), you are experiencing exhilarating joy, and you would even consider giving all of that up because of one teaching? You are expecting these people to be fully self-realized saints. That is unreasonable." He added that if the congregation ever became uncomfortable with my presence, I should leave as the church was *their* home. His comments helped me to immediately put the situation into perspective.

As the days passed, I realized the enormity of the opportunity I had been given. My pattern with my father was to get angry and leave (I lose) or tell him off through word or deed and then be thrown out (I lose). Now I had the opportunity to stay and develop a constructive relationship with a father figure whose beliefs differed from mine. I knew I had much to learn from Pastor Jenkins and that any influence I would have on him would be from the silent witness of living my own faith.

During the spring, I had begun preparation for a four-day fall trip to Bryce Canyon. I invited many friends to come along. Several agreed to join me but then, one by one they backed out. Eventually, I realized this was a trip I was supposed to make alone.

At one point, I considered canceling the trip, as some part of me feared taking the journey alone. I also felt conflicted because I wanted to spend some time at the California ashram and knew there was no way I could go both places. Over time, it became clear that the Bryce trip was to be the priority.

Bryce Canyon, Utah.

I left for Bryce mid-September. The canyons were awe-inspiring and I loved being there. I took a six-hour hike down into the canyon, a hike that was labeled strenuous. I do almost no physical exercise, other than occasional yoga, so was very excited that I was able to complete the hike without any significant difficulty.

On my second night, as I lounged in my hotel room, my inner voice started saying, "Go to church tomorrow." My response was, "You have got to be kidding, I have only dirty blue jeans and tennis shoes." Nevertheless, the voice continued. I searched the phone book but could not see any reasonable way to follow the direction.

I awoke Sunday with the same imperative running through my mind. I turned on the television, assuming I would find a station broadcasting a church service. I did not. Next, I turned on the radio and immediately located a church service in progress. The minister was saying that the voice of God is most often the first voice we hear inside. What usually follows is a flood of discounting messages telling us why God's message will not work, "You can't do that," "That's wrong," "It will never work," "Do this instead." He said that the quiet voice of God may make another attempt or two, but if we ignore it, it will eventually fade. The pastor said we must learn to follow the direction of the first voice. I believed that this was the message I was supposed to hear. As I pondered the sermon, I realized I could identify numerous examples of the quiet voice followed by the distracters in my life and in the lives of my clients.

Later that year, a COGIC missionary taught additional information about responding to God's directives. I will share it here, even though it is out of sequence. She said when God directs us to do something, our response is to be, "Yes, Lord." If, however, the instruction seems in our judgment to be inappropriate, such as being told to go to church when all we have to wear is dirty blue jeans, our next statement should be, "Make the way, Lord." She taught that God will inevitably create the opportunity for us follow His direction.

I had not planned to return to Seattle until late Monday, but this year's trip to Bryce seemed complete. I had no desire to spend a day in Las Vegas, my port of departure, so called to check on the possibility of an early morning flight. I discovered a flight from Las Vegas to Seattle that allowed me a half-day layover in San Francisco, thereby giving me the opportunity to spend several hours at Ammachi's ashram in San Ramon! I believed I was being given my original desire, that of traveling to Bryce *and* the ashram, as a reward for being willing to follow the direction of my inner voice on each step of the journey.

During my first trip to India in 1990, the thought, "Michael is supposed to be here" flowed through my mind continually. (You may remember is that Michael was Sreejit's birth name.) I mentioned him so frequently that many of my ashram friends did not even realize I had a daughter. Sreejit had shown no interest in accompanying me on my previous trips, so I was astounded when, after spending a day in deep meditation, he said, "I'm going to India." Therefore, as fall arrived, Sreejit and I started planning a trip to India!

Sunset in India.

PART 4

Kali danced vigorously, the sounds 'jhilam, jhilam' of her anklets resounding everywhere. Then Bhairavi shook Her body; She brandished Her sword, and then with a roar, She cut away the last vestiges of my mind.

She waved Her trident in front of me, then exorcised the "me" in me. She made me selfless and catapulted me onto the path of the Self. What I had been holding onto as something dear was lost forever. Durga laughed at me, who was totally nonplussed!

I bowed down, confessed all to this ferocious form of the Divine Mother, who was standing in front of me, eyes rolling, tongue sticking out. Kalika smiled at me; it was like the full moon flooding me with its cool refreshing light. Ambika filled my mind with clarity, with ineffable peace.[1]

Lessons in My Lap!
December 1991- February 1992 India visit

As I looked back at my previous sojourns to India, I realized that Ammachi had in each case given lessons that pushed my traveling companions to the absolute limits of their tolerance. Lynn had a difficult time even being in a third world country and Christine's episode with the train station nearly sent her packing. This year, I found myself guiding seven members of the Seattle satsang[2] to the ashram. My hope was that the challenge of group travel would be challenge enough. Our trip to the ashram was uneventful, although several travelers felt momentarily over-

---

[1]Excerpts from "Jhilam Jhilam Chilankakal," *1994 Bhajan Supplement*, San Ramon: Mata Amritanandamayi Center, p. 38-39.

[2]Satsang - a spiritual discourse by a sage or scholar; a spiritual gathering. In this case, satsang refers to a group of Ammachi's devotees who meet weekly to sing and meditate.

whelmed by the intensity of their introduction to India. The trip had flowed so smoothly, I had the rather absurd thought, "Maybe this year my whole visit to the ashram will be relaxed, peaceful and joyful."

As you might remember, when I arrived at the ashram the previous year, Ammachi had given me a very special greeting, enthusiastically pointing out to others that I had arrived. I knew better than to expect that level of welcome again, but was not prepared for what was to come.

I was carrying a shell someone in Seattle had asked me to give to Mother. I was filled with many negative judgments about the gift, part of me not understanding why anyone would send Mother a shell when the earth at the ashram is made of shells. At the same time, I was aware that this particular shell meant a great deal to the woman and was therefore a special gift. I knew also that the woman had no way of knowing how many shells were imbedded in the ashram land, and like any other mother, Ammachi would appreciate any gift given to her with love. Regardless, I could not shake the negative judgments. When I arrived at the front of the darshan line, Ammachi showed no sign of recognition. She took the shell and pulled me across her lap. She then laughed and talked to everyone else in the room before proceeding to greet the next person in line without giving me so much as a glance or a hug.

I had no doubt that she knew me, so was not jolted by her seeming lack of recognition. What disturbed me was my belief that she had been laughing because she thought that the shell was from me. I could endure being ignored but being made the fool was intolerable! I sat in the back of the darshan hut with tears streaming down my cheeks. Later, when Sreejit sat down beside me, I asked what he had witnessed as Mother held me. As expected by the wiser part of me, her laughter had nothing to do with me. As she held me, she had been laughing and talking with some boys in the audience! So much for this being a trip of peace and relaxation! I had been given immediate entry into my weak points.

My second night in India was a Devi Bhava night. I was so exhausted that I found it impossible to attend the whole program. When I could stay awake no longer, I went to my room and collapsed into bed. That year, I was staying in the women's dorm, located on the second floor of the temple, directly above the area where Ammachi was sitting. As the bhajans flowed one into the other, I drifted in and out of consciousness. At one point during the night, I woke up with my face drenched with tears. The song being sung in that moment was *Krishna Madhava*. I

discovered my heart felt massively full of bliss. In fact, I felt so full and so complete in that moment that I knew if I died right then and there, I would leave the earth with no regrets. I wept for hours. Even though that sense of complete fullness did not last, I felt graced to have experienced it at all. The moment was one of the peak moments of my life.

I mentioned earlier how, when in Mother's presence, many situations occur to bring up negative tendencies. For example, if a person has competition issues, he can be assured he will find himself in an abundance of situations where he will have to decide whether or not to be competitive. In this way a person can observe his negative tendencies and determine the degree to which his issues have been resolved. Ammachi may also behave in a way that directly provokes our negative tendencies. On that trip, Sreejit had several of those experiences with Mother.

Prior to meeting Mother, Sreejit was very interested in heavy metal rock music. Even now that his life was spiritually focused, he wore his hair in a multitude of long braids, a style compatible with his heavy metal interests. Wherever he went, the Indian people stared at him. They often surrounded him, asking questions such as, "Is that how people wear their hair in America?" and "Does your hair grow that way naturally?" He hated that kind of attention. The only privacy he found was in his room. Soon, he learned that the best way to prevent such conversations, other than staying in his room, was to look at the ground and avoid eye contact.

One of Sreejit's greatest desires was for Mother to spontaneously give him spiritual guidance. She did initiate a discussion with him one day, but it was not the conversation for which he longed. Her questions, "How long did it take you to get your hair like that?" and "Who braided it for you?" Needless to say, his vasanas[3] flared!

At this point in his life, Sreejit was spending a great deal of time doing spiritual practices. I was quite concerned as his schoolwork was suffering. Since Mother was not spontaneously giving him spiritual advice, he decided to ask her directly. When Sreejit handed the brahmachari his written question, he was told to wait. He sat next to the brahmachari the remainder of the morning. The brahmachari never even shared the question with Mother! Towards the end of the trip, Sreejit decided to make one more attempt. When the brahmachari translated the question, Mother directed him to write down his daily schedule. Sreejit enthusiastically left the darshan hut and did as he was told. He returned to the hut at the same time I entered the darshan line. After he gave Mother his itemized schedule, she instructed him to sit nearby. I slowly proceeded through the darshan line. When I reached the front of the line, Mother finally responded to Sreejit. Normally, other devotees cannot hear answers to personal questions, but I heard the answer loud and clear. She responded, "You do enough spiritual practice, spend more time on your studies." I was thrilled that she had supported his education and marveled at how she had masterminded the whole scene!

Sreejit turned into a stereotypical adolescent during that trip, angry with me, and angry with her. I was used to having a very quiet, cooperative child, so this time was very difficult for both of us. I knew enough child development and developmental psychology to know that this rebellion was normal and healthy, but since I was also in emotional turmoil most of the time, I found it very difficult to deal with Sreejit's adolescent behavior. I flip-flopped from being angry with him to feeling empathic to feeling responsible for his pain. After all, I had introduced him to Mother!

When Sreejit first arrived at the ashram, he hated it. Sometime during the trip, his original distaste of India was converted to such a deep love of the ashram that by the time we were ready to leave, he was furious that I would not let him stay. I felt like I could not win. We were both on a seemingly never-ending emotional roller coaster.

---

[3] Vasana - latent tendencies. Negative vasanas are dense emotions such as anger, jealousy, competition, etc.

I spent some time each morning, meditating on the temple roof. One day, I made an interesting observation. I recalled that when I meditated in the church in Seattle, I usually visualized myself sitting on the temple roof in India, looking over the endless carpet of treetops. Now I was in India, looking over the treetops, and as I meditated, I was imagining myself sitting in front of the altar in the Seattle church. I enjoyed the way in which my two worlds were blending.

While I was in India, the brahmachari in charge of the European programs visited the ashram. For a few weeks, he gave daily lectures to the western visitors and the ashram residents, sharing insights into how to connect with Ammachi. One day, he was asked, "What does Ammachi know?" Sometimes it seems that Mother knows everything about us and other times not. He told us that Ammachi knows what she needs to know or what she wants to know. If she needs or wants to know something, the information is simply there. She, therefore, is not continually inundated by all of our useless mind chatter.

He remarked that devotees frequently ask Ammachi for advice or direction and then don't follow it. They often come back at a later time and ask the exact same question. In this instance, Mother will frequently say, "Do as you wish." He cautioned us to recognize that in all likelihood, her first answer was her true advice. When people choose to not follow her original suggestions, Ammachi will support them in exploring their own way.

The brahmachari urged us to "drink in" every moment of attention from Ammachi, to forget how much we know and let ourselves become childlike. He said that in the empty space of innocence, Mother's love would flow in.

He also pointed out how often our minds create blocks which prevent us from receiving the love that is available. For example, our minds counsel us that we should expect Ammachi to remove all obstacles, that is, she should make the path, sweep the path clean and then call us to her. When I shared this information with a friend, he added, "Actually, we want her to make the path, sweep the path clean, take us by the hand and accompany us every step of the way, dealing with any remaining obstacles that present themselves." A COGIC minister made a similar point when he said, "We expect to be rescued from the lion's den without ever having taken the risk of going in." The brahmachari stated Mother will reveal to us what work we need to do, but we must put in the necessary self-effort.

During the summer of 1991, my hands had started spontaneously forming mudras[4] during bhajans. That summer, I had asked Swami Ramakrishnananda to tell me about the hand signs. He explained a few of the basic principles and then told me there was an excellent book about mudras in the library in India. Upon arriving in India, I looked unsuccessfully for the book. I asked Swami Ramakrishnananda for help. When he could not locate it, I asked him to repeat the principles he had shared with me during the summer tour. He did not know what I was talking about. Aha! This was going to be one of those situations where any active attempt to get intellectual desires met was going to be blocked. I let go and simply let the mudras be.

One day, a brahmachari told us that as the meditation process progresses, events start happening which are interesting but distracting. He said he found it helpful to take the attitude, "God, take it back, I want only you." I wondered if the mudras were one of those distractions and if so, should I make them stop? When I asked Mother, she responded, "No, they are a sign your meditation is working, hold them close to your heart." I was relieved to know the mudras were not unhealthy distractions and pleased to be told that their presence

Swami Ramakrishnananda, Mother, Swamiji

---

[4] Mudras - hand signals indicating spiritual truths.

meant my meditations were working. Actually, this information surprised me as I considered myself a "flop" at meditation. I decided she must have been alluding to the states I reached during bhajans. There was no way she could be referring to my feeble attempts at more traditional methods of meditation.

I had often wondered what Ammachi would think about my type of psychotherapy practice. I especially wondered what she would think about our having clients use methods such as beating pillows to release their anger. During this trip, I received the answer to my question. One day, the woman ahead of me in the darshan line was very angry with Ammachi. Mother acknowledged her anger and then took the woman's hand and struck herself (Ammachi) with it. Later, a brahmachari referred to that interaction saying that of course one could not physically hurt Mother, but that it was fine to visualize hitting her if you were furious with her. Since then I have even heard Mother say that if we cannot find another way to release anger, it is acceptable to hit a doll or some other inanimate object that represents the person with whom we are angry. She says what is most important is that we not hurt others with our anger. I could not have asked for better validation of my work.

While I still experienced grief at the thought of leaving India and during certain songs, my grief in general was less pervasive than in previous years. I discovered, however, that I was no longer willing to limit my trips to India to three weeks a year. I committed to do whatever it took to stay two months a year in the future.

Towards the end of our time at the ashram, one of the Seattle satsang members asked Mother if she would meet separately with our group. We wanted her to give us advice about strengthening our satsang and to tell us more about her charitable projects. She agreed, so one night as we sat under a blanket of stars, Mother chatted about the projects that were already underway. She also told us of projects that were still in the planning stages, ones that would help the many young girls who sought refuge at the ashram. In Kerala, if a woman does not have a dowry, she cannot marry. Women who are not married may be forced into prostitution. Mother said many of the girls who come to the ashram asking to be brahmacharinis[5] lack the disposition to make that lifelong commitment. Ammachi was developing a program that would allow them to live at the

---

[5] Brahmacharini - female celibate student of a Guru.

ashram while receiving education, training and meaningful work. When they chose to reenter the world, they would have the skills needed to enter successfully. I loved being in that informal setting with Mother, hearing her plans and once again seeing evidence of her never-ending compassion.

On the day we were to leave the ashram, Ammachi attended the morning meditation being held on the temple roof. Her mat had been placed in such a way that the sun shown directly into her eyes. Ammachi, when disciplining her devotees, will occasionally take on the fierce energy of the Goddess Kali. She glared at a brahmachari, nonverbally chastising him for being careless when placing the mat and for not repairing the thatched roof. After scowling, she turned her back towards him. As he struggled to maintain a sense of inner peace, I had a clear view of Ammachi's profile and noticed that as she looked out over the ocean, she was giggling. I was very grateful to witness this leela and to experience a living example of how her display of anger is for our good and not founded on her own inner rage. (Ammachi teaches that if we can learn to maintain inner tranquillity when she is disciplining us, we will be able to stay grounded in any situation the world presents.)

As I prepared to leave the ashram, I was aware of two thoughts. The first was the desire to have Mother give me an extra goodbye, something like putting her hand on my head as she walked by. (I had said my farewells during my darshan the previous day.) I wondered whether my leaving would be like my coming, that is, would she completely ignore me. As Mother left the roof of the temple, that morning, she walked directly up to Sreejit and put her hand on his head. Then she draped her sari over his body as she walked on. Later, I discovered that when she left the temple roof, she went to the women's dorm to give a special goodbye to the other person with whom I was traveling. She never even looked at me! I laughed and thought, "Mother, you are an incredibly good provocative therapist!" I patted myself on the back for my growing ability to laugh off these provocations.

As we had prepared to return home, we had experienced yet another series of travel leelas. When I called to confirm our return flight, I was told there was no record of our reservations to fly from Madras to Singapore. The agent insisted we come to Trivandrum to obtain new tickets. Frustrated with India and its inefficient and ineffective bureaucracy, we left the ashram for Trivandrum. Eight hours later, we returned to the ashram with new tickets in hand.

Now we were ready to leave the ashram. Would there be any more travel leelas awaiting us? Fortunately, the trip from Trivandrum to Madras was uneventful. When we checked in at the Madras ticket counter, however, the agent looked at us quizzically asking, "Why have you all booked two tickets from Madras to Singapore?"

Gifts From My Family
Winter-Spring 1992

Shortly after my return from India, I received a message that my mother was near death. She had been comatose for most of the last few days, yet whenever the coma lightened, she called for me. This was not only a surprise but also a dilemma. Years before, she had instructed that when she reached the end of her life, I was not to visit her in the hospital nor attend her funeral as she knew my presence would upset my father. Now the time was here and she was calling for me.

When I shared my concern about a possible "run-in" with my father, my brothers told me not to worry about it, saying they would handle the situation if the need arose. Our mother wanted me with her and my brothers were committed to doing whatever it took to see her wish fulfilled. This was the first time I could remember anyone ever considering standing up to my father. (The only exception was my mother's refusal to cut me out of her life when I married Al.) I felt protected and wanted.

My brothers chose to surprise my mother with my arrival. When I showed up at her bedside, she wept with joy and relief. Since my father's schedule was entirely predictable, I was able to visit my mother daily without him knowing. My brothers wanted to prevent any unnecessary confrontation. They were justifiably afraid that he would refuse to see my mother again if he knew I was in town.

I wondered if there was any way for me ease my mother's passing. We had never been close, and as a result saying the loving things that I believed a mother should hear would have been hypocritical. Several days before I was to return to Seattle, I felt drawn to buy her several items, a teddy bear to remind her "inner child" that I was thinking of her even when I was in Seattle, a audio cassette tape player and two tapes, *Alleluia* and *Om Namah Shivaya*, both by Robert Gass and the Wings of Song.

My mother kept the bear in bed with her until she died. When she first listened to the *Alleluia* tape, she started to cry. Her immediate reaction to *Om Namah Shivaya* was, "I've heard that before." From what I knew about my mother and her life, I thought it highly unlikely she had ever, at least in her conscious mind, heard the song before. I wondered if Ammachi had been near, preparing her for her journey Home.

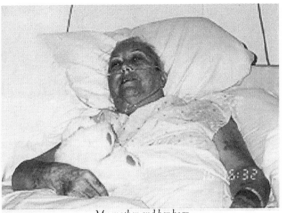

My mother and her bear.

Upon my return to Seattle, I discovered that while I was in Florida, my children had written beautiful letters to my mother. My aunt told me my mother wept when she read them. I was happy that my children were able to say the things I wanted her to hear, but could not say. My mother and aunt shared those letters with many people, both before and after her death.

When my mother died about a month after I returned to Seattle, my brothers asked me to attend her funeral. They had already informed my father I would be there and that he had no say in the matter. He agreed to stay socially appropriate provided I promised not to sit next to him during the funeral. In fact, I was not to approach him at any time. When I sat down on the family pew, he leaned forward and looked across the people sitting between us. The eye contact that happened in that moment was the first in twenty-one years. Even though he later made disparaging remarks about me to my brothers, in that moment his look did not seem hateful, but rather one of curiosity. What I beheld was a very old, tense, unhappy man.

The information I was given about my mother's last days filled me with awe. She had apparently listened endlessly to the *Om Namah Shivaya* tape. The nurses would wheel her into the atrium of the hospice, tape player and headphones accompanying her, and there she would sit for hours. She and my brothers would listen to it together in her room. I was told one of the nurses would sit by her bed and together they would sing along with the tape. She died listening to *Om Namah Shivaya*.

I was immensely grateful I had been able to contribute to my mother's dying in a meaningful and significant way. While I felt sad that I was not grieving the ending of a close relationship, I was content to be able to experience an ending in which I felt complete, without anger or resentment. I was happy she was finally at peace and free from pain.

In late spring, I told my co-therapists and clients of my decision to extend my India trips to two months per year. Without exception every co-therapist and client fully supported my decision. They saw how important the experience was for my development and how much they benefited from my learnings. They also appreciated that I was modeling that each of us has the power to create the life style we want. I felt tremendous gratitude for the support in my life.

I had believed for some time that my mother and brother would die within a close time span. It seemed that each of them was "holding out" so that neither contributed pain to the other. A month after my mother's death, Bill's health began to quickly deteriorate. As I had spent time with him when my mother was in the hospital and later at her funeral, I decided I would not visit again. It was very important to his wife Cindy that I attend his funeral, so I planned to go to North Carolina when that time came.

In the subsequent months, I talked to Bill on the phone from time to time. As he came closer and closer to death, I began to feel immense gratitude towards his wife. My brother, being the third child, was even more unwanted by our father than I was. My mother's love was limited since she placed such a high priority on keeping my father happy. Therefore, until Cindy entered his life, he had never experienced being unconditionally loved. Now he was in constant pain. Cindy curled up in the bed beside him and held him day after day, week after week, long after he was nonresponsive.

Learning Through Loss
1992 Summer Tour

I expected Bill to die weeks before the beginning of the summer tour. As the time for Ammachi's arrival approached, however, it became clear he would pass *during* the summer tour. I would definitely leave for Bill's funeral when the time came, but I felt sad to have to miss even a second with Mother.

I believed I was being given another lesson in letting go and not being attached to plans. The uncertainty about my brother's living and dying was not the only form in which this particular lesson presented itself. That summer, the first stop on the tour was Vancouver, Canada. A few days prior to Mother's arrival, my car started having mechanical problems. First the head gasket died, then a wheel was ripped to the rim, and next the wiring began to fail. As soon as one thing was repaired, something else malfunctioned. Even on the eve of my anticipated departure, I was uncertain that my car would be driveable.

The next morning, another series of "follow inner direction" and "do not be attached to your plans" lessons began. As I prepared to leave, the thought, "Get the lip balm," went through my mind. I internally answered, "I think it is already packed." Again I heard, "Get the lip balm." "Okay," I responded as I went for the lip balm. (I rarely used lip balm so this entire scenario was more than a little bizarre.)

I left Seattle without incident. I stopped briefly in Mt. Vernon, Washington to use the restroom, and then drove for another hour. On the outskirts of Bellingham, I noticed my lips were feeling very, very dry. I spontaneously reached for the lip balm, only to discover my purse was gone! I had left it in the restroom in Mt. Vernon! I turned around and frantically drove back to the gas station. I had been within a half-hour of reaching Vancouver, and Mother, and now once again there was a possibility I would be unable to be with her. There was no way I could leave the United States and enter Canada without money and identification. I worked to accept the attitude that whatever happened was for my own good. I was able to reach a state of calmness and acceptance much easier than I would have expected. When I drove into the Mt. Vernon gas station, the attendant was delighted. He reached behind the counter and pulled out my purse!

One of my wishes for that summer tour was to re-experience the feeling I had had in India, of being so full and complete that if I died in the moment I would have no regrets. As the bhajans began that night, I started having similar sensations, though not quite as intense as before. I was able to stay in that frame of mind throughout most of the Vancouver program. There was one notable exception. One day when my eyes fell on Nirmalamrita (then called Suneethi), a brahmacharini who seemed like a sister to me. I thought, "She gets to live in India and I don't." Moments later the California ashram group began to sing and I noted, "They get to live in the ashram in California and I don't." Next, I noticed my son had been invited to sing along with the California ashram residents and I whined, "He is going to live in India with Ammachi some day and I can't." My being exploded into familiar grief. After some moments of self-pity, I thought, "Wait a minute, I could live in California, I have chosen not to. I could live in India, I have chosen not to." As I claimed those choices, the grief stopped. Later, when I processed the incident, I realized the grief had replaced the bliss when I allowed my mind to leave the present moment, and when I focused on what I was lacking instead of what I had. I knew the experience was an important demonstration of how I, and others, sabotage happiness.

I experienced another memorable moment during the Vancouver Devi Bhava. As you might remember, clients in my therapy practice have the opportunity to make parenting contracts with their therapists. One of my therapy daughters, Katherine, had come to the Vancouver program. We had had no contact during the evening, and, as far as I knew, Ammachi had never seen us together. I proceeded through the darshan line first and then sat down near Mother. When Katherine came through the line, I saw her whisper something into Mother's ear. Ammachi whipped her head to the side and looked directly at me, a huge smile crossing her face. I was more than a little curious to know what in the world Katherine had said to her. I wondered if she had said something about me! Later, I discovered that she had asked Mother for a mantra. I knew then that Mother had been sharing her delight with me. Once again, I marveled at the Mother who knows more than it seems possible she could know.

I left Vancouver and drove to the Seattle retreat. For the first time my daughter, Chaitanya, had decided to attend the retreat. Watching Chaitanya's journey towards Mother had been, and still is, very fascinating. During the first two years, she accompanied me to the California ashram several times. She loved being in the community setting and helping with activities such as cooking and office work. She enjoyed hearing the music, from a distance, but wanted no part of the spiritual programs. She had no interest in meeting Mother. She was angry about how much her brother and I had changed since becoming involved with Ammachi.

During the third summer, Chaitanya had agreed to attend one of the Seattle programs. She quickly became bored and went to a remote part of the auditorium to do her homework. Again, she liked the music, especially *Arati*, but as soon as the music ended, she demanded to be taken home. Although her attitude towards Mother did not shift following this experience, I began to notice sheets of paper around the house on which Chaitanya had repetitively written "Mata Amritanandamayi." When questioned, she responded that she simply liked writing Mother's name. I chuckled to myself, wondering where this story would end.

Therefore, this year's retreat would be Chaitanya's first real contact with Mother. She spent most of the retreat sleeping and reading in her room. She attended the music programs occasionally, but refused from the onset to go for darshan.

Chaitanya wanted to ask Ammachi for permission to come to India, with the caveat that she not have to participate in any spiritual programs. Sreejit and I described the process of getting a question answered. We giggled to ourselves knowing that if Chaitanya did go through the question line, she would likely get a surprise hug. The morning that she intended to ask the question arrived. She requested that I once again describe the process of going through the question line. As I repeated the process, a look of alarm crossed her face. "I can't do that," she said. "If I do that, she'll get me!" I laughed and responded, "That's right!" She decided she would have me ask Mother her question later in the tour!

To my surprise, on the last morning of the retreat, Chaitanya announced she was going for darshan. With joy, I watched as she melted into Mother's arms. Later when I asked what being held was like for her, she replied, "Well, I didn't feel *any* energy or *any* power. But she was *so* soft, and she smelled *so* good. It was just like being held by a *big* teddy bear." I smiled to myself and silently reflected, "Well you may think you didn't experience any power or energy, but you got it!"

On the last day of the retreat, as I was sitting out in an open field listening to my *Guru Gita* tape, Sreejit approached, informing me that

Bill had died. He put his arm around me and I wept. I felt very close to my son in that moment. During the next few hours, I realized how much God had taken care of me in Bill's dying. I had most wanted to attend the Seattle retreat. Bill had died when the retreat was almost complete, at a time and place where I could have the support of my friends and when I could be in Mother's arms. Later, when I made plane reservations, I felt even more cared for. While I would miss the regular programs in Seattle, I would be returning to the Seattle-Tacoma airport at exactly the same time that Mother would be in the airport awaiting her flight to California. I could and did go directly from the funeral into her arms. I was so grateful for her presence in my life.

While it had not seemed important to take Sreejit and Chaitanya to my mother's funeral, it was important to me that they go to my brother's. For the second time in twenty-one years, my father and I were about to see each other. This would be the first time he had ever seen my children. When that moment finally arrived, it was fascinating to watch him observe them, when he thought no one was looking. As before, he made no attempt to speak to me, and I respecting his wishes, did not approach him.

Attending Bill's funeral was a profoundly moving experience. His friends related stories from their lives with him and read from his journal. One anecdote described his efforts in cooking his first meal for Cindy. As a way of ensuring the meal was prepared correctly, he served a duplicate meal to friends the day ahead. Bill's friends spoke of his love for music, his love of life and his love of God. I saw that he had developed a family of friends who loved him immensely. I was grateful to know that, like me, he had been able to create a healthy family for himself.

Bill, who had trained for years to become an oncologist,[6] had been in private practice for only two years before he was diagnosed with colon cancer and became so ill he could not continue to practice. At the funeral, the wife of one of his friends approached me, saying her husband had been one of my brother's professors. The husband later told me he had left teaching in order to follow Bill to Arden, North Carolina. He said he wanted to learn from a physician who had the depth of empathy my brother exhibited. I wept to hear how loved Bill was and to see how in such a short time, he had become the teacher of the teacher. Tears fall

---

[6] Oncologist - physician who specializes in treatment of cancer.

even as I write this, from gratitude for the love he received and also from the sadness for what I missed in not really knowing him.

I spent most of that night reading and copying parts of Bill's journal. I read about what it was like for him to grow up in a house where no touch was allowed, where our father chanted, "Momma's boy, Momma's boy" any time my mother showed him any affection. Bill wrote about how on the day friends brought him dinner when he was sick, he curled

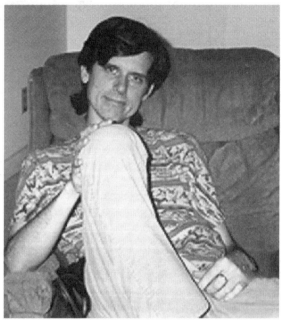

My brother Bill shortly before his death.

up in the corner and cried like a baby, not understanding why anyone would care enough about him to do such a thing. Reading on, I learned how he attributed both his love of nature and his desire to know how nature and machinery works to our father's insistence that we look up the answers to all questions in the encyclopedia or the dictionary. (Bill's home was always filled with snakes, fish, bugs, and frogs. Whenever a bird was hurt, he would take it in and nurse it back to health. He loved watching eggs hatch and cocoons open). He attributed his capacity for empathy to our mother, who spent day after day sewing clothes for migrant children and making knickknacks for church bazaars. Whenever there was work to be done, our mother was consistently the first to volunteer. I considered the possibility that my craving for knowledge of psychological and spiritual process resulted from my father's modeling and my compassion from my mother's. I was thankful to have the opportunity to try on this way of thinking. I was also a little in awe that my brother could have had such profound insights.

There was one entry in the journal that was so important to me that I am going to present it in its entirety. Keep in mind this was written by a young man who developed terminal cancer two years after he had married and started a private practice and who was only thirty-eight years old when he died.

❀ ❀ ❀

Truth I Live By
(William John Smith 1953-1992)

Everything makes sense. This can be paraphrased many different ways, although many attempts are less accurate. One of Voltaire's characters stated, "All is for the best, in the best of all possible worlds. This is unnecessarily optimistic. My phrasing doesn't imply that everything that happens to us is good either in the short or the long term. Everyone experiences moments or long periods of unpleasantness. One can hope that over the long period of a lifetime these sad times may not add up to much overall, but most persons with a little thought can think of individuals whom "fate has treated unkindly," i.e. who have received more than their share of agonies. I think this is one of the hardest things for you, Cindy, that what has happened is just not fair. I'm not sure how long ago I came to believe (or realize) that fairness isn't the issue. There is nothing fair about life, either in distribution of rewards or unhappiness. And what's to say that it should be fair. If each of us had an opportunity to create a world, then maybe that's an attribute that we would build in. But this world is not of our making, and all of the mental checklists that we might make comparing who's got-

ten more breaks than we have, etc., will never change the
fact that we have to make the best of what we've got, not
despair over what we perceive as inequities. So life isn't
fair. How do we cope with that? One way might be to
remind ourselves that no matter how bad things seem to be
at any one time, a little time spent flipping around the TV
channel or reading a news magazine will serve as a reminder
that we should be embarrassed to be heard complaining about
the vast majority of things that concern us. I don't doubt for
a second that I have lived a very privileged existence compared to 90% of the world's people.

I'm not sure that that is the best way to approach a new
tragedy, though (i.e., making ourselves feel better by thinking of others doing worse). I would appreciate a more optimistic approach. The best way to greet each unpleasant
event is to grab it by the throat and make the best of it.
Cindy and I have both had our share of suffering, almost all
of it, I'm happy to say proceeding our first date. There is no
doubt that led to a degree of maturity that made our time
together (pre-diagnosis and post-diagnosis) much more meaningful than the lives of those growing up "with the silver
spoons."

Is cancer unfair? Is it fair that we should expect billions of
cells in our body to reproduce over and over again, over an
entire lifetime, and always get it right? Doesn't it make more
sense to recognize the initial miracle of our birth, the mag-
nificence of our growth into feeling, loving, praising adults,
the privilege of experiencing enough of life that we can despair over not having the time to spend longer doing the same?
One of the things I am most grateful for is that many, many
years ago I learned to be grateful for what I've been given. I
didn't, as occurs with many, only get shocked into this realization by a terminal tragedy. This type of appreciation often does begin in the midst of despair, and for that reason I
am actually glad that I had enough hard times as a young
man, to allow me to think hard about what things are and

are not important. Accordingly, for the past 15 or 20 years, I've been able to ignore aspects of 20th century American living that are of no consequence to me (parties, cars, frivolous chatter, clubs, etc.) and concentrate on things that touch me personally. I am forever grateful for what it was that dropped the blinders from my eyes so many years ago.

I am very sad that people seem to see so little of the world around them. I can't walk outside without seeing the beauty of our created world, from the rainbow in a line of earthworm slime, to another visible ring on Jupiter. We have been given this magnificent world to study and enjoy in limitless detail at any level, microscopic to cosmic. Even though I have enough things to interest me another 10 lifetimes, I must take solace in knowing that, at least compared to others, I've had much more than my share even in half a life time.

I appreciated having been given such a glimpse into my brother's world. I am thankful for the love he received and the love he gave. Even though he did not know Ammachi, at least in a conscious way, there is no doubt in my mind that he was blessed by God and the Divine Mother energy with which she is joined.

After reading Bill's journal, I started identifying the themes that had been running through that year's lessons. So many lessons were a reminder that I continually have the choice between living in gratitude or resentment, joy or suffering, abundance or scarcity, in the present moment or in the past or the future, and in harmony with or in opposition to God's will. My choices are made moment-to-moment as I decide where to focus my attention.

I once was told that wherever there is a poisonous plant, the antidote is usually located nearby. Likewise, it seems that when lessons come, the answers and the help needed to learn the lessons or solve the problems are all around us. I marveled at the many ways I had received the answers to lessons during that year. I remembered a minister in San Francisco teaching me another way out of suffering when he said, "I'm so tired of people talking only about bad news, don't they know there is good news? Why don't they just switch the channel?" Another minister had reminded the congregation that that with which we fill our minds, we will see everywhere. For example, if we fill our minds with negative thoughts, we will see negative things everywhere. Ammachi taught that we should be like the honey bee who wastes no time in going for the honey. She also pointed out to us that if you put an ant in a bowl filled with salt and sugar, the ant heads immediately for the sugar.

I also noted how the concept of gratitude had become a dominant theme. One of the most frequent sayings in the Church of God in Christ is, "When the praises go up, the blessings come down." All services are centered on offering praise and gratitude to God. My yoga teacher had recently sent his students an article about respect that stated:

> We respect nothing until we are grateful, until we take nothing for granted. There may be no quality which causes as quick a transformation from sorrow to joy, from depression to elation, from dejected futility to awakened usefulness than overflowing gratitude.[7]

Years before, I had been present when Jean Wiger, a psychotherapist from the Midwest, was asked what she considered to be the best predictor of success in therapy. Her response, "The client's capacity to experience gratitude." I was thoroughly convinced that if I accepted the lessons that come with gratitude and a spirit of adventure and excitement, I would learn what I needed to learn quicker and with less pain than if I accepted the lesson with reluctance and resistance.

As I reviewed the lessons I had learned over the past few years, I remembered another of Ammachi's teachings and saw how it held true for me. When I have been able to hold my mind silent by focusing on solving the problem, seeing the positive qualities in each situation, and accepting each lesson with gratitude, I have most often been able to stay calm even when I am in the middle of chaos. When I focused on the negative, letting my mind run rampant or when I resisted the lesson, I would usually feel chaotic even if everything and everyone around me were calm and peaceful.

I had been inundated with so many lessons that year. Since two of my family members had died in the last three months, I thought perhaps

---

[7] Aadil Palkhivala, *Yoga Centers Newsletter*, Bellevue: Yoga Centers, 3(1): January-August 1992.

I would be allowed to "rest" or "coast" during the remainder of the tour. Once again, I was wrong! A few days after my return from North Carolina, I departed for five days of Mother's programs in the Bay Area of California. I scheduled my itinerary so I would arrive at the ashram before the beginning of the morning program. When I found my rental car, I noticed that one of the tires was slightly flat. I reported the problem, expecting to be directed to another car. Instead, the attendant asked me to drive the car to the shop, assuring me they would have me on the road in a "few minutes." An hour later, I was on my way to the program, frustrated and irritated at the delay.

Two days later, when I walked to my car, I discovered the same tire was completely flat. I had allowed only enough time to drive to the ashram, so once again I would be late. I walked to a pay phone, called the rental agency and was told a taxi would pick me up. They instructed me to leave the keys in the ignition of the rental car. I was given a new car and proceeded to the program, arriving very late. Later in the day, as I was driving to Berkeley, the location of the evening program, I realized that I had left the key to the apartment in which I was staying in the ignition of the original rental car. The friends who owned the apartment were gone for the weekend, thus if I did not find the key, I would have nowhere to stay. I phoned the rental agency, located forty-five minutes away, in San Francisco. They said they would have to retrieve the key from a parking lot located some distance away and that I could pick the key up at their San Francisco office in an hour or two. I shook my head, not believing this was happening yet knowing at the same time that I was being forced, once again, to practice letting go, staying focused and calm, and giving up expectations. I did what I needed to do and felt very successful at my ability to stay calm and centered. As I drove back to Berkeley, I assumed that I would once again arrive late to the program. As I approached the church, however, Ammachi was just walking in! I believed I had passed a significant test and was euphoric that it did not require that I miss time with Mother!

The following week, Sreejit and I were to attend the San Ramon retreat. As I spend two months in India each year, I try to miss as few therapy groups as possible during the rest of the year. Therefore, during the summer tours I fly between California and Seattle several times. This allowed me to attend my weekly groups. That year I had been very successful in flying standby, so Sreejit, who was seventeen at the time, and I decided to take a flight to San Francisco that was earlier than the one we had booked. When we arrived at the airport, we were told it was highly unlikely that a seat would be available as the flight was overbooked. At the last minute, however, we discovered there was one empty seat. Without thinking, I told Sreejit to take the seat. As soon as the plane departed, I realized he was going to arrive in San Francisco with no phone numbers, no addresses, and no mother (me!). I knew there would be other devotees arriving in San Francisco at the same time, so I tried to convince myself he would be fine. My mind, however, was anything other than calm and centered. How could I, his mother, have allowed such a thing to happen! I was given a seat on the next flight, an occurrence that could only have been divine grace as the airline, due to overbooking, had paid numerous people to wait for a later flight. I arrived in San Francisco hoping Sreejit would greet me at the gate. As he was nowhere to be found, I picked up my rental car and drove to the ashram. He was not at the ashram either. Just as I began to panic, a van drove up and there he was. He had not been the slightest bit flustered by the situation. I asked many "What would you have done if...?" questions. I discovered my son was a lot wiser than I had given him credit for.

As I relate these experiences, I am reminded that people frequently ask why I put myself in situations that trigger such emotional pain. What is true is that there is a great reward for going through the challenges. I constantly notice differences in myself. I am happier, more content, more flexible, more centered and a lot more intuitive. It seems now that so much of what I want and need is given to me with a minimum of effort on my part. Many of my questions are answered without my even verbalizing them. I continually experience myself as a clearer and more effective therapist. Likewise, my ability to parent grows. My nurturing spirit continues to bloom. I continually see my clients and my children benefiting from the lessons I learn. Therefore, I believe that even though the journey is often hard and frustrating, the payoff is well worth the effort. In addition, the ecstatic bliss I experience during the bhajans is worth enduring untold amounts of pain.

Several weeks later, Sreejit and I attended the public programs being held in New York City and Boston, and the Rhode Island retreat. As the crowds in New York City tend to be very large, those of us who regularly spend time with Ammachi usually do not go for darshan during the

evening program.[8] Sometimes we would go for morning darshan, sometimes not. One morning on this trip I found myself in a quandary, debating back and forth as to whether or not to join the darshan line. As the
line shortened, I decided to simply go for it! Just before I arrived to the
front of the line, however, Mother stood up. I took her action to mean I
should not have joined the line. I left immediately, criticizing myself
profusely for having made a mistake. (The fact that Mother stood up
when I arrived to the front of the line in all likelihood had nothing to do
with me!) The next day the crowd was even larger, so I made no attempt
to go for darshan.

As we were driving to that morning program, we had passed a very
large cathedral, Cathedral of St. John the Divine. I knew immediately
that I wanted to go back to the cathedral when the morning program
ended. When I entered the building later that day, I felt a strong mag-
netic pull to the back. As I walked, I began to enter a profoundly altered
state of consciousness. When I arrived at an altar located near the rear of
the church, I practically collapsed on my knees, my hands beginning to
form mudras. There were pews on both sides of the room and a speaker's
podium in the middle. I could *see* and *hear* the priests and nuns of long
ago as they sang from the side pews. I could *hear* the priest as he preached
from the pulpit. Prior to this time all my altered state experiences had
been kinesthetic, this was the first time I had ever had a visual or auditory
experience. Next, I was aware that part of me was *seeing* even more,
although there was no actual vision. What kept going through my mind
was, "I am seeing what Saint Bernadette saw! I am seeing what Saint
Bernadette saw!" I did not know what I was seeing. Saint Bernadette saw
the Virgin Mary. My sense was that some part of me was *seeing* Jesus or
Mary or some other aspect of the Divine Mother. I remained in that state
until a friend who had come to the cathedral with me asked if she and my
other friends should stay or go. I said, "Go." Simply making that statement pulled me out of the altered state and with that came a flood of
tears.

During the next two days I cried incessantly, unsure exactly what
had happened to me. I felt it possible I had tapped into past life experiences. At one point a devotee said I should go to Mother, reminding me
that it is always acceptable to go to her when I needed her, no matter how

---

[8] Our attempt to help the program end by the curfew.

big the crowds were. I was very shaken by the experience and in addition was still criticizing myself for having made the "mistake" of entering the line the day before. Instead of asking for help, I sat as far away from her as possible. (The fact that I did not even sit close to her was a good indication I was becoming well-entrenched in self-indulgent suffering!)

The next day I was in a similar frame of mind. By now, I was fully immersed in self-pity. Eventually, I decided I was willing to sit closer, so I moved to the steps directly behind Ammachi. At one point Mother glanced to the space in-between the woman sitting beside me and myself, beckoning that one of us could come for darshan. We looked at each other wondering whom she had called. The other woman said she felt no need for darshan. I remained seated there thinking, "If you want ME, you'll have to let me know directly." Needless to say, her offer was not repeated. Oh, the price we pay to be righteous!

That night when I went for Devi Bhava darshan, most of my agitation and grief faded away. I felt so calm and complete that when the time came to receive the flower petals Ammachi showers on devotees at the end of each Devi Bhava, I decided to stay seated near the singers rather than joining the line. After Ammachi sprinkles flower petals on the passing devotees, she usually throws petals towards the people sitting in front of her, singers included. That night she tossed the petals on everyone, except for the people in the area in which I was sitting. I plummeted right back into my negative thinking, sure she was angry at me for not getting up and walking around with everyone else, thereby expecting something for nothing. As a result of my action, everyone around me was now suffering. Later my friend, Joan, who was seated next to me, told me she believed Ammachi had not thrown the flowers because she, Joan, was not satisfied with what she had already been given. Still later, another friend informed me she felt sad that Ammachi's arm had been in so much pain, she had been unable to continue throwing the petals.

The next day we took a taxi to the New York airport to see Mother off as she departed for Boston. As Mother walked down the airport corridor with Joan on one side and me on the other, she was so friendly, loving and open that it was abundantly obvious that she was not at all angry with either one of us. The whole experience was such a good example of how we all project our thoughts and feelings onto Mother's actions and of how we all get the lessons we need. In all likelihood, none of us had interpreted her action correctly.

I felt that I had barely survived the New York City program. I longed for Boston where the crowds would be smaller and I could finally be close. I approached the Boston program with great excitement. As I entered the building, I discovered I had more lessons in store. In an attempt to give new people more contact with Ammachi, a huge portion of the room was blocked off (at the time it seemed like three fourths of the room, although that could not possibly have been reality) and only newcomers could enter that zone. I had previously "survived" with no physical contact with Ammachi by sitting close, now even that was not available. This seemed like "the last straw." I was frantic and wanted to run. Instead, I sat against the back wall, as far away as possible, and cried. For the first time in four years, I experienced no altered state during bhajans, feeling instead that I was an observer watching a concert given by singers from a foreign country.

I did not want emotional support from anyone in Boston, thinking they were all part of a "conspiracy" keeping me away from Mother. I called friends in Seattle, only to reach a steady stream of answering machines. It was as if the entire city of Seattle had been wiped from the face of the earth. I experienced deep despair and a terror that I would not be able to convert these feelings by the end of the tour, which was rapidly approaching.

As I sat in the first program of the Rhode Island retreat, the last location on the 1992 United States tour, I pondered my next step. Nothing I had thought of so far had worked. I came upon an idea, one I hope I remember much sooner next time! As I went through the darshan line I carried the attitude of, "Mother, there is nothing I can do with these feelings, please help me." As she held me, I melted into her. The tension, sadness and scare all drained from me and I left her arms feeling totally peaceful.

At the beginning of the summer tour, I had silently asked Mother to help me feel connected to her when she was in Devi form, something that is more difficult for me than when she is in her "normal" state. She had connected with me in special ways during almost every Devi Bhava during the tour. In one city, the line monitor had asked everyone to keep their hands on Ammachi's chair while she was holding them, rather than holding on to her body. That time she had lifted my hand from the chair and put it around her. Other times she had connected with a glance or by "playing" with me with her foot.

As the last Devi Bhava approached, I wondered what, if anything, would happen this time. Sreejit was becoming more and more depressed about the tour ending. He not only refused to go for darshan, he would not even enter the program hall. My heart hurt to see him in so much pain and while I understood his dilemma, I believed that staying away was not the way out of the pain. As she held me, I felt the sorrow of knowing this was the last time, for now. I took my Hershey's kiss and sat nearby. I wept a little and then settled into a relatively peaceful state. After awhile, I realized the objects she had placed in my hand felt different from their normal sensation. I opened my hand and there, in addition to the flowers, sat *three* Hershey's kisses! I had no doubt that one was for me, one was for Chaitanya who was in Seattle, and one was for Sreejit who would not come to her that night. I sat, tears streaming down my face, grateful to and in awe of the Mother who can take millions in her arms, yet know and meet the needs of the individual.

There is Much I Do Not Know
Summer/Fall 1992

I had for years been a major skeptic about the field of astrology. I saw no possible validity in it. That year, Mother started making frequent astrological references. I rationalized that since she had entered the world in India, she *had* to use their concepts, whether or not they were valid. I decided, however, to check it out for myself, going primarily to prove it was indeed nonsense. I found a person who was an internationally known Vedic astrologer. I prepared for the session by taking off or covering everything I thought could reveal information about me, that is, rings, necklaces and bracelets. I was sure I had covered all of my bases.

As usual, I discovered there is much I do not know. The astrologer related major events in my life, at times identifying the exact month the occurrence had taken place. He talked about my being pulled between the enjoyment of living in the world and the desire to live an ashram lifestyle. He said my job was to experience both, to learn to live in the world but not be of it. He said I was not to live in an ashram, but suggested I spend time in one as often as possible. He talked about 1989 having been a year in which a profound spiritual transformation had begun. (1989 was the year I met Ammachi!) He said it was time for me to take on more responsibility for my spiritual practice and to continue to learn to live more simply. He suggested I start studying yoga. He said it would be helpful for me to find a spiritual teacher who had a lot of shakti[9] and who emphasized seva. He suggested I would find chanting helpful. I laughed silently as he described everything I already had with Ammachi. He commented that I learned a lot of lessons when I traveled. I really laughed (internally) at that one! I left his office that day, much less skeptical about astrology and feeling very validated about my choice of path.

I visited the California ashram over the Labor Day weekend. My experience that weekend was different from any of my previous visits. While I thoroughly enjoyed my stay, I felt no need to be there and had no sense of grief when it was time to leave. I believed this was evidence that I was living in a state of spiritual fullness instead of a state of spiritual starvation.

Later in September, I took what had become my yearly trip to Bryce Canyon. I decided to invite two friends. While we had fun, it was not the spiritual experience I had had in the past, it was a vacation. I now understood the importance of keeping the Bryce trip spiritually focused and resolved to plan differently in the future.

In November, I decided to attend the Church of God in Christ convocation being held in Memphis, Tennessee. Two friends and I attended four days of the eight-day convocation. Up to 40,000 people came together each day, primarily for the purpose of praising and worshipping God. Meetings sometimes lasted twenty hours a day. Even though only about a dozen white people participated, we were, as always, welcomed warmly. I was overjoyed to be able to immerse myself in the electric devotional energy. I was also extremely impressed by the spiritual power and the vision of the church's leaders.

On the last day of the convocation, Bishop Ford, leader of the denomination, angrily stated that much time had been wasted collecting offerings during the previous week. He said that if everyone tithed as the Bible directed, that is, paid ten percent of their income to God's work, there would be enough money available to pay for all of the service projects (providing food, shelter, jobs for poor, handicapped and elderly), and for necessary church expenses. In fact, there would be money to spare. I had already been impressed by the importance this church placed on tithing.

---

[9] Shakti - spiritual energy.

The bishop's confrontation was a powerful reminder. He added another thought-provoking statement when he said it was unlikely God would grant us our personal visions if we were unwilling to help others obtain theirs.

Leaving the convocation was much more difficult than I had expected. Once again I experienced the grief that comes when I leave an intense level of devotional energy.

On the way home, an exciting event occurred. Since I began attending Power House Church of God in Christ in 1991, it had seemed very important that I simply be there, as opposed to talking about or debating doctrine. I had honored that internal directive, but longed to share and discuss the similarities and differences in our beliefs. Sitting behind me on the plane were two COGIC ministers from Tacoma, Washington. When I made it known that I had been to the convocation, we talked for a while. Later, one of the ministers leaned forward and with great curiosity said, "How in the world did you get here? What is your story?" I shared about Ammachi and my spiritual path. Still later, the other minister leaned forward and said, "I'm dying to ask you questions. Are you willing to talk?" He then asked me what I thought about his church and its doctrines, about the Bible, and about Jesus. I answered his questions and we had a lively discussion. It was the conversation I had always wanted to have at Power House. Even though he did not agree with me on everything and had some concerns, he was very open and accepting of me as a person. As we were nearing Seattle, he told me more than once how much he had appreciated our talk. I told him I felt similarly.

At one point in the fall, I discovered I was becoming increasingly concerned that parishioners would think me a liar because I raised my hand when Pastor Jenkins or one of the other ministers asked who in the congregation had been baptized in the Holy Ghost. This church has very narrow guidelines for that condition, among them are speaking in "tongues" (in an unknown language) and spontaneous dancing. I had experienced neither, but knew that the spirit of God was alive and well within me. To not raise my hand when asked if I "had" the Holy Ghost would mean I was not being true to myself, but I did not want to be considered a liar.

I called Swami Paramatmananda in California to ask how he defined "tongues." He told me they were a sign of God's presence and that part of their importance was that they were totally out of the control of

Swami Paramatmananda.

the individual. The "tongues" could not be made to come, and they could not be explained away.

My fear of being considered a liar was so disturbing that I finally decided to discuss the topic with Mrs. Jenkins, even though I feared she would say, "If you don't have the tongues and the dance, you don't really have the spirit." On the contrary, she told me that the spiritual journey is a soul's journey, a journey totally between the individual and God. She said only I could know what was true for me. She cautioned me to stop worrying about what other people thought. She used the example, "If someone told you that you did not have a hundred dollar bill in your pocket when you knew it was there, would you change your belief?" Besides, she said, it was abundantly obvious to anyone who knew me that God was pulling me towards Him. I was shocked to hear how closely her beliefs matched mine and was very appreciative of her help in relieving my concerns.

I started feeling sad because, even though I felt and acted as if I was a member of Power House, it did not seem appropriate for me to join the church since I did not believe their statement of faith. I told Pastor Jenkins I was handling the dilemma by considering myself to be an unofficial member of the church. He seemed comfortable with my solution.

Many friends and acquaintances had accompanied me to church during my year and a half of participation. Pastor Jenkins and I were both watching the process occurring in front of our eyes as the races and religions mixed. We shared the attitude that God was working and that we could watch and facilitate the process, but should not interfere.

One day, after a particularly powerful service, Pastor Jenkins said from the pulpit, "Sister Karuna, we claim you and your friends as members of this church. We claim *you!*" As I cried in gratitude, I realized that yet another of my stereotypes about the fundamentalist portion of the Christian Church had just dissolved.

PART 5

Ambike, ... amazing are the ways adopted by Thee to get rid of my fears and hopes. O Mother, please guide me in all ways and remove all obstacles which may arise in my path. O Embodiment of Mercy, I bow down to Thee for all the blissful moments that Thou has showered on me.

Mother, the hummingbird of my mind has come flying to Thy lotus-like Feet. Now please fold the petals so as to prevent it from flying away. O Thou who art greater than the greatest, enjoying that nectar of bliss, let me dive deep into it. O Quintessence of all the four Vedas, I bow down to Thee.[1]

Seeing Beyond Myself
December 1992- February 1993 India Trip

Towards the end of the 1992 summer tour, I asked Mother about Chaitanya's request to come to India without any expectation that she would participate in spiritual practices. Mother laughed, responding that it was fine for her to come even under those conditions. That year Kristin, another one of my friends, decided to travel with us.

We journeyed to India without incident. After spending a night in Madras, we flew to Trivandrum. The taxi ride was its normal high-speed adventure. I was surprised that Chaitanya, who was sitting in the front seat, was not overtly reacting to the experience. I learned later that she had kept her eyes closed most of the trip. She described the ride as a never-ending game of "Chicken!"

[1]Excerpts from "Katutta Shokamam," *Bhajanamritam Volume 1*, San Ramon: Mata Amritanandamayi Center 1992, pp. 249-50.

We arrived at the ashram after dark, a first for me. As we boarded the canoe and traveled over the backwaters, the sound of singing wafted down from the temple. It was a wonderfully moving experience. We were shown to our room. After showering, Kristin and Chaitanya went to sleep and I walked to the temple for Devi Bhava darshan. When Mother saw me in the darshan line, she pointed out my presence to the Seattle friends who had come to India earlier in the month. I laughed to myself thinking, "Oh good, you are not going to play the same game as last year!" I was overjoyed to be home again.

I had wondered if this trip to India was even necessary, given my sense of spiritual fullness. I even had the fantasy that I might want to return to Seattle after a few weeks. I quickly discovered that though my experiences at Power House had substantially contributed to my spiritual growth and to my ability to maintain a sense of fullness, the ashram was my spiritual home.

While in Seattle, I felt closest to Mother when I was in church. I had become increasingly reluctant to go to satsang, yet I felt a responsibility to contribute to that group as well. I decided to take this dilemma to Mother. After hearing my concerns, she talked to the translator for a long time. As usual, she answered in a way that took me through every possible emotion! The answer came in three parts. First, she reminded me that whenever a devotee follows two paths, there inevitably is competition between them, that is why Mother suggests we focus only on *one* path. My internal response was a defensive, "But Mother, I'm *not* following two paths!" Secondly, Mother said that if people leave the satsang, there will be no satsang. By now, I was really getting frightened. I did not like the direction this was going! I thought Mother was done and started to leave, wondering if I was willing to let go of my church experience. The translator then pulled me back and said "So, Mother says you should go to satsang Friday night and then go to church the rest of the time." I was so relieved. All of a sudden going to satsang did not seem to be a problem at all!

Sharing the ashram experience with Kristin and Chaitanya was wonderful. Chaitanya and I engaged in many deep discussions, enjoying each other's company more than ever before. Chaitanya started sleeping on top of the temple and invited me to join her. Each night, we would sleep together under the glorious blanket of stars. Sleeping on the temple roof was, for her, the most memorable part of the trip.

Chaitanya and Kristin.

Chaitanya started working in the ashram school. She loved this work and as a result her decision to become a teacher was reinforced. Kristin went to help at the orphanage. She loved being there but found the experience to be grueling, both emotionally and physically. We cried together, more than once, as she shared her despair over the children's living conditions. When Ammachi had accepted responsibility for the orphanage three years before, there were no sanitation facilities, and the children were starving, uneducated and undisciplined. That was no longer true as there were now functioning showers and toilets as well as roofs on the buildings. The children had suitable clothes, were well fed and were known throughout Kerala for their educational achievement. Nonetheless, the living conditions at the orphanage were still quite primitive compared to what would be considered minimum standards in the west. For example, at that time all of the children still slept on the floor.[2]

Although I was remaining in India for two months, Chaitanya and Kristin were staying only three weeks. As their departure date neared, they decided to relax for a few days at a nearby resort. About that time

---

[2] The conditions at the orphanage have continued to improve. Now all of the children sleep on bunkbeds.

riots began escalating in Bombay, their port of departure from India. When I asked Ammachi what should be done, she advised me to send them via another route. Shobana, a Seattle friend who would be leaving at the same time, and I decided to travel to Trivandrum to change the tickets.

The day before we left for Trivandrum, I had had one of my most powerful darshan experiences ever. I felt Ammachi's love deeply and intensely. I remember thinking, "This will be the last darshan you will have for awhile." As I intended to only be away from the ashram for twenty-four hours, the thought did not make any sense.

Chaitanya also had a memorable darshan before she left for the resort. She had given Mother a letter saying that even though she was not spiritually drawn to Mother, she saw the love Mother had for everyone. She thanked her for letting us stay in her home. As the translator read the letter, Mother started laughing, saying that even though Chaitanya did not feel connected to her, it was too late, she had been connecting to Chaitanya!

Once at the ticket office, Shobana and I discovered we could not change the route due to the occurrence of strikes all over India. We decided the three would stay in India another week. I had planned to spend one day at the resort with Chaitanya and Kristin before they left the country. Due to our last minute decision to change the airline tickets, however, I arrived at the resort twenty-four hours before I was expected.

An unwelcome surprise was in store for me, as Kristin and Chaitanya were nowhere to be seen. It was late, so I knew there was nothing I could do then to find them. While part of me was frantic, another part knew that Kristin, who was in her mid-twenties, was quite capable of taking care of my daughter and herself. During the night, I became feverish. I had nightmares of the two being separated, one sleeping on the beach, the other in the trees! I had lost my daughter in India. What was I to do?

When I awoke the next morning, Shobana said she had a surprise for me. In walked Kristin! They had connected in the hotel lobby when Kristin was delivering a note informing me she had found better accommodations.

Later that day, Shobana returned to the ashram and I joined Kristin and Chaitanya at the new hotel. I still planned to return to the ashram after twenty-four hours. My plans abruptly changed, however, when all three of us became violently ill with vomiting and diarrhea. Day after day, we re-evaluated our condition. Was this the day to go to the hospital? Was this the day to call for help? We were afraid to go to an Indian hospital, so as long as we saw ongoing improvement, we decided we could hold out. The hotel staff members were keeping a watchful eye on us and were helping us in any way they could. We also knew we could call Mother's branch ashram in Trivandrum or the main one in Amritapuri if we needed help.

We discovered the only way any of us could relieve the severe abdominal cramping was to listen to one of Ammachi's bhajan tapes. We only had one tape, so passed it from person-to-person, depending on who needed it the most.

After a week, Chaitanya, Kristin and Shobana took off for the United States. Kristin and Chaitanya were still weak, but were much improved. I was not so lucky. Several days later, with the help of an Ayurvedic physician, I was able to stop the diarrhea. My twenty-four hour trip to Trivandrum had ended up being a two-week trip into Hell. I returned to the ashram much thinner and tired, but glad to be home and proud that I had survived the sickness, staying centered and grounded most of the time.

Ammachi gives blessed ash to Indian visitors fairly routinely. She rarely gives it to western visitors, however, unless they are ill.[3] I had been quite surprised, therefore, when Mother handed me a packet when I first arrived in India. After all, I felt fine! When I went for my first darshan after my momentous trip to Trivandrum, she handed me another packet of ash! I looked at her startled, thinking, "Oh, no! Not again!"

The very next day, I developed symptoms of chronic fatigue syndrome. As I mentioned earlier, I had had little trouble with the disease since I met Mother in 1989. The symptoms came on so fast and were so intense that I was unable to go to dinner that night and had difficulty finding the energy to walk to meals the next day. The second night was a Devi Bhava night. I decided I was going for darshan regardless of my condition. As I proceeded through the line, I thought, "Mother *please* look at me." When I reached her, she looked deeply into my eyes. I felt as if she were looking deeper into me than ever before, right to my core. I felt loved and cared for and firmly connected. By morning, all symptoms of the disease had disappeared.

During darshan a few days later, Ammachi handed me yet another packet of ash. I breathed deeply and thought, "Whatever will be, will be." I felt willing to accept whatever was to come, but was anxious and tired. That night when diarrhea began, someone gave me an Ayurvedic

---

[3]When Mother travels in the west she will occasionally hand out ash to everyone.

remedy. The diarrhea was gone by morning. I was developing a new-found respect for Ayurvedic medicine.

The next week, Remya, one of my friends who lived at the ashram, asked Ammachi why she (Remya) was always sick. Ammachi responded that it was because she would not get close (to Mother) any other way. I assessed my own situation, but Mother's response to Remya did not seem to fit. I did not feel resistance to Mother and was more willing than ever to be close. As I reviewed each of the illnesses, however, I discovered each had enhanced my connection to her. During the first illness, I had called out to Mother and received her comfort through the bhajan tape. During the second, she had merely looked at me and I was healed. During the third, I had surrendered to God's will and became well almost immediately. I believed these healings were manifestations of the power of love and concluded that I knew next to nothing about love. I renewed my commitment to my path with Ammachi and resolved to learn all I could about how to love the way she loves.

For years I had taught that there were four reasons for sickness, 1) poor self-care, 2) contact with a virus or bacteria that is extremely virulent, 3) a lesson to be learned, and 4) purification. Even though I acknowledged all four, I emphasized only the first two. My experiences that year taught me how important the other two were as well. After my return from India I sought massage and integration work with two different practitioners. Both were amazed at the degree of purification that had occurred within me. They told me it was as if I had returned with a new body, similar on the outside, but very different on the inside.

One day, Renuka, another ashram resident, became very sick. She had a high fever, severe headaches, and was delirious. As I watched the physician and nurses go in and out of her room, I felt very helpless. Even though I was a nurse, my medical skills seemed long gone. I wished that Mother would provide a way for me to be of service. Not long thereafter, I discovered that due to Renuka's illness, Remya, her roommate, was plummeting back into memories of childhood traumas. That I knew a lot about! I helped her to understand what was happening and to work through the terror of the flashbacks.

Later that night, I discovered Remya in her room, depressed and almost non-responsive. Devi Bhava darshan was well underway in the temple below us. I asked Remya if she was willing to be held the way I hold clients in my Seattle therapy practice. She answered, "Yes." As I held her, both of us experienced Ammachi coming into me and holding her through me. It was an awesome experience.

Earlier that day, Renuka had been sent to the government hospital in Alleppey, about two hours from the ashram. Two days later, three of us decided to relieve the friends who had accompanied her. As I walked into the hospital, I discovered a maze of concrete corridors leading past a variety of wards. There were no doors to the wards, all were open to public view. Renuka was in a room with nearly twenty other patients. There were no partitions between the beds and unbelievably, some beds had more than one patient. Many beds contained family members as well as patients. The beds were metal and sagged to a V-shape due to years of being overloaded. If there was a mattress on any given bed, it was an unbelievably filthy and rotten piece of foam.

I never saw a nurse or a doctor. If a patient needed a nurse, someone had to find one and bribe them to do what needed to be done. Renuka's arms were covered with bruises from their attempts at inserting IVs.[4] If a patient needed medicine, they were given the entire supply and the family was in charge of administering it.

There was no source of food available in the hospital. Family members had to leave the property to find necessary sustenance. The toilets were simply holes in the floor. Rats waited nearby, sometimes attacking, to get the waste products.

The staff did not appear to consider the type of disease the patients had when assigning beds. Renuka, who had an unknown virus that could have been contagious, was placed next to a child. Across from her was a woman dying of pneumonia. Next to that woman was a dehydrated pregnant woman who was in tremendous pain. Who knows what diseases the other sixteen patients, as well as their families and friends, carried?

While I was overwhelmed and numb from witnessing that scene, I was also overjoyed to see that Renuka was now fever-free and well enough to walk the halls! Thankfully, we were all able to return to the ashram the very next day.

In the days that followed, the picture of that hospital ward was in my mind constantly. I could not stop crying. When I went to Ammachi, she asked why I was crying. I said I cried because of what I had witnessed at the hospital. She looked at me with what I describe as her "Miss Inno-

---

[4]IVs - intravenous infusions.

cent" look and asked, "What did you see?" When I described the horrific
scene, she matter-of-factly told me the government did not care about
the hospital or its patients, they would do nothing about it. I could only
guess why this lesson had been given Renuka, but I could easily recognize

Karuna and Renuka.

at least some of the lessons learned by those of us who accompanied her.
This had been a significant life experience for me. I told Ammachi I
looked forward to the day when she would have hospitals in India that
provided the type of care patients deserve to have. (At some point the
next year, Mother announced plans to build an 800 bed tertiary care hospital near Cochin!)

As I thought of everything I had seen and felt, I remembered Bishop
Ford's statement about tithing, that if all of us tithed ten percent of our
income to God's work, there would be enough for everyone to have what
they needed. I also remembered the message of a movie I had seen the
previous year, *The Power of One*, a reminder that one person cannot fix
the world but each person can make a substantial difference. I started
thinking of ways I could contribute when I returned to Seattle.

As I neared the end of my stay in India, I reviewed the goals I had
made for this particular trip. I had desired to have the willingness and
energy to participate in seva activities. I had been able to accomplish
that goal. I had served food in the canteen, washed and sown mattresses
for the orphanage infirmary, worked in the print shop, carried sand for
the landfill and made beaded earrings to be sold on the next world tour. I

had actually enjoyed many of those activities. I had learned to take the attitude that whatever I did was enough. Even though I may have carried only three sacks of sand to the landfill, they were three sacks someone else did not have to carry.

Another of my goals was to meditate, and to enjoy the process. I had meditated in the past, but had never enjoyed it unless it was the state that came spontaneously during bhajans. That year, I decided to try a new tactic. I sat on the top of the temple each morning and meditated while listening to gospel music on my tape player. The effect of combining my two worlds was incredibly powerful. My hands consistently formed spontaneous mudras. I found myself truly looking forward to the meditation times.

There were two songs that were particularly important to me during that time:

The first was a traditional gospel melody:

Yes, Lord, yes
To Your will and to Your way.
I'll say Yes, Lord, Yes
I will trust You and obey.
When Your spirit calls to Me
With my whole heart I'll agree.
And my answer will be
Yes, Lord, Yes.[5]

The second was based on Psalm 51:10 which states:

Create in me a clean heart, O God
and renew a right spirit within me.[6]

Even though we say we are committed to our spiritual process, there is still a large part of us that resists. A brahmachari once taught that

---

[5] Traditional Gospel melody.
[6] *Psalm 51:10, Holy Bible*, King James version 1611.

when one hundred percent of us wants Self-Realization, we would have it. As I prepared to leave India, I asked Ammachi to help me to adopt the attitude these songs conveyed.

I had not been sure what Mother would think of me using my tape player during meditation. I avoided asking because I did not want to hear, "No." Before I left India, however, I decided to ask if it was acceptable for me to meditate with music or if I should learn to meditate in silence. Her response, it was fine for me to use the music!

Another of that year's goals was to maintain a consistent yoga practice. I had done well until I became ill. Afterwards, I had become quite lax in my self-discipline. Something on which to focus after I returned to Seattle!

My final week in India was to be spent at programs rededicating a temple Ammachi had opened in Trivandrum the previous year. During the rededication, archana[7] is performed five times daily. In addition, twice a day Mother lectures, leads bhajans, and gives darshan.

I attended five days of the eight-day program. I had chanted the archana before but never more than once a day. I was amazed at the intensity of my experience. I discovered a steady stream of insights and new ideas emerged during the altered states created by the archanas. I remembered a brahmachari once stating that when he teaches meditation techniques to other brahmacharis, he instructs them to stay focused on the meditation, not allowing their minds to be captivated by the thoughts that emerge. My response was, "Well, I'm not a monk. This is wonderful!" At the end of each program, I rushed to my journal to jot down the insights and new ideas.

I was aware that I had experienced almost none of my usual grief during this trip to India. As my departure date neared, I found myself filled with excitement about the new projects I would set in motion upon my return to Seattle. I recognized there was so much to be done that the time between my departure from India and Mother's next visit to the United States would seem brief. I also reasoned that the lack of grief must indicate I was filled with her love.

I knew I would be able have Mother's darshan the night before I left, no matter how large the crowds were. I was taken by surprise, how-

---

[7] Archana - chanting of the 1,000 names of the Divine Mother.

ever, when forty-eight hours before I was to leave, Ammachi announced that all western devotees could come for darshan that night.[8]

During that day I attended all of the archanas, entering deeper and deeper altered states of consciousness. The bhajans that night further intensified my meditative state. All of a sudden my grief hit full force. I was so overwhelmed by the waves of sorrow, I ran for the dorm, curled up

Food preparation.

Food lines.

---

[8] When Mother travels in India the crowds typically are 7,000-15,000. The western devotees who travel with her do not go for darshan unless they are just arriving or are leaving.

into a ball and wept uncontrollably. From my room I could hear a brahmachari begin to sing a song that sounded like a lullaby. I could take no more. I dove for a friend seated nearby, cuddled close and let the tears come.

I could not stop crying and soon realized I needed Mother's help. I returned to the program, only to discover that even though Ammachi had indicated the western devotees could come for darshan, they were not doing so due to the size of the crowd. Several devotees told me to get in line anyway, but I refused. Soon I realized I was acting like some of my clients who insist on staying unnecessarily miserable. I forced myself to enter the line.

When Ammachi saw me from afar, a momentary look of alarm crossed her face. (Later when someone asked if I had requested Mother to cure my eye infections, I realized I must have looked dreadful. I certainly had no eye infections!) When I finally reached Mother, she asked what was wrong. I responded I was sad because I was to leave India in two days. She started laughing, telling the people around her why I was crying. When she held me, the experience was different from any other time. I had the feeling of blacking out for a few seconds. When I "came to," I was holding her tightly, which is not to be done. I panicked because I also realized I was not willing to let go! I thought quickly and decided that what I needed to do was to simply relax into her. When I did that, all of my grief washed away. As I thought about that experience during the weeks that followed, the word surrender kept coming into my mind. I realized I had surrendered at a new level.

The next day, I attended all of the archanas. That night, during bhajans, I sat near the back of the hall near an Indian family who had a small baby. The baby appeared to be about eight months old, although it was hard to tell for sure as she seemed to be extremely malnourished. The family was intent on making the baby pay attention to me. When she indicated she was hungry, they distracted her. Eventually, they pulled out a bottle that contained a very strange looking brown liquid. The baby stopped crying as they prepared the bottle, so once prepared, they set the bottle aside. The next time she started crying, they again tried to distract her. This time she was not willing to be distracted so they took the nipple off the bottle and put it in the dirt. The mother then put a small amount of the liquid in her hand and let the baby lick it. The baby sucked eagerly. The mother then replaced the nipple on the bottle, and put the bottle back in the bag. The baby had not received more than a quarter of a teaspoon of fluid. My heart ached. I believed I was seeing the result of western technology (both the bottle and the formula) having been given to people who had no idea how to properly use them. This experience had much the same impact as my earlier hospital visit. Once again, I felt committed to do whatever I could do to rectify the situation.

As we prepared to leave India, my friend Joan joked, "You don't need to worry about travel leelas this time, I'm with you!" (She had experienced a remarkably smooth journey to the ashram.) I cringed, thinking she might be challenging the universe in a way we would soon regret.

Although we were concerned about the rioting in Bombay, we were able to leave the country without delay. As we flew to Bangkok, Joan and I discovered the same song was "playing" in both of our heads, one we had heard only once before. That song played non-stop during the rest of the trip. It helped vastly in aiding us to maintain a sense of calmness during the events that followed.

At first, the routine in Bangkok seemed normal. The crew was ready for the 11:00 p.m. departure, but the plane did not leave. First, we were told there would be a one-hour delay. Since there were many empty seats available, Joan and I lay down and went to sleep. When we woke up some time later, we realized if we did not leave soon, we would miss our international connection. Eventually, we were told the plane could not be fixed, we would have to spend the night at the airport hotel. Further, we were told there would be no more flights leaving for Tokyo that night, on any airline. For reasons unknown to us, we were detained even longer. When we were finally led through the airport, on the way to the hotel, we noticed the television monitor indicated a flight would be leaving for Tokyo in an hour. We broke the rules, darting for the other airline, soon discovering we could easily be accommodated. The only problem, we must have the written approval of our airline staff. We searched both on-foot and by phone, but could find no one to approve the flight. At that point we gave up and found our way to the airport hotel.

When we checked into the hotel, we were told that except for meals we were to stay in our room. The written instructions stated that the airline would see that we were booked on another flight. We were to be prepared to leave with an hour's notice. We waited the better part of the day, checking in occasionally with the airline's office. After hours of waiting, we realized we were being given another "run-around." We believed the staff had no intention of booking us on another airline. We left the hotel room and started looking for a flight ourselves. Once again, we were able to easily find a way out of Bangkok. The problem, we needed the approval of our original carrier.

We contacted the agent and were instructed to come to the office at 8:00 p.m. When we arrived, we were very rudely instructed to go to another location. Once at that location, we were directed back to the office. No one was in the office the rest of the night. What followed was a series of "two steps forward and one step back" experiences. We were able to retrieve our passports, which had been taken when we arrived in Bangkok, only to discover that since we had the passports without immigration papers, we were in the country illegally. There seemed to be no way to retrieve our baggage from the other airline. The original airline would give only verbal travel authorization, and the new airline would take only written. We were told we had to pay airport taxes even though the other airline was responsible for our delay. The problems seemed never-ending. Each step was practice in staying grounded and focused and sticking to the process. We persisted and as a result were one of only five people from our original flight that left the country that day.

Insights and Gifts
Winter/Spring 1993

I readjusted to the United States easier than ever before. I came back full of creative energy, so quickly started implementing the service projects I had planned in India. I found that many people were interested in helping in one way or another, they simply needed to know ways to contribute.

I was constantly aware of how much the hospital visit had impacted me. Soon after that experience, I sensed I was not to sleep on a bed when I returned home. Therefore, when I arrived in Seattle, I turned my bedroom into a meditation room, and began sleeping on a straw mat.

I was unsure why I had been internally directed to give up my bed. I knew it was not, "If they can't have it, you can't have it either." I watched for the purpose of the lesson to emerge. The first reason that became evident was that sleeping on the floor helped me to remember all I had seen and experienced. I sensed that my experiences might have been relegated to a dream state had I not had a tangible reminder. After a few weeks, I discovered that I slept on the floor as easily and as deeply as when I slept on a bed. I then understood why Ammachi had not made a top priority of obtaining beds for the children in the orphanage, there were many more important needs. Sleeping on the floor also gave me an incredible sense of freedom. I realized if I could sleep here this easily, I could sleep quite comfortably almost anywhere. Soon thereafter, I recognized that when I slept on the floor I did not sleep as long, so I had more time to do what I needed or wanted to do.

For years I had said that japa[9] was not meant to be part of my spiritual path. I had no idea how I came to that conclusion, probably it was one of the ways I had avoided the Krishna mantra. Towards the end of my stay in India, however, I decided that once I returned to Seattle I would give mantra japa another try.

In India, Ammachi had the ashram residents use a tally counter to count their mantras. I purchased one and started saying 1000-5000 mantras a day, occasionally more! I noticed that I soon had more energy than normal and found it extremely easy to stay centered and calm and take whatever lessons came. Several weeks after I started japa, I woke up with the mantra going nonstop through my mind. I realized that this process was probably continuing throughout the night. In that moment of realization, I felt incredibly peaceful and filled with devotional energy.

It occurred to me that since the mantra process worked so well for me, it might also be a helpful tool for clients. For years my clients had used affirmations to help change belief patterns, but as they tended to say the affirmations only one to ten times a day, I had been doubtful for some time about the efficacy of that technique. I decided to challenge each client to, using a tally counter, say his or her affirmations a minimum of 1000 times a day for twenty-one days. We were all astounded by the results. They were able to change dysfunctional belief patterns at a rate I had never before witnessed, filling me with a renewed respect for the teachings of the Masters.

On Easter Sunday, a new development in my process occurred at Power House, my feet began to dance on their own! Those manifestations of Spirit I had not previously exhibited were suddenly happening to me! As I let go of more of my inhibitions over the next few months, I

---

[9] Japa - mantra repetition.

became freer and freer in the dance until I found myself experiencing episodes of what could only be called "getting drunk" in the Spirit. At times I was so intoxicated with bliss that I found I could not even walk without support.

New Worlds Open!
1993 *Summer Tour*

That summer was filled with new experiences. It was as if a new world opened up to me. For the most part, the old grief was gone, replaced by joy, adventure and new skills to learn.

The first incident occurred during the Seattle retreat. Starting with my first trip to India, whenever I was with Ammachi I had experienced pain in my back muscles due, I had supposed, to long hours of sitting. More recently, along with the back pain, I had pain along the sides and back of my neck. This led to shoulder tension and headaches. Not only was this a problem when I was with Ammachi, but also when in the powerful energy at Power House.

The second day of the retreat, while meditating alone in a field, I noticed my body beginning to move spontaneously. I soon discovered that these movements released all of the built up pain-producing energy. Some of the movements I knew to be yoga postures, some were totally different.

I was used to my hands spontaneously forming mudras. Also, following my first days with Ammachi, there had been several occasions when my arms and hands moved spontaneously when in a meditative state. At that time, the entire process was so new and foreign to me that I was too afraid to allow the movements to continue. This time, however, I simply let go and observed. I discovered that as I sat cross-legged on the ground, my head, neck, arms and trunk moved in ways that intricately stretched each muscle group needed to release the backache and headache. In the next few days, I discovered that I could depend on my body releasing those energies in that way. If I began to feel the familiar tension in my neck or back, I would go to a private spot and let the movements emerge. They never failed me, the energy was always released.

One night, I found the movements to have another benefit. I had gone to bed, feeling a particularly nasty chest cold coming on, my chest filling fast with fluid. I was exhausted and wanted simply to lie there, but my body let me know that I needed to get up and let it exercise. By the time the movements had run their course, about fifty minutes, all traces of the lung congestion and cold were gone. The next day all that was left was fatigue.

I was enthralled by this new discovery and its potential implications. Perhaps our bodies have the ability to heal themselves in minutes, no matter what the problem is. Maybe we just have to get out of the way and let our bodies do what needs to be done!

The energy in my body had increased vastly since Ammachi had arrived in the United States. I needed to allow the movements to come at least three times a day in order to prevent head and neck pain. Each process took fifteen to fifty minutes, usually stopping by my decision that I had had enough. Since the movements seemed to always be immediately accessible, I couldn't imagine how long they would last if I let them run their own course unimpeded.

That year, Chaitanya attended the Seattle retreat. One of the joys of being around Ammachi is watching her play with people. Chaitanya and I experienced one of those playful moments ourselves. While she had interacted with Ammachi more this year, she still kept her distance. One day at the retreat, Chaitanya came into the program area looking for me. Ammachi saw her and beckoned to her. Chaitanya ducked behind me, acting as if she did not know Mother had called. Ammachi kept looking towards her, raising her eyebrows much like a mom playing "peek-a-boo" with her child. Finally, one of my friends laughingly said, "Karuna, take your daughter up to Mother!" Chaitanya and I grinned and went forward together.

Sreejit had continued in his serious renunciate path. This year, he asked Mother for permission to move to India. Ammachi is very concerned that young people receive education and training, so it was no surprise to me when she said, "No," she wanted him to continue with his schooling, suggesting religious studies. While he was very disappointed to hear the "No," he was pleased she had given him some direction. As it is very important to me that Sreejit learns the skills of living in the world before he moves into an ashram, I immensely appreciated the structure she gave him.

A week after the Seattle retreat, I attended some of programs in the Bay Area of California. During one of those programs, an event occurred which was very meaningful to me. While watching darshan, I looked to my left and saw Swamini Amma[10] (then called Gayatri), looking more radiant and happy than I had ever seen. As I looked around, I noticed one brahmachari after another becoming excited. I soon discovered that a brahmacharini who had left Mother three years before had returned. I found myself flooded with grief that was way out of proportion to the situation. I knew the brahmacharini also, and was very happy to see her back, but knew something also was going on within me. I soon realized what I was observing was what occurs in a healthy family when a child who has run away returns home. The welcome she received was so different from that given by my father the previous year. The reason for my profound grief was obvious.

Prior to the first evening program of the San Ramon retreat, I was in my room allowing the exercises to occur. My body went into a yoga posture I had adamantly avoided during my years of studying yoga. Whenever I had performed that particular posture, I had become nauseated and my body filled with terror. As the familiar terror soared through my body, I realized that this exercise process would not be solely for the purpose of ending physical ailments, it was also going to take me into blocked memories such as the unknown terror this particular yoga posture accessed. I said, "No," I'm not going there, at least not now," and lay down.

I attended the evening program, my body still reeling from the terror. I decided it was time to notify Ammachi about my recent experiences. Over the years, I had read that many of the patients in mental hospitals have had spiritual emergencies misdiagnosed as psychosis. A guru can lead you through these experiences safely. I knew I was entering an unknown and perhaps dangerous process so I resolved to keep her *fully* informed!

At the first opportunity, I told Mother about the spontaneous body movements and about the nausea and dizziness that were the frequent side effects of the sometimes rapid movements. I told her that when I felt overwhelmed, I simply lay down. I asked, "Mother, isn't there something I should know about what is happening to me?" hoping for a fulfilling discussion of the process. "Yes," she responded, "that sometimes happens when meditation patterns change. If you are overwhelmed, lie down." My response was frustration, relief and amusement. Ammachi is so consistent in her refusal to feed the minds of western devotees!

---

[10] Mother's personal attendant.

Two days later, as I was waiting for darshan, a friend rushed up to me requesting that I come to the ashram to help Remya who was once again dealing with traumatic memory flashbacks. After we had completed some energy release work, I held her for a while and once again we both experienced Ammachi coming to her through me. I felt tremendous surges of energy soaring through my body as well as overflowing love and compassion. The same thing happened again that evening. I wondered if I was being allowed a tiny glimpse of what the third stage of spiritual development would be like, that is, merging with Ammachi.

While I was very excited about these experiences, on a physical level I was close to burnout. I felt as if I had been plugged into a wall socket. All of my nerve endings felt exposed and vulnerable. In the past, I had attended one or more church services in Seattle in between my summer trips with Mother. This time when I stopped by Power House to find out what church programs were planned, I described to Pastor Jenkins the sensations that were occurring in my body. He told me I was like a rubber band that had been stretched to its breaking point. He reminded me of the importance of balance and suggested I rest rather than attend church that night. I appreciated the fatherly advice protecting me from my own enthusiasm.

My next "unusual" experience happened the following weekend at the Los Angeles retreat. I was in my room, allowing the exercises to come. Up to that point, I always had let them occur seated, never changing the position of my legs. I kept my eyes closed throughout the process. This time, after a few minutes, I was startled when my arms hit the wall. For a moment, I felt jolted and off balance and then realized there was no way my arms could have hit the wall from where I had been sitting. My eyes flew open. Somehow without my knowing it, my body had rotated ninety degrees! As nothing of the sort had ever happened before, panic tore through my body. I breathed deeply and worked to ground myself. I wondered if I should, once again, tell Ammachi what was happening. As I calmed down, I realized nothing bad had happened, the process was simply evolving. I sensed Ammachi was watching me closely, so decided there was no need to talk to her about this particular development.

The day after I returned from the Los Angeles retreat, while allowing the exercises to run their course, I sensed that my body wanted to go lower than the floor would allow. I decided to see what would happen if I stood up. The exercises that emerged were remarkable, whole body lunging, Edgu, yoga, and some of the Chinese processes, perhaps Tai Chi, that I knew nothing about. The exercises were much more strenuous than I had experienced before. When I tired, I lay down and rested. As I stilled, my arms started making spontaneous clockwise and counterclockwise movements over various parts of my body, particularly over my third eye.

This pattern of active physical exercise followed by more gentle, passive energy-moving motions continued. The yoga exercises grew in intensity. Aadil, my yoga teacher, had been known for his zeal in pushing his students, but I realized this internal "instructor" was even harder on me than Aadil. It knew the location of *all* of my weak points!

A few days later after the heavier exercises were over and I was lying down, my hands started circling over my stomach and I became nauseated, over my heart and I developed heart pain, then over my third eye. I started dry heaving and sobbing. The energy inside of me felt chaotic and totally out of control.

I remembered two stories Mother had shared in the past. One story related how Krishna had come to a devotee only when she called out solely to God, forgoing all human assistance. The other was the story of a person who died because he insisted on God's direct intervention, rejecting the doctor and anesthesiologist God sent to help. I felt caught between the two teachings. I chose to meditate rather than call friends for help.

The sensations passed, but I felt miserable. The next day I experienced many involuntary altered states of consciousness. I made appointments with two body-workers who do varying forms of energy work. The first one intuitively placed my body into some of the same positions that my own body had tried to create the day before. He was able to push my body parts further than I could by myself. Once those motions were completed, I again felt in balance.

The second body-worker reminded me of the importance of breathing and taught me some new techniques for grounding. Later that day, when I let the exercises come, they once again became very chaotic. I felt dizzy and panicky. When I remembered to breathe, the movements became rhythmic, almost like a dance. I remembered all of the times Aadil had tried to teach me breathing techniques and I had internally responded, "Aadil, I can't even do these positions, I don't care about any breathing." I knew I was now paying the consequences for refusing to learn earlier lessons.

Over the next few days I speculated, "If I am willing to go through this perhaps there might be a point in time where I can sit in my home in the United States and at the same time 'go' to the nightly bhajans in India." The very thought of that possibility created motivation enough to go through just about anything.

I continued having trouble with spontaneously triggered, uncontrollable altered states. One day, when heading to a meeting, I started "fading out." I arrived at the meeting teary and feeling out of control. On the way there I had spontaneously slapped my arm, reminding me of a therapeutic technique we call "pons stimulation." In this procedure clients are "clapped" with many cupped hands over the length of their body. The therapeutic procedure is used to help re-awaken the bodies of clients who have become numb due to years of childhood abuse. When I arrived at the meeting, I asked my friends and colleagues to do the procedure on me. The intervention brought me immediately back to full consciousness.

The next day, I again started slipping into an altered state process while shopping. When I returned to my car, I put an Ammachi tape in the cassette recorder, something I would not normally do when in that condition. My hands began spontaneously clapping my leg in time to the music, in much the same way that we "clap" during bhajans. I immediately returned to full consciousness. I laughed when I realized that Ammachi must use the music to help us enter altered states and then uses clapping to keep devotees "grounded!"

The next week, I decided to attend an initiation that the Dalai Lama was conducting in Seattle. When he entered the room, I immediately went into an altered state and stayed there most of the morning. My hands started forming mudras, more rapid and more intricate than I had ever experienced. I would occasionally "come out" of the altered state, just in time to hear an important remark, and then would "go under" again. The Dalai Lama informed us that only people who had received a variety of previous Buddhist initiations would actually receive this initiation, the rest of us could take a nap or simply enjoy the meditation. During the initiation process, my hands moved in continual mudras and I noticed a variety of sensations in my body. It seemed to me that my body was moving in conjunction with what he was saying and doing. I had the distinct impression I was actually receiving the initiation that day, even though, at least in this lifetime, I had never had the prerequisite initiations.

At one point during the day, the Dalai Lama talked about the concept of emptiness. It occurred to me that it was when I went into the
state of emptiness that the mudras and exercises emerged. I had learned
to create emptiness without even knowing what I was doing!

A few days later, during a meditation, I had the distinct feeling
another being was present in the room with me. Simultaneously, my
mind started spontaneous chanting of the Krishna mantra, a mantra I
had not thought of for years. I *knew* that it was Krishna who was present.
My being exploded with love and devotion for Krishna. I experienced his
presence on and off for the next three days. I felt and acted like a woman
who was madly in love. While at one level this experience seemed very
bizarre, at another it felt perfectly normal. Once again I had evidence
that my receiving the Krishna mantra during that first week with Ammachi
was no accident. Still later, it occurred to me that Ammachi had granted
my 1991 request, to be taught to love Krishna. She had certainly met my
desire in a far different way than I had expected!

On the third day of this experience, I felt an intense scare that if I
allowed this connection with Krishna to develop, I would lose Ammachi.
Even though there was no evidence for such a conclusion, I consoled my
"inner child" by telling her I would consult Mother during the New York
program.

We flew to New York in time to be able to greet Ammachi at the
airport. When she touched me during airport darshan, my consciousness
became so altered I forgot to reach for the candy she was handing me,
staying erect was of more concern!

During the first program in New York, I handed the translator a
note that briefly stated the events of the previous few days. I asked
Ammachi to tell me she would stay with me, no matter where my path
might lead. The translator took the note, read it to himself, and seemingly did nothing. I was pushed to the side by the crowd and immediately
entered an intensely altered state. One of my hands started spontaneously tapping my shoulder in a way that I had come to realize was to keep
me somewhat present in the room. The altered state lifted only once in
the next forty-five minutes. At that moment, I discovered Ammachi to
be looking directly at me. I had the sense that she was going deep inside
of me to find out *exactly* what had happened. Soon thereafter, the altered
state ended. The translator leaned over to me and said, "She says it's
fine." I looked at him, irritated, thinking, "That is not what I asked for."

He repeated, "She says it's fine." Later, I realized that once again I had been given what I needed, instead of what I wanted.

I decided while I was in New York City I would go to a Church of God in Christ service. There was a COGIC church in West Harlem, just a few blocks from Ammachi's program. The church service was very different from what I was used to. There were only twenty-five to thirty people at the service, the average age being around sixty-five. The songs were soulful and melancholy rather than celebratory. I could feel the spirit energy present, although it seemed so muted. When the offering was taken, I noticed many people would give coins or would put a dollar on the offering plate and then take back change. As always the people were extremely friendly and saw that I was included in everything.

As I left church that day and walked through Harlem, the signs of poverty were rampant. There were rows and rows of buildings full of graffiti, their first story windows bricked over. People were living on the streets. Empty alcohol bottles and drug paraphernalia littered the streets and parks. Two blocks away, luxury apartments rented for $1,500 a month. I cried as I saw all of this. I sensed that the lack of young people and the lack of funds in the church reflected the fact that the streets with their drugs and crime were winning.

Only about ten blocks from the Harlem church stood the Cathedral of St. John the Divine. This was the cathedral in which I had had such a powerful vision the previous year. As I walked in, I once again felt the powerful draw to the rear of the church. The tunnel vision of an altered state experience began. Since there was a wedding about to take place in the back portion of the cathedral, I was not able to go to the same area as the previous year.

I soon discovered this was to be no ordinary wedding. As I moved towards the rear of the church, I passed members of the wedding party dressed in brightly colored African garb. When I was as far to the rear as I was allowed to go, I knelt at an altar rail. As organ music began in some part of the cathedral, I started to weep. In another area of the cathedral an organ played the song, *I Believe*. Next the huge pipe organ began to sound, its magnificent notes filling the cathedral. My body spontaneously prostrated, my head moving to touch the floor. My tears began to pour. A wedding procession of people playing African drums marched through the cathedral. At that moment, my tears became so profuse my contact lenses were washed away. I started quietly murmuring "Ma Ma

Ma" and then started "speaking in tongues." This was the first time that manifestation of Spirit had ever happened to me! The tongues and the tears lasted for close to an hour. When at last they faded, I noticed there was a stream of my tears dripping down the altar rail into a puddle on the floor.

I stumbled outside, blinded by my lack of glasses. I walked most of the way home before finding a taxi. Energy raced through my body. When I arrived at my apartment, I tried to lie down but the energy inside of me was too intense. After a while, my body started flailing around with the chaotic energy. Luckily, my friend Shobana was available to help me get grounded.

As I reflected on that experience, I marveled at the synchronicity of all that had occurred. The wedding began minutes after I had arrived from the service in Harlem, a service that ended on flextime as opposed a particular set time. The experience contained elements that had touched me at a soul level throughout my life. Africa, the destination of my original missionary zeal and the subject of two movies that had profoundly impacted me during the previous year, *At Play in the Fields of the Lord* and *The Power of One*. Drums, the common denominator between the poem Shelley had written for me after my first trip to India, tabla lessons, bhajans in India, Tribal Therapy band, and Power House church. The appearance of tongues seemed like a new thread being woven through a fabric long under construction.

For the rest of the tour, I experienced the sensation of "speaking in tongues" whenever I was around Ammachi. Usually the words came too fast to recognize. A few times, however, I was able to identify the words as they slowed down. Once I heard "Sita, Sita, Sita,"[11] another time "Sharade, Sharade, Sharade."[12] Weeks later I read the story of the life of a Hindu saint. This saint experienced vocalization of spontaneously occurring mantras. I wondered if the "tongues" experienced by Pentecostal believers might be Sanskrit mantras. I marveled at even the possibility the religious experiences of the east and west might be joined in that way.

Another important event occurred during the east coast tour. On my last morning in New York, I decided not to go for morning darshan. I would go instead during Devi Bhava that night. At one point, I glanced up and thought I saw Ammachi look at me. Simultaneously I *heard*, "Do

---

[11] An incarnation of Lakshmi, Goddess of Abundance.
[12] Sharade was a name for the Goddess of Wisdom.

not go to darshan during Devi Bhava, come NOW." I immediately joined the line.

This experience of feeling directed was very different from any previous experience. It seemed more like a direct communication from Ammachi to me, via telepathy, than the "knowings" or sense of receiving inner direction that I commonly have. I could find no words to describe the difference, I simply knew it was different.

When Mother touched me during the darshan that day, my consciousness shifted immediately. Once again, I forgot to take the candy she held out to me. When the program ended, soon thereafter, Shobana and I headed out for lunch. As we were walking through New York City streets, I experienced a chaotic energy rush through my body and with it came a tremendous surge of fear. I later concluded the fear might have been a past-life flashback. I was overwhelmed and panicky but luckily, Shobana was again available to help me get grounded. The overwhelming fear came in unpredictable surges throughout the next hour. I was thankful Mother had called me for "regular" darshan. I felt much too brittle to handle the accelerated energy of Devi Bhava darshan. I once again felt seen and protected.

A few days later in Boston, I experienced another series of travel leelas. Something happened each day that prevented Shobana and me from resting between the morning and evening programs. On the final day, we left the morning program only to discover that the rental car had electrical problems and could not be driven. I was frustrated and slightly amused. Would this type of lesson ever end?

That evening, I decided not to go for darshan. I had to drive to Rhode Island the next day and wanted to ensure my mind would be clear and my energy stable. I looked up at one point during the evening and noticed Remya was in the darshan line. When Ammachi touched Remya's third eye, I felt energy surge inside of *me*! I was amazed. Afterwards someone told me I looked drunk, that is, drunk in Spirit. Indeed I was! The process that was happening between Remya and me was fascinating. I thought getting double darshans was a splendid side effect. I wondered if we could also find a way to receive the benefit of each other's lessons without having to endure the pain of going through them ourselves!

Years ago, Swamiji had taught that during the early part of spiritual process, we have to make most of the effort. He said that later on God starts pulling us. I felt that transition happening. I realized that by simply "going where the Spirit said go" and "doing what the Spirit said do" I was doing everything I believed was important in a solid spiritual practice. I was meditating, doing yoga, japa, singing, and service work. Ammachi has said one's whole life should be a prayer. I felt that was more and more true for me. I also discovered I had incorporated the belief that everything I owned, as opposed to only my ten-percent tithe, was God's. I did not know when or how I had made all of these shifts, it seemed as if they had just happened. I remembered one of the church's sayings, "Let go and let God." I think I had finally created the space and the willingness to let God take over.

Throughout all of the east coast programs, I experienced my questions being answered prior to my asking them. For example, I would be sitting at dinner and people at the table would be discussing a subject I had been contemplating. This has always happened to some extent, but the occasions had increased dramatically and as a result my concerns were rapidly diminishing.

My one outstanding question concerned when to rely solely on God and when to use the of support others. I asked Ammachi that question in Boston. She uncharacteristically gave a long and detailed answer. She started by saying that in the east the brahmacharis turn over all their money and property to God, and rely on God for everything. She said that is not the way of the west. Here we are expected to use our discrimination, relying solely on God only when circumstances require that attitude. She told me the story of a disciple whose job was to take care of the cows. One day the disciple took the cows off to pasture and then returned to the guru. The guru asked what he was doing there when he was supposed to be taking care of the cows. The disciple's response was "God will take care of the cows." Ammachi looked at me and said that the disciple's attitude was not appropriate. I thought, "But Mother, I'm talking about what to do when the energy gets out of control and chaotic." She looked at me intensely and said, "You are not to call out *only* to God, unless you are in a life-and-death emergency and you have no other choice." That was what I needed to hear. I understood I have been given a tremendous amount of support and as I proceed through this process, I am expected to take advantage of what I have been given. She will be there to help me, but I am to use *all* of the tools I have been given. I was grateful for the *very* direct and detailed answer.

The Rhode Island retreat, the last of the year, was a time of stabilization. The mudras and "tongues" continued. I experienced both joy and grief during bhajans. At one point, when the grief was particularly intense, I was sitting cross-legged with my head resting on the floor. My hands moved forward spontaneously and held my head. I felt as if Mother had taken over my hands and that she herself was gently holding my head in her hands. I relaxed at the touch. Over the next few days, that happened several times. This was not what I had imagined she meant when she said, "I am closer to you than you are to yourself," but I enjoyed the experience all the same. So many new processes had begun this summer, I wondered what would happen next.

Perhaps the most important event of all took place during my last regular[13] darshan with Mother. As she held me, I was in an extremely altered state of consciousness. When she looked into my eyes I saw her smile at me and heard her say the word "mukti." Later, I asked what the word meant and was told it meant "liberation."

---

[13] as opposed to Devi Bhava darshan.

AFTERWARD

Mother
Sing through me
Mother
Play a song
So sweetly with these hands
Let me see with your vision
Let me feel with your boundless heart
With these feet of mine walk the earth
And with my life, give birth.[1]

Would I wake up the next morning and find everything different? Would she touch me at Devi Bhava, changing my whole world? I had been in an altered state. Had I heard the word incorrectly? Had she said anything at all? Not surprisingly, nothing dramatic happened. In the weeks that followed Ammachi's departure from the United States, my process slowed down. The spontaneous exercises continued but were shorter in duration and less intense. The speaking in "tongues" occurred both in church and in my private meditations. My personal challenge continued to be to balance my spiritual process and living in the world. I had to learn how to live with the increased level of energy running through my body and with the hair-triggered altered states. As I write this, I am still unable to listen to either Mother's bhajan tapes or gospel music in the car.

As mentioned earlier, during the New York program I had felt inner direction to write this book. When the tour was over, I started working on the book in every spare moment. My writing was a major tool in helping me to "ground" and reenter my everyday world. I don't know what is next. What I do know is that I love Mother, I love my journey with her and I love the changes occurring in me and in my world. Wherever she leads, I hope I have the strength to follow.

August 1993

---

[1] Kathy Zavada, excerpts from song, "Serve the Mother," *Mother's Song*, Mount Shasta: Precious Music.

BOOK 2

Ammachi

INTRODUCTION

E ver since *Getting to Joy, Book 1* was released in the summer of 1997, a steady stream of people requested that I write a sequel. Book 1 covered a period that ended in 1993. When I reflected on all that I experienced between 1993 and 1997, I realized I had many more stories and lessons to share.

This book will begin where the last one ended. I have used the same structure as in the first book. The only major difference is that I will share considerably less of my children's spiritual journeys. Their stories are theirs to share.

PART 1

Let us dance and dance along with the Lord Krishna and sing gaily His glory forever and ever. Seeing the face of the Blissful One, let us get ourselves immersed in the ocean of bliss, forgetting everything else in seeking His refuge.[1]

I Find the Dance!
Summer/Fall 1993

In the months following the tour, the sounds in my head, which I still labeled as "tongues," became a frequent companion. They were often accompanied by massive amounts of energy. One day, so much energy came with the tongues that I was afraid to deal with it alone. I called Mrs. Jenkins at Power House Church of God in Christ and asked if I could be with her while I allowed the sounds and feelings to emerge. She said she would be happy to support me in that way. The sounds, which continued for about fifteen minutes unabated, were accompanied by gut-wrenching grief.

One day, the tongues started during a meditation. This time there was no accompanying emotion. The "words" were primarily repetition of the syllables "ba" and "da." The pitch of the sounds began to change, becoming higher and higher. All of a sudden, my arms spontaneously extended from my sides and my hands clapped together. Immediately, the sounds stopped and I returned to full consciousness.

On yet another day, the tongues started shortly before a client appointment. I began to panic because I could not control them and there was no way I could meet with a client in that state! Pastor and Mrs.

[1]"Atituvom Namum Atituvom," *Bhajanamritam Volume 3*, San Ramon: Mata Amritanandamayi Center, 1997, pg. 43.

Jenkins were not at church, so I decided to call the California ashram and talk to Swami Paramatmananda. I described what was happening and asked him for advice. He asked if I had told Mother about this process. I told him that I had not informed her specifically about the tongues, but that I had shared other unusual experiences with her. Her response to me at that time had been, "It's fine." "Then it's fine," said Swami Paramatmananda. "It is NOT fine," I exclaimed. "I have a client coming in half-an-hour!" He recommended that I take a cold shower and if that did not ground me, I should go for a walk. If I was still having problems after the shower and the walk, he suggested that I cancel the client appointment and instead spend time with someone who would understand. I thanked him for the structure. I was soon pleased to discover that the cold shower grounded me immediately.

So much energy was coursing through my body that it became necessary to spend many hours a day finding ways to ground myself. By then I had collected many suggestions for returning to a normal state of consciousness.

- Breathe, slowly and deeply
- Lie down, send excess energy to my heart
- Lie down, send excess energy into the earth
- Cold shower
- Pons stimulation (deep massage and/or clapping of body)
- Chocolate
- Pace - ten steps, turn, ten steps, turn
- Wrap myself tightly in a blanket
- Put my right hand on the top of my head
- Jump up, land on my heels with knees bent
- Take a walk
- Sit down outdoors, focus on the sky, trees, etc.
- Sit down outdoors, rub my hands on the gravel or sidewalk
- Talk on the phone
- Be with friends
- Walk barefoot outdoors
- Visualize growing roots into the ground as I walk
- Go jogging or jog in place
- Cinnamon essential oil (one small drop applied to the gums)
- Write
- Apply ice packs to head, neck, base of spine and/or feet

I also created the time and space needed to allow the energy to move through me using spontaneously occurring exercises and yoga postures. With this multitude of interventions, I was generally able to stay on top of the process.

One day, I woke up with a tremendous amount of energy surging through my body. Allowing the spontaneous exercises to come did not relieve the head and neck pain I was experiencing. As the day progressed, the energy continued to increase. I sensed something was going to happen. While lunching with colleagues, I started feeling terror and grief. Next, the tongues started blaring inside of my head. After leaving the restaurant, I told my colleagues what was happening and asked if they would support me in letting the words become vocal. With one friend sitting in front of me, I "talked and talked," tears streaming down my face. While I was speaking, another voice came into my head saying, "Do you understand? Can you see my pain?" Next came the knowing, "This is what the women in Bosnia are feeling." I believed some part of me had tapped into all of the grief being experienced by the rape victims in that country.

Late in the summer, I attended a women's retreat. The retreat ended with each woman having the opportunity to dance to accompanying drums. The last person to dance was Connor Sauer, one of the retreat leaders. As her dance progressed, Connor began to move with what could only be called "wild abandon." Every cell of her body was involved in the dance. A knowing came, "*That* is inside of *me* somewhere, and *I'm* going to find it!"

Some time later, in Gabrielle Roth's book *Maps to Ecstasy*, I read a passage that closely mirrored my experience with Connor. The chapter that contains this passage is called "Invitation to the Dance of Life."

> *La Chunga bursts onto the stage with the first strum of the guitar. She is total. She is raw passion, unbridled power. She has crystal ball eyes and the posture of a statue that has been standing at the gates of the Mediterranean for a thousand years. She is a many-faceted jewel, flashing multiple depths. She is a total presence, a bolt from beyond, commanding the unadorned proscenium with bare feet and bare soul.*

La Chunga rips me open. Her trance is electric. It fires me with ecstasy. Her overflowing energy releases me to dance with abandon. She burns away my guilt-ridden, diminished, negative, ambivalent persona, the wimpy role-player I so readily become. She stamps out my "original sin" with her blazing feet, and I'm whisked away to the Silver Desert, drenched in the blood-red glow of a Mediterranean sunset. I'm thrilled and terrified to know the power of unleashed passion, and there's no turning back.[2]

I assumed finding that part of myself would be a major undertaking as I had no rhythm, no coordination and was stiff as a board. Much to my surprise, only days later when I tried dancing to a newly purchased tape of African drum music, my body began to take over, moving in what were obviously African dance steps. My dance had that same quality of wild abandon I had seen when Connor danced. I was excited and amazed. I began to dance more and more often. I discovered I now had a way to move energy though my body that was faster and more effective than yoga, and a lot more fun!

One evening in the fall, I decided to see what would happen if I let the spontaneous dance emerge as I listened to tapes from different cultures. It seemed to me that the movements that came forth were consistent with the music, that is, the movements seemed to be African when an African tape was played, Tibetan with Tibetan music, and so forth. I found the whole process fascinating.

After my initial experience with the spontaneously occurring African dance, I decided to take African dance lessons in an attempt to bring the conscious and unconscious processes together. For the same reason, I registered for a belly dance workshop that was being offered by a dance instructor named Delilah. I was disappointed with my performance in both classes. When experiencing the spontaneous dance, my body moved in rhythmic and flowing ways. While the classes taught me some techniques, my movements for the most part remained as stiff and uncoordinated as always.

---

[2]Excerpted from *Maps to Ecstasy* by Gabrielle Roth ©1998 (original version published 1989). Reprinted with permission of New World Library, Novato, CA 94949.

Days after taking the belly dance workshop, I danced at home to Gabrielle Roth's tape, *Initiation*.[3]   As I moved, my body began to take over, reacting differently to each shift in the music. At one point, the energy inside of me was so intense that I became frightened and shut the process down. Not only was I afraid of the energy, but I also felt unsafe as I could not allow my body to do what it wanted to do and protect myself at the same time. I needed someone who could both be a witness and protect me from hitting furniture or walls. As soon as I stopped the dance, the floodgates of grief within me opened once again. It was as if I had promised a long suppressed part of myself that she could come forth, and then reneged on my promise

Frequently when I experience energy this massive I feel frightened, afraid that I might "blow a circuit." Don Juan, in Carlos Castaneda's book, *Power of Silence*, taught that when energy assemblage points move, a person may experience an amplification of energy that is felt as a "killing anxiety." He said that nothing needs to be done, one must simply wait for the energy to subside. He went on to say that there is no danger, once the person understands what is happening.[4]   My anxiety did indeed feel like a "killing anxiety." I was comforted to find my experience described in a book.

As I stood in my fear, Delilah, my dance instructor, came to mind. I found her phone number, called her and asked if I could have an appointment with her, NOW. "Now?" she said, sounding surprised. "Yes," I responded. She agreed, and I drove immediately to her house.

With Delilah present to witness and support me, I once again danced to the *Intiation* tape. I was fascinated by the movements that emerged. I was able to dance beyond the point in the tape where my fear had previously overwhelmed me. My body assumed many shapes and postures, my hands forming mudras. When the tape ended, I asked Delilah what she had witnessed. She said it looked to her as if I was beckoning a lover. "Krishna" my mind immediately responded. She said one particular mudra had appeared repeatedly. In this mudra, the thumb, index finger and the small finger were extended. The two remaining fingers were folded against the palm. She did not know what the hand formation meant as a mudra, but knew that it was the deaf sign for "I love you." Someone later told me that mudra was associated with Krishna.

---

[3]Gabrielle Roth and the Mirrors, *Initiation*, Red Bank, The Moving Center, 1988.
[4]Carlos Castaneda, *Power of Silence*, New York: Washington Square Press, 1987, p. 149.

A day or two later, a client asked if I would be willing to barter in exchange for artwork. I was not interested and said so. The artist was persistent, asking if I would at least look at his work. I relented. I was astounded when I discovered that the theme of one of his paintings was the very same mudra I described above. He had no idea what the hand formation was, stating that it had "appeared" in a meditation, years before. He had named the painting "The Never-ending Song." Needless to say, I was now more than interested in a barter agreement!

Going Deeper
India 1994

In 1994, I traveled to India with several Seattle devotees. While in the Singapore airport, the tongues started blaring in my head. I asked Amrita, one of my fellow devotees, to sit with me in the privacy of the airport chapel, so I could allow them to become vocal. I felt as if someone else was relating her story through me, a story full of sadness and pain. It seemed as if "she" had been waiting to speak for so long that she was desperate to get the words out as fast as possible. The resulting "talk" was so rapid that it came out mostly as single repetitive syllables. I wondered if this was a past life memory or if I was accessing some kind of universal pain.

Recently, I asked Amrita to describe her memory of this event. She said:

> I was shocked at first because Karuna had never told me this kind of thing was happening to her. The first thing I noticed was a quality of expansion, similar to that which occurs during meditation. It was as if a crack was opening in creation and something was coming in, bringing with it Divine possibilities. I felt like creation was crying through her, a heart-wrenching sorrow. With the sorrow came a sense of the potential of freedom from sorrow. I felt that in addition to the larger grief, some of Karuna's own grief was contained in the experience. When it was over, the energy in the room had been transformed from a dead place where people fall asleep into a real prayer room full of spiritual energy.

I had a horrific headache for the next twenty-four hours. I was supposed to be guiding the devotees who were coming to India for the first time, but the truth is I had a hard time moving myself from one location to the next. I longed to be able to lie down and sleep.

When we finally arrived at the ashram, I experienced more of a sense of "coming home" than ever before. I thoroughly enjoyed investigating the many changes that had occurred since my last visit. During the next few weeks, the tongues were a frequent companion, particularly when I was near Mother. Almost daily, I climbed to the top of the temple roof and let the exercises and dance "come forth." Immense joy flowed through my body. I felt as if I was in Heaven!

From the time I arrived in India, I experienced my attention continually being pulled to Swamiji. When he sang with Mother, my eyes were consistently drawn to him rather than her.

Mother and Swamiji

This process intensified when we attended programs in Calicut. There were times on that trip when I sat between Mother and Swamiji, Mother sitting directly in front of me and Swamiji sitting behind me. At those times, I literally had to stop myself from turning my back on her so I could gaze at him. This felt very much like the pull to watch Mother, which I had long experienced. Swamiji began to show up in my meditations and in my dreams. I was confused and a bit frightened by these occurrences. I feared that Mother was going to leave her body and was preparing me to be devoted to *him*. Since worrying about that was use-less, I tried to let go and simply witness the process as it unfolded.

My attention was frequently drawn to Swamiji's feet. One time in Calicut, he was sitting behind a balcony curtain, only his feet being vis-ible. I felt an intense rush of devotion, as well as a desire to bow to him the way the Indian devotees do. That desire manifested other times as well, but I could not force myself to bow. I assumed that my reluctance came from my western upbringing, which taught that such behavior is inappropriate. Somehow I was able to rationalize that bowing to Mother was different. It was to be another four years before I would bow to Swamiji other than in a ritualized way at the beginning of one of his classes. When I finally did bow to him, my tears poured.

One day, after returning from Calicut, my friend Madhuri and I took an evening stroll through the nearby village. As we reentered the ashram grounds, we passed Swamiji, who smiled as we walked by. Sec-onds later, I was overcome with a grief so intense that I had trouble stay-ing erect. After walking a bit further, I leaned against a tree and let the tears come. I did not have a clue where this grief came from.

Devotion was only one of the types of energy I experienced that year in relation to Swamiji. At other times, he seemed more like a father

Swamiji and me![5]

---

[5]Stephen Perringer, Arist.

to me. Once a three-year-old blond girl walked up to Swamiji during bhajans and sat down beside him. She assumed a position similar to his, much like a little girl trying to imitate her dad. I was very touched and imagined myself being that three-year-old. That scene impacted me so deeply, I burst into tears. Later, I asked an artist to draw it for me, substituting a picture of myself when I was three. I sent Mother a copy of the artwork. I am told she laughed as she shared the drawing with the people sitting around her.

There was yet another form of energy to emerge. One day as I passed Swamiji, a teenage voice surfaced from within me, saying internally, "Nice shoulder Swamiji!" I was mortified. I believed that at times he, like Mother, could read minds. I hoped he did not "hear" that one! While I knew it was best not to judge my thoughts, I shoved that particular one down as fast as possible and prayed it would never come back! It may have been an acceptable thought, but it was not acceptable to me!

One of my personal goals for that trip was to develop a workshop to teach clients how to stop victim feelings and behaviors such as self-pity, guilt, and living in scarcity. On the day I decided to start planning the workshop, I spent the morning reading Wayne Muller's, *Legacy of the Heart: The Spiritual Advantages of a Painful Childhood.*[6] I was very excited about the material he presented. Mother, however, apparently decided to strengthen my workshop by providing me with experiences of my own to share.

I had come to India bearing sixty sets of clothes that people in Seattle had made for the children at Mother's orphanage. Many sets of clothes were completed before the summer tour but any attempt I made to send them to India at that time was blocked. I asked Mother what to do and was instructed to bring them to India the next time I traveled to the ashram.

Even after I arrived in India, I was unsuccessful in any endeavor to have the clothes delivered to the orphanage. I decided to ask Mother if I could deliver them myself. She responded that unless I had brought 400 sets of clothes, the orphans could not have them. I could not believe it! For the first time ever, I was furious with her. I felt she had betrayed me and had caused me to betray all of the people who had helped make them. Since many of these people had never even met Mother, I worried about judgments that they would have when they heard what had happened.

---

[6]Wayne Muller, *Legacy of the Heart: The Spiritual Advantages of a Painful Childhood*, New York: Simon and Schuster, 1992.

I internally ranted and raved. "You could have told me this when I talked to you about the project last summer." During the next hours, there were four tracks going on in my mind at the same time. One track was thoroughly immersed in victim thinking, "How dare you do this to me? What are people going to think, about you and about me? You made me waste so much time!"

The second track was very reasonable, "You are getting a good lesson in not being attached to the fruit of your actions. Others will have the opportunity to learn the same lesson. Everyone had fun at the work parties, that is enough." I remembered reading in *Mutant Message* that if you give someone a gift and then have negative feelings when you later discover that they destroyed or gave it away, then the gift was not truly a gift.[7] I was certainly receiving a lesson in gift giving.

The third track was contemplating what to do with the clothes. That part thought about the intent behind the gift. I decided I would deliver the clothes to the ashram store, asking that the proceeds be given to the orphanage.

The fourth track was monitoring the whole process and giving advice as to how to work through the anger. At first, that part told me to move close to Mother. In my therapy community we have a saying, "When in doubt, get closer." That behavior tends to promote problem resolution even when a person is angry. When staying close did not work, this fourth track advised me to find a friend and gripe about our mean Mother. I was careful to pick a friend that I knew would understand I was using griping as a way to release energy. Consciously playing a Transactional Analysis game called "Ain't it Awful" can be a very effective way to shift energy. This course of action is very different than gossiping about people behind their backs. When I felt the energy shift, I returned to the temple and sat close to Mother. Later, I was excited to discover that I had moved through the entire process in less than an hour! The clothes were on display in the store soon thereafter.

My anger was not totally gone, however. During the next few days, whenever I saw the ashram children wearing the clothes, I thought, "You look nice, but you are NOT the children who are supposed to be wearing those outfits." Continuing to see the clothes gave me the opportunity to be aware of and work through the remaining anger.

During that trip, I also received a powerful lesson on attachment. One day, a thought entered my mind, an awareness that I felt no attach-

[7]Margo Morgan, *Mutant Message Downunder*, Lees Summit: MM Co., 1991, p. 138–139.

ment to anything I owned in Seattle. As I reflected on the thought, I concluded that my only attachment was to my children. Soon thereafter, a series of events occurred which proved that my lofty self-assessment was quite incorrect.

First, I loaned several different people a knife my children had given me for Christmas. On one of those occasions, the knife disappeared. I had never had the chance to use it myself. Next, someone used a bucket of water I had stored. Water was a very scarce commodity in those days. Each morning, we would fill a bucket of water to use for bathing and toilet flushing throughout the day. I was angry that something of mine had been taken without my permission, and I was afraid that there would be no water available for me when I needed it. Soon thereafter, someone borrowed my spoon and instead of returning it to me, placed it in the big container of ashram utensils. I was very annoyed. When I reflected on all of these experiences and my reaction to them, I realized that the reason I did not feel particularly attached to my belongings in the United States was that I could easily replace them when necessary. It was much more difficult to replace items in India. I recognized that what I was feeling about my belongings back home could not be described as nonattachment!

Throughout that entire trip, I used spontaneous dance and exercise to facilitate movement of energy through my body. I would dance on the temple roof, in my room, and on hidden balconies. I found dancing effective in keeping my energy balanced. From time to time, I experienced tremendous surges of energy, especially during bhajans. At times these surges were very frightening. I continued to rely on my friends for support when necessary.

On several occasions during that trip, I experienced burning and drainage in my eyes, which I assumed was due to an infection. I began to have difficulty wearing my contact lenses. I wondered if the eye movements that occurred whenever I was in an altered state were the source of the problem. One day, after going to the morning archana, I decided to meditate and dance on the roof. I left my glasses in my room to ensure their safety. After two hours of dancing, I noticed a tremendous improvement in my eyesight. Was it possible that the eye trouble I had been experiencing was because I was not supposed to be wearing my glasses? Since I did not have to drive in India, I decided I would stop wearing the glasses for awhile and see what happened. (There will be more to this story later.)

One day, towards the end of my trip, Dr. Michael, the ashram physician, asked if I would like to listen to music he had written. His compositions combined eastern spiritual words and concepts with western rock-style melodies. I was interested and agreed to listen. Almost from the instant I put on the head phones, energy shot through my body. The dancing part of me wanted very much to dance, so I asked Dr. Michael if that would be possible. He agreed, but the dance which emerged was too big for his small room. (His room housed both a sound studio and a pharmacy, glass bottles lining a good portion of one wall.) When I shut down the dance, my entire being exploded with grief. The tongues erupted. The energy and the grief were more than I could handle alone, so I asked Dr. Michael to find a particular friend of mine. When she arrived, I let the grief come. Soon I felt like a very tiny infant, full of despair. After some time, the infant crying changed back into the tongues. My body began to shake and the grief intensified. The entire process lasted for more than an hour. My friend and I talked at length after the energy and grief subsided.

Devi Bhava was occurring during all of this, so I went to sit next to Mother, feeling very agitated. At one point, when I stood up to put a garland on the Shiva statue, a woman took my seat. I left the temple and unexpectedly walked past Swamiji. Once again my tears started to pour. I felt completely overwhelmed.

The next day, I felt as if I had been run over by a truck. My control of the energy was tenuous. Just prior to the evening bhajans, Mother called us for an outdoor meditation. A mantra started inside of me, going

Mother interacting with devotees prior to meditation

faster and faster. Soon the energy within me surged and became chaotic. My hands started tingling, and my heart pounded. One of my hands began to tap my knee over and over again and then formed a mudra. My head descended to the ground. After some time an ant bit me, bringing me instantaneously back into full consciousness!

A few days later, Dr. Michael asked if I wanted to have a tape of his songs. With some trepidation, I said "Sure." When it was ready, I took the tape and my audio tape player to an empty room. (Finding an empty room in the ashram was a small miracle in and of itself.) I listened to the first song and let the dance come. During the second song, my body started walking rapidly in a big circle around the perimeter of the room. Simultaneously, my right arm started rotating, using full range of motion. Next, both of my arms rotated at the same time. Then, the right arm stopped and the left one continued. After circling the room about twenty times, I decided to start counting. Once I had walked the perimeter another fifty times, the circles started becoming smaller and smaller, until at last I was standing in the middle of the room in a very quiet and peaceful state. The process that had just occurred amazed me. When I told Dr. Michael what had happened, he suggested I have someone else present the next time I listened to his tape. He believed there were songs on the tape that would affect me even more than the first two. I was intrigued!

Soon thereafter, I tried listening to the tape in my room, with Madhuri there to witness and protect me. The dance that emerged with the first song was gentle enough. Then the music shifted and the energy increased in intensity. My body felt as if it had been plugged into an electrical socket. I spontaneously began to pace, circle, and spin. I realized I was getting into trouble and took off the headset. As the energy continued to grow, my arms flailed. I tried jumping up and down as a way of grounding. I attempted to control my breathing. Then the grief hit, lasting nearly an hour. Madhuri said she could feel heat radiating from my body three feet away.

Even after the grief had subsided, the energy still flared inside of me. I knew I needed to walk fast. I went to Dr. Michael's room and somewhat jokingly said, "Your music did this to me, you are going with me for a walk, NOW! We went to the beach and walked as fast as one could without running, until the energy dissipated.

While dancing to Dr. Michael's music felt very right, the level of energy frightened me. Michael suggested I should tell Mother what was happening and ask if this was in my best interest. I responded that asking her was unnecessary. Surprisingly however, between the time I dropped him off at his room and returned to my own, I had changed my mind. I prepared my question, found someone to translate it into Malayalam and then took it to Mother at the first possible opportunity. When she heard what was happening, she laughed in delight and said "No problem." She then talked to the translator for some time. The translator said Mother had responded that it was good for me to dance, but added that when the "meditation" was over, I should lie down but not go to sleep.

The sense of having been plugged into an electrical outlet lasted for days. I continued to use the exercises to help move the energy through. I noticed I was eating endlessly, perhaps another means of grounding.

I decided not to experiment with Dr. Michael's tape anymore while in India. I knew I needed to prepare for my rapidly approaching return to Seattle by concentrating on stabilizing the energy within me. Also, when I allow myself to go into this state, I close my eyes and give my body permission to do whatever it wants to do. The ashram is made primarily of concrete. I did not feel steady enough in the dance to protect myself from hard floors or tall columns. It was also difficult to find a room that was both large and private. I decided to wait and explore his music in the United States where I could have space, people to support the process, and a softer environment!

About the same time, I noticed that skin tags and moles that had been on my body for years had begun to dry up and fall off. I had no doubt this was due to the energy coursing through my body. I was impressed with the healing process that was occurring within me.

During this period, I still felt intense devotion, love or grief whenever I was near Swamiji. At the temple rededication program in Trivandrum, I stayed in a house close to the ashram. From my bed on the roof, I could hear the music emanating from the temple grounds. One night, I awakened to hear Swamiji singing a song that sounded like a lullaby. I cried with grief for the loving father I never had and imagined myself a tiny infant being held by Swamiji. I felt so happy and peaceful.

Mother offers three pujas during each of the rededication programs. The pujas are for the purpose of alleviating problems caused by the negative influences of Mars, Rahu and Saturn. Even though these are pujas Mother has designed, when I participate in them I feel as if I am taking part in rituals that are thousands of years old. The Saturn puja has always been my favorite. That time, as we filed into the temple for the puja, I found myself sitting back-to-back with one of my roommates, Daya (who was then named Clancy). Since we knew each other a little, we allowed our backs to rest one against the other, thereby providing each of us with some back support. At one point during the puja, Mother started singing an *Om Namah Shivaya*[8] chant. I immediately went into a deep medita-

---

[8]*Om Namah Shivaya* has many translations. The one I like best is in actuality a combination of three translations. The translation, *I bow to the universal God, I bow to the God within me, I bow to the aspect of God that is Shiva.*

tive state. As the mudras began, my right hand started raising horizon-
tally, palm facing upward, stopping at upper chest level. Daya's body started
moving in a manner that led me to believe she was experiencing deep
grief. I had no idea how much time passed. After what seemed like a long
time, the altered state lifted and my hand quickly descended. Simultaneously, Daya's movements stopped and Mother ended the song. I opened
my eyes and saw Mother looking directly at us, smiling broadly. I was
convinced that Mother had purposely continued the song until our experience had come to conclusion. When Daya and I talked later, I discovered she had not been crying, she had been laughing. Sharing what seemed
to me to be a joined energy event was both meaningful and exciting.

Several days later, in my room at the Amritapuri ashram, I allowed the spontaneous yoga to occur while Daya slept in the upper bunk. The yoga postures were accompanied by mudras. Since my eyes were closed, I was unaware that Daya had awakened and was having an experience of her own. When she had opened her eyes, my hand, held in a mudra formation, was pointing directly at her. In that instant, she heard, in some internal way, a man speaking in an unfamiliar language. When, at a later time, she shared this with me, we both wondered exactly what was happening in these beyond consciousness experiences.

In *Power of Silence*, Castaneda said that events which happen during altered states, states he called heightened awareness, are often not recollected after return to normal consciousness.[9] In reviewing my journals of that time period, I found an experience recorded of which I have no conscious memory.

The experiences I had with Krishna during 1993 are etched forever in my memory. Until I reviewed my journal, I believed I had been graced with His presence only on those three summer days. A journal entry, however, indicated otherwise. Apparently, during the last Devi Bhava on my 1994 India trip, the energy within me started flaring. I knew I needed to dance but I could not find any suitable place, so asked Dr. Michael if I could use his room. As the dance emerged, I witnessed that a part of me was calling Krishna through the dance. I wrote that Krishna appeared and danced with me. The experience ended when I bowed before him. I am excited to know that he came to me once again, but sad that I have no conscious memory of the event.

---

[9]Carlos Castaneda, *Power of Silence*, New York: Washington Square Press, 1987, p. xvii.

New Ways of Managing the Energy
Winter/Spring 1994

For months after returning to the United States, my energy was brittle, the tongues and altered states once again occurring at unexpected times. I spent a considerable amount of each day managing the energy, making appointments with body-workers as necessary to help open painful energy blockages.

One of my goals upon returning to the United States was to dance to Dr. Michael's music. I asked my friends, Lee and Joan, to be present to witness and keep me safe, that is, keep me from falling over furniture or hitting walls. The movements that emerged were a combination of dance, mudras and other body postures. It took two sessions to dance to the entire tape. The second session was the most unusual. My body tried balancing on one leg, did a shoulder stand, and then moved into a position where my feet went backwards over my head. You would have to see my feeble attempts at yoga to understand the wonder of this occurrence. I was not performing the postures with confidence but they were considerably stronger than if I had attempted them in a normal state of consciousness. My sense was that if I had fully let go, I could have executed each of the positions with strength and confidence. My fear, combined with the belief that I could not really do what my body wanted me to do, kept the postures somewhat tentative.

Next, my body decided to do a somersault. I stopped the process momentarily, thinking, "You have got to be kidding" and then "Oh, what the hell" and let it happen. We all burst out laughing. I shook my head as I laughed. I was a forty-five year old woman. Somersaults were not in my normal realm of experience!

One day in March, I woke up unable to tolerate wearing my glasses, they were much too strong. You may remember that I had noticed a change in my eyesight during my last trip to India. I had set the glasses aside for awhile after that shift, but started wearing them consistently again when I returned to the United States. Now, overnight, there had been a remarkable change. I called my optometrist and told him what had occurred. He was very skeptical, saying eyesight does *not* change in that direction. He was more than convinced by the eye exam, however, as my eyesight was three levels better than before I had traveled to India. I chose to share this story during a testimony service at Power House church that weekend. The congregation responded with lots of *Amen's*, *Hallelujah's* and *Praise God's*. I enjoyed seeing how Spirit was showing people at this church that my path to God was indeed a valid path.

The next weekend, while participating as a staff member at a therapy intensive, the tongues started within me. Since they occurred during a break time, I asked Sandra, another staff member, for support as I let them come. I sensed I was trying to share another gut-wrenching story. I "talked and talked," tears pouring down my face. The energy within me began to flare. My body started forming postures similar to those that had happened when I "danced" with Lee and Joan. The energy continued to intensify. All of a sudden I executed three somersaults in a row! I had a vague sense of this happening but my awareness was minimal, my "witness" part being much less present than normal. When I asked Sandra if I had indeed turned three somersaults, she confirmed my perception. As I reflected upon the incident, I concluded that my body must have turned the somersaults as a way of stopping the flow of chaotic energy, that is, as some kind of stabilization process.

The next day, still at the therapy intensive, I felt myself being quickly pulled into another altered state. As this was not an appropriate time for exploration, I asked Connor, who was also on staff, to help me ground myself. I appreciated that I had enough control over the process to decide when it should be allowed and when it needed to be stopped.

During that period of my life, the energy inside of me was so massive and so unpredictable that I often felt very alone. I knew I appeared normal on the outside but inside I was screaming, *"Does anyone know what it feels like to live in a body with all of this happening?"*

One Sunday in May, I noticed a change in the spontaneous dancing which I experienced at church. While my dance had included whirling for awhile, I often felt cautious and a bit tentative. Now, with my eyes focused straight ahead, the whirl became faster and faster, my body staying steady and confident. When the dance ended on its own accord, I found myself in a very deep meditative state. I was thankful to be in a setting where dance was an acceptable part of spiritual practice. I was also thankful for the ushers that ensured my safety, their presence allowing me to let go and let each process unfold.

Generally, whenever the church choir sang, the energy within me soared. I found that spontaneous spinning often occurred to stabilize the energy. In addition, I noticed that the whirling frequently happened when I came to church already experiencing pain from energy blocks. I was gratified to see, yet again, that our bodies know what we need.

Another development occurred that May. As I was standing in my living room playing around with my conga drum, I entered an altered state. All of a sudden, my hands began to drum on their own! My heart started beating rapidly and as my body filled with terror my breathing became shallow and fast. I reacted as I often do when new processes emerge. I stopped, backed away and said, "No, not now." I slowed my breathing and my heart and assessed the situation. After a few minutes, I tentatively re-approached the drum, put my hands above it and allowed the altered state to come. Once again, my hands started playing on their own. This time I allowed the drumming to continue. My hands played many rhythms and tempos, some sounding African, some Native American. At one point, my hands even tried playing tabla beats on the conga!

I noticed that the "tongues" in my head matched what my hands were playing on the drums. The previous week I had attended a concert by Zakir Hussain, a world renowned tabla player. Each note on a tabla has a vocal name. During part of the concert Zakir "played" songs using only the vocalizations, as opposed to actually drumming. I recalled my tabla teacher of long ago telling me that during the first six months of his training, he had been allowed to learn only the vocalizations. Only when he was skilled with the vocalizations was he permitted to touch the drums. I now recognized that many of the sounds I had labeled "tongues" were actually "tabla talk," the vocalization of tabla notes.

I was still more than a little unnerved by this process. I decided to call my drumming teacher, Kofi, and ask if I could have an appointment with him, NOW. When he arrived at my home, I allowed the spontaneous drumming to come once again. This time, I permitted the process to continue until it stilled on its own. I was amazed by my experience. Sometimes the drumming was slow and serious. At other times, my hands moved high above my head before they came down on the drum. At those times, it was if I was being really silly and playful with the drum. The process pulled me into such a deep meditative state that I had a hard time "coming out." Kofi remarked that I had a very playful spirit inside of me.

I told Kofi, whom I discovered was also an African dance teacher, about the spontaneous dance I was experiencing. Two weeks later, I asked if he would watch that process as well. I played an African drumming tape and allowed the dance to begin. I expected he would tell me my dance came from a particular African tribe. After watching for about fifteen minutes, he told me he saw dances not only from a variety of African tribes but also from Hindu, Tibetan, Middle Eastern and Spanish cultures.

I do not really remember Kofi's interpretation of these events. What I do remember is that he was not the slightest bit shocked or concerned. Instead, he inferred he knew what would likely happen next and was excited and happy for me. His support made it possible for me to let go of the fear and to eagerly anticipate what was to come.

Several years earlier, I had sensed I was supposed to meditate in the magnolia tree in my back yard. I asked a friend to build a platform in the tree. He built the platform, but since sitting meditation was not my style of sadhana,[10] I almost never used it. Sometime later, I had the sense I was

Tree House in Springtime

---

[10]Sadhana - spiritual practice.

supposed to sleep outside. It was almost as if the constraints of being in the house were deadening, I needed to be outside and free. I thought about sleeping on my backyard deck, but I did not feel safe there. Even though I had experienced no significant problems in the twenty-one years I had lived in my house, I was still aware I lived in a large city. Sleeping outside seemed unwise.

About that time Connor encouraged me to read the book, *Sorcerer's Crossing*. It is the story of a woman who was part of Don Juan's lineage (Carlos Castaneda's teacher). At one point in the book, the author, Taisha, was told she was to become a tree dweller, that is, she was supposed to live in the trees.[11] Some part of me screamed "Yes." I knew I needed to build a tree house and to sleep in the trees. The six-foot by six-foot tree house I built has served as my bedroom for six or seven months a year ever since. It is not usable in the winter months as there is no source of heat or electricity. The lock on the door helped me feel safe in a way that I could not previously imagine when I thought about sleeping on the deck.

The tree house was completed just before the start of the 1994 summer tour. Prior to that point, I rarely remembered dreams. During my first few months in the tree house, however, I remembered four to six dreams a night! I loved waking up during the night and being able to watch the sparkling stars and the occasional airplane through the skylight. I also loved waking up in the morning to the chirping of birds and the sight of the tree and the sky. I had such a sense of expansion and freedom.

Longing for Krishna
Summer Tour 1994

For several weeks prior to the summer tour, I felt toxic with repressed grief. The instant I saw Mother, my tears began to pour. I was relieved. I believed that being with her was going to help me access and release this unknown, trapped sorrow. When the bhajans started that first night, my grief intensified. I waited for clues as to its source. Having an understanding of the nature of the pain can relieve the sense of crazi-

---

[11]Taisha Abelar, *Sorcerer's Crossing*, Middlesex: Penguin Books, 1992, p. 193.

ness that may accompany an unnamed pain, thereby making it feel safer to enter. As I let the grief come, it became obvious that the sorrow was related to my childhood desire to have a father who wanted and loved me. Inside, a tiny voice silently cried, "Daddy, daddy, daddy."

One of the highlights of the Seattle retreat occurred when the brahmacharis and swamis danced for us. When Mother had first told them to dance, one had responded, "No," remarking that he was too shy. Mother laughed and said she had been joking, but now she was serious, they needed to get over their shyness. I enjoyed watching Mother continue to teach and challenge her senior disciples. I was also very moved by the dance itself.

One of the major challenges given to me at that retreat occurred when I was asked to be a line monitor during darshan, a job requiring considerable concentration. When sitting near Mother it is easy to drift into a meditative state, which makes for a very ineffective line monitor. At a point when I was feeling a bit proud and cocky about what a good job I was doing, someone put a tape of Dr. Michael's music on the sound system. The energy within me soared, immediately becoming chaotic. Inside I screamed, "MOTHER, you are NOT playing fair!" It took everything I had to stay focused. If Mother had decided I needed more of a challenge, she had certainly found an effective means!

That year, a particularly memorable event occurred during one of Seattle's public programs. At the beginning of the evening, I was asked to be one of the two people who circle the camphor flame in front of Mother during *Arati*. I could not believe that I was being given this privilege. As I stood in front of Mother, moving the flame around and around, my heart was moved to the core. I found myself saying, *"Thank you, Thank you, Thank you"* with everything that was within me.

Mother's swamis have asked Mother to confront any behaviors that keep them from their goal of Self-Realization. Therefore, Mother will point out and sometimes scold them for any wrongdoing. This scolding also helps them learn to stay calm in all situations. She has said if her disciples can face *her* anger with equanimity, they will be able to deal with anything they encounter in the world.

It is not uncommon to see Amma[12] angry in India. Rarely, however, do we see that side of her in the west. A notable exception occurred at the end of one of the San Ramon Devi Bhava programs. As the Devi Bhava

---

[12]By the time I wrote Book 2, I had started referring to Mother as Amma instead of Ammachi.

neared its close, the swamis made one mistake after another. First, some had fallen asleep during their break and as a result showed up late for the last set of bhajans. Next, they failed to adequately prepare the devotees for receiving their mantras. Therefore, one person after another was reaching Mother without having identified the deity that was to be the focus of their mantra. Then, no one effectively facilitated the flow of devotees as Mother threw flower petals at the end of the Devi Bhava. Finally, when *Amma, Amma Taye* was sung at the end of the program, the swamis made yet another mistake when they missed Mother's cue to speed up the music.

It seemed to me that Mother's skin color became blacker and blacker as the swamis' mistakes multiplied. When she threw five handfuls of flowers on them at the end, I fantasized the flowers were filled with venom. (Remember that my fantasies and projections may have no relation to reality.) I was glad I was not in *their* shoes.

Normally, after Mother completes a Devi Bhava, she walks through the crowd slowly and then, along with the swamis, gets into the ashram van. This time, however, she stormed out of the temple, entered the van and took off, leaving the stunned swamis in the dust.

Many of the Seattle devotees were staying in the room next to Mother's at the East Ashram. Needless to say, we were in no hurry to get back to our room. We lingered in the temple, wondering what was occurring at the East Ashram as the swamis returned to their rooms, which were located in Mother's suite. After some time, we tentatively and quietly tiptoed to our room, only to discover that the swamis had been ejected. They were now sleeping in the hallways of the main part of the building!

The whole process fascinated me. I was heartened to see that even swamis make mistakes. I was intrigued to see that Mother could be so angry and the world did not end. The following day, I was relieved to see that she did not hold grudges, she had reprimanded them and let the anger go. I was also impressed that the swamis could survive such an occurrence and be happy and at ease the following day.

I find that devotees often discount Mother's anger, thinking that she is simply testing or provoking them. While that may be true, in the years I have been with Mother, rarely have I ever seen her display anger without obvious cause.

That year, I attended the programs in Santa Fe for the first time. The fact that this was the state of my birth seemed to heighten the power of the program for me. Also, I heard that Mother once said that seventy percent of the people who come to the Santa Fe programs maintain on-going spiritual practices. It made sense to me that the level of energy would be more intense than in cities where less sadhana occurred.

During the Santa Fe program, my son, Sreejit, asked Mother if he could move to India. I was a bit surprised when she said, "Yes," as he had not yet finished college. Nevertheless, her response seemed very right to me. I was pleased she supported him in following his heart.

Soon thereafter, I felt compelled to enter the darshan line. I had not even considered going for darshan as the crowd was so large. When I came within fifteen feet of Mother, the floodgates of grief within me opened. Even though some of the sadness was because my son was going to be so far away, the grief seemed more related to the abrupt nature of his leaving. I had tapped into grief about all of the other abrupt endings I had experi-enced in my life. When I was one person away from Mother, she looked at me with her "Miss Innocent" look. With great concern she said, "Aller-gies?" I laughed internally knowing she knew full well I was not suffering from allergies. When I said, "No," she then asked, "Crying?" I told her I felt some sadness because Sreejit was leaving, but mostly I felt very happy for him. As she talked to me, she was holding someone else. The look she gave me in that moment was the experience of a lifetime. Through her face and eyes, she expressed immense gentleness, love and compassion. While she held the other person, she stroked my hair and my face. She held my gaze for some time and then took me into her arms, and said, "Don't worry." I was bursting with gratitude. Several people told me they had cried as they witnessed our interaction. For days, I cried as I remem-bered her look and touch. Even now I become teary at the memory.

During the Santa Fe program, I agreed to work on a sewing project. I was amazed to discover that I could sew eight or more hours a day with-out becoming tired. Normally I would have experienced a significant amount of back pain. My "workroom" was a small hallway next to the stage, which meant I was able to hear all of the music. Since it was the hallway where the swamis and others gathered before and after programs, I was able to witness a lot of spontaneous interaction. I felt like I was in the hub of things and was quite happy. I was aware that sewing during music was keeping me from having altered state experiences and won-dered if this was Mother's way of keeping me grounded.

I received another gift during the Santa Fe program when a new song was introduced:

TEACH ME THE LANGUAGE OF YOUR HEART

Teach me the language of Your heart
Only Your love will bring peace inside me.

Teach me the language of Your smile
Looking at you all my sorrows vanish.

Teach me the language of Your voice
Help me to speak only words of kindness.

Teach me the language of Your eyes
Deep in Your gaze is the Truth I long for.

Teach me the language of Your light
Feeling Your strength I will fear no darkness.

Teach me the language of Your touch
Please let me stay in Your arms forever.

Teach me the language of Your heart
Only Your love will bring peace inside me.

Promise me that You will always guide me,
I need to know You are right beside me.
Teach me the language of Your heart.[13]

The song so expressed what was in my heart. The impact was even stronger when a few days into the program, Swamiji began to sing the song. Knowing he had taken the time to learn an English bhajan moved me deeply.

Later, during Devi Bhava, Mother was very playful with me. I had a strong sense that she was somehow different, but had difficulty identifying that difference. I noticed her skin seemed darker and there was an impish quality about her behavior. Something else was unusual. What was it? When I ran the experience through my mind's computer banks, I

---

[13] "Teach Me the Language," *Santa Fe Bhajan Tape #1*, Santa Fe: AMMA Center of New Mexico, 1995.

got it! Krishna had come to me through my guru! My heart filled with gratitude for the grace I was experiencing during this program.

Mother during Devi Bhava

I once heard that the difference between shock and embarrassment is that shock drains life force energy whereas embarrassment may enhance it. The person experiencing shock turns white and "death-like." With embarrassment, the fear is joined by a bit of pleasure. Instead of turning white, the person experiencing embarrassment turns red from the increase in blood-flow. I had such an embarrassing moment when I rejoined the tour in New York City.

For several years, whenever I went to Mother's New York city programs, I also attended services at a black church in Harlem. This time, my friend Kristin decided to come to church with me. The church was similar to Power House in Seattle, but seemed more restrained. I had not seen anyone dance during my previous visits.

At the beginning of the service, the minister welcomed Kristin and me and told us to have a good time. As in previous years, we were the only white people in the church. During the time since my last visit, I had begun to experience spontaneous dance almost every time I went to church. I looked around this church and saw the ushers were children. I concluded that dancing was probably not a regular occurrence here and decided to restrain the dance.

I was not prepared, however, for the fact that all of my recent contact with Mother had opened up my energy pathways. The minute the music started, my body began to dance. As I had almost no ability to control the dance, I acquiesced and let it come. Kristin said people looked at her, concerned that I was okay. She just stood there helplessly indicating I was fine. The energy was more than I could handle so I fairly quickly dropped into a position of prostration. While I knew that it was fine that I had danced and that people would probably for years enjoy telling the story of the day the white girl came to their church, I was embarrassed to have made such a spectacle of myself. At the end of the service, the minister said, "We told her to have a good time, and she did!" I knew they were delighted, but at that point I could not share their pleasure. Now, I can mostly laugh and enjoy the leela.

Another important lesson occurred later that day. When we left the church, Kristin went her separate way, and I walked to the Cathedral of St. John the Divine. Having had such interesting experiences at the Cathedral in previous years, I wondered what was in store for me this time.

Once inside, I noticed the sensation that my feet were moving on their own. I decided to let them go where they wanted to go, provided that they did not want to do anything too outrageous. First, they walked to the back of the church, then all the way around the inside perimeter. I wondered if they would walk around the cathedral three times, as often happens in Hindu tradition. That did not occur. Next, they went to an altar in the back of the cathedral. Once there, my body spontaneously sat down. For awhile, I experienced a gentle meditation. As I continued to allow my body free reign, it stood up and turned three times in front of the altar. I insisted the turning be slow so it would appear that I was viewing the cathedral. I did not want to draw anyone's attention! My feet then continued walking throughout the cathedral in a very purposeful manner. First, they stopped briefly at an AIDS memorial, then at a "Making a Difference" display. Next, I stopped at a Bosnian sculpture focused on genocide. My feet then walked around a column three times. I stopped in front of a few other displays, one being another piece of

Bosnian artwork, another a huge stained glass mandala. Then as my feet picked up speed, I walked swiftly out the front door of the cathedral! I laughed. That had certainly been an unusual experience, even for me! The entire process had occurred within a fairly short period of time.

After taking back full control of my feet, I started walking towards a friend's apartment. I was thirsty and decided to buy some fresh juice at a corner store. Once inside the store, a beggar approached me and asked for money. I was shocked and indignant that he had the nerve to approach me there. I could not understand why the store would allow such behavior. I said "No," disdainfully, took my juice and left the store. As I exited the store, I glanced in a mirror and noticed that the beggar was continuing to look at me. There was something about his eyes that really caught my attention. Some part of me wondered, "Was that Mother? Had she come in the form of a beggar to test my compassion?"

As I walked down the street, I continued to think about the interaction I had just had with the beggar. If it had been a test, I certainly had failed. Being compassionate with beggars was an area I had been working on for the last year or so. For many years I had walked by beggars in Seattle, avoiding eye contact, either ignoring the fact that they had spoken to me or saying "No" and continuing on. During those times, my mind was often filled with judgments such as "You would only use it for alcohol," "How do I know you really need it?" or "If you really needed it you would not be smoking."

I had even carried my judgmental attitude to India, where one is continually inundated with beggars. One year, however, I felt as if blinders were taken off my eyes. I suddenly realized that the situation in India was not the same as in the United States. In India, if the homeless, malformed, and starving did not receive money by begging, they did not eat. In addition, many holy men and women eat only what they are given. My attitude began to change and I started to give more consistently when asked.

As I reflected on what had just occurred in the juice store, I felt sad and ashamed. I wondered if Mother was disappointed in me. Then I remembered that Bhai Sahib, a Sufi master, once told his devotee, Irina Tweedie, that a good Teacher is never displeased with a disciple. The teacher will give the student opportunity after opportunity to learn necessary lessons.[14]

---

[14]Irene Tweedie, *Daughter of Fire*, Nevada City: Blue Dolphin, 1989, p. 119.

I wondered if I should go back and buy the beggar a sandwich and some juice but intuited that if I returned to the store, he would be gone. I reminded myself that when Ammachi gives tests, it is not about passing or failing. I believed the purpose of this incident was to show me inner work I still needed to complete. Mother had exposed one of my negative qualities and given me an experience I was not likely to ever forget.

Some months later, I dreamed that a group of beggars approached me several times. Each time I sent them away. From inside me came a voice saying, "So you *still* have not learned what you need to learn." I then noticed that one of the beggars had light and joy in his eyes and I knew that he spread that light and goodness throughout the world. I sensed that once again, Mother had come to me in the form of a beggar. This time the visit not only highlighted unfinished work, but also reminded me that even beggars can be servants of God.

I was still experiencing grief or devotion whenever I was around Swamiji. While part of it was obviously due to my unfinished work with my father, it seemed so much more than that. The grief was so massive that at times I felt crazy. I decided I would ask Mother for an explanation. The answer came before I even asked the question. During my morning meditation, I realized that all of my feelings were projection. I was projecting all of my feelings for Krishna onto Swamiji! As I write this now I am quite intrigued. I remember well the overwhelming feelings towards Swamiji but I had totally forgotten this "answer" until I read it in my journal. Once again, I remembered Castaneda's statement that when in heightened states of awareness our ability to understand Spirit's instruction is greatly enhanced, while our ability to describe or even remember the event afterwards is impaired.[15] As I reflect now on that time period, I realize that the exaggerated feelings lessened after this insight.

I now see how longing for Krishna was the central theme of that time period. I am reminded of the translation of one of my favorite Krishna bhajans.

> Please come, O Krishna. I, your Radha[16], am calling out
> to you. Without You, My Lord, I cannot survive. I lose
> my consciousness, quite often. Am I not most dear to You,
> Krishna? Please do come back, O Murari![17] I am melting,

---

[15] Carlos Castaneda, *Power of Silence*, New York: Washington Square Press, 1987, p. xvii.
[16] Radha - consort of Krishna.
[17] Murari - another name of Krishna.

*dwelling in Your thoughts. I have been crying continuously
for you. Please do not delay any further, O Lord, Please
put an end to all my sorrows.*[18]

Throughout the remainder of the 1994 tour, I continued with my
sewing seva. When I was asked to sew during the Rhode Island retreat,
the last retreat of the year, I was dismayed to discover that the workroom
was far away from the program hall. I appreciated being trusted to do that
particular job, but grieved being away from the music. I accepted the job
as a test of surrender and struggled to keep a positive attitude. I finished
just in time to attend the last Devi Bhava. I was satisfied that I had made
correct choices, but sad that I had missed so much time with Mother.

Devi Bhava

---

[18] "Avo Mere Nandalal," *Bhajanamritam Volume 3*, San Ramon: Mata Amritanandamay Center, 1997, p. 44.

My darshan during that Devi Bhava was wonderful. When I thought back on all of the darshans I had received during that tour, I realized every one had been so very personal. Was she being different, or was I?

There was one more shock in store for me. Madhuri, Shobana and I had changed our plane tickets so we could leave Boston early the morning after the retreat. As the Devi Bhava proceeded, I began to realize we were going to have to leave the hall before the end of the program. I was devastated. In the weeks that followed, I repeatedly told people I had made the biggest mistake of my life. While I knew even at the time that was an overstatement, it certainly described the extent of my despair. I was not going to *ever* make that "mistake" again!

The Spirit Continues to Guide
Summer/Fall 1994

I loved returning to my tree house. Each night I fell asleep quickly, waking the next morning thoroughly rested. My vision improved daily. I was thankful I had asked the optometrist for a prescription that would allow for the possibility of ongoing improvement in my vision.

Towards the end of July, I sensed I would soon be creating a new workshop. Even though I had no clue as to the nature of the workshop, I scheduled it by reserving space at a retreat center, a sure way to prevent procrastination!

One day, my daughter asked me to drive her to her volunteer job at the Veteran's Hospital. As we prepared to leave, my gaze fell upon the book, *Celestine Prophecy*. As we drove to the hospital, my attention was pulled to a scene occurring in front of a church. There was a black man dressed in colorful priest's robes standing on the stairs in front of the church. He was conversing with a white man who was standing next to a bicycle that was locked to the hand railing. I never before noticed this particular church. I recalled that a major lesson in *Celestine Prophecy* was that there is no such thing as a coincidence. The author stated we should pay attention to anything that catches our attention.[19] I elected to return to the church once I had dropped my daughter at the hospital.

---

[19]James Redfield, *Celestine Prophecy*, Hoover: Satori Publishing, 1993, p. 187.

As I entered the church, the priest was walking towards the door. I sensed he had been about to lock up, so I told him I would come back another time. He encouraged me to stay. I sat down in one of the pews and immediately entered a light meditative state. I felt uncomfortable about delaying the priest from his planned activities, however, so I left soon thereafter. I decided I would attend the next day's mass.

When I entered the church the next morning, I was pleased to discover that a very pleasant meditative state washed over my body. Having never attended a mass before, I was dismayed to find that it involved repetitive standing and sitting. Being in an altered state of consciousness, I found this experience jarring and uncomfortable. I did love hearing the chanting of the mass so decided I would return the next morning and find a way to resolve this dilemma.

The following morning, I arrived shortly before the mass began. I explored the church and found a nook near a side altar that would be out of sight of the priest and the congregation, yet within earshot of the mass. I sat down cross-legged on the floor, and allowed the altered state to emerge. In the half-hour it took to complete the mass, my mind was flooded with ideas. By the time the mass was over, I knew the name of my new workshop (*Lessons on Lessons*) as well as half of the content. As I exited, I noticed that I felt no need to return to the church.

After the Santa Fe program, Sreejit began preparing to move to India. By the middle of August, he was ready. The weekend before he left, a Seattle satsang family gifted him with a homemade Kali doll. He carried the doll in a gift bag, separate from the rest of his luggage. When he landed in Madras, the customs agent examined the large bags he was carrying for the ashram and informed him he would have to pay a duty fee. Sreejit did not have the necessary money. As the agent continued his search, he came across the Kali doll. He took one look at the doll, crossed himself and then escorted Sreejit through the customs area, no questions asked, duty forgotten. Mother Kali works in interesting ways!

Ever since the spontaneous drumming had begun, I used it as a way to move the energy through my body. I found drumming as effective as dance in stabilizing and moving energy. About that time another process began. It seemed like some part of me was being given "tabla lessons." I frequently woke up at night knowing it was time for a lesson. I would get out of bed, hold my hands above the tabla and let the unconscious pro-

Kali murti that is installed in the Amritapuri inner temple[19]

cess begin. Sometimes I would play for hours. As the months went by, my tabla notes became clearer and clearer.

While my talk with Kofi had provided me with some information about the drumming, I was very aware that his explanation came from an African frame of reference, a frame very different from my own. I wondered what an East Indian explanation would sound like. I decided to make a trip to Mother's ashram in California so I could show Swami Paramatmananda what was happening.

When the time for my appointment arrived, I collected the tabla drums from the puja room and carried them to the room in which we were meeting. Swami Paramatmananda looked at me quizzically saying "You are going to play the tabla for me?" "Sort of," I responded.

I told him what was occurring in my life and then allowed the drumming to emerge. The hand style was tabla, but the beat was Native American. I played for ten to fifteen minutes and then asked what he thought was happening. Without hesitation, he responded that all of the ways I had found God in past lives were opening up to me and blending together. I told him I was feeling overwhelmed by all that was happening,

---

[19]Murti - an image or icon of God used during worship.

the dance, the drumming, the tongues. I shared that I had taken dance lessons as a way of trying to bring conscious and unconscious processes together. Was I also to pursue learning the tabla? He said this was not about taking lessons. I was being given access to various forms of meditational processes, but I was not being directed to develop or use all of them. I felt a great sense of relief.

I decided to attend a weeklong women's retreat in August. I had an experience during that week, that has stayed with me ever since. Someone led a guided imagery session in which we were requested to wave a magic wand, an action that would make all of our desires and wishes a reality. While most people were delighted with their experience, I felt fury. *I had been robbed of the joy that comes with the journey!* As I thought about it, I realized that putting together the puzzle of life, planning, testing, experimenting, finding the way, was what brought me joy. As far as I was concerned, that was the purpose of life. I had no interest in having all of my desires spontaneously manifest. I also realized this is why I felt so little affinity with the attitude of some of my friends, who say "Mother, help me learn what I need to learn so I do not have to come back to this world." Why would I not want to come back? There is much that needs to be done. Living and learning is fulfilling, invigorating, magical, and joyful, even when it is difficult.

There was one more memorable event that occurred during that time period. Each fall, Pastor and Mrs. Jenkins took the entire church congregation out to dinner. That year, I rode to the restaurant with an elderly woman who is a street evangelist. She told me she loved to watch me dance in church because in the dance she sees me "humble myself before God" and because people say that blacks dance in the Spirit because they are emotional. She saw my dancing as validation that the phenomenon was beyond race and emotion.

During that dinner, I sat between two women who were discussing the church's position on homosexuality. The women said even though they thought homosexuality was a sin, they did not believe Jesus would treat homosexuals in the mocking, demeaning manner their church promoted. They were unwilling to engage in that type of behavior themselves. I felt heartened to hear that church members were making their own decisions in matters such as these, not blindly taking on the attitude of the church hierarchy.

PART 2

*In my distress I called upon the Lord; to
my God I cried for help.*

*From his temple he heard my voice, and
my cry to him reached his ears.*

Psalm 18:6

A Multitude of Lessons
India 1995

For the first time ever, Chaitanya, Sreejit and I were to be at Mother's
India ashram at the same time. I looked forward to sharing such an
important life event with them. Prior to that year's trip, I had written
Mother that I was willing to offer psychotherapy services while at the
ashram, if she so desired. I asked if there was a way for individuals to do
bioenergetic work, that is, physical release of anger and fear, on the ashram
grounds. Since this work can be quite noisy, I was unsure how to adapt
that style of therapy to the setting.

Within fifteen minutes of my arrival, three people asked if they
could make therapy appointments with me. I took this as Mother's way
of answering my first question. This still left the second, one she would
answer in a far different way.

A few hours later, I learned of something that had happened in
Seattle that infuriated me. I went to bed, seething with rage, a very un-
usual state for me. I woke up about 3:00 a.m. feeling as if my body would
explode with the anger. My mind scrambled to find a technique by which
I could release the rage, without waking up all of the sleeping residents.
Shortly thereafter, I was sitting on an outside balcony twisting a towel,

screaming silently. While I offer that particular technique as an alternative to my clients, I had never used it myself. I was amazed at its effectiveness. With each twist, I could practically see the energy leave my body. I started laughing to myself. I had asked Mother if clients could do anger work at the ashram. Could she not have simply said, "You may use that room to do your work?" No! She had to let me discover the way myself. As always, she taught that the best way to learn is through experience.

One of my goals for that particular trip was to plan the *Lessons on Lessons* workshop. Going to India with that intention was like holding up a sign saying, "Mother, send me LOTS of extra lessons." That year's temple rededication program in Calicut provided the setting for a multitude of lessons.

The story of the Calicut lessons actually begins earlier. Shortly upon my arrival at the ashram, two devotees enthusiastically said, "I can not wait until you hear Swamiji's new song, *Jai Ma Ambe*." One added, "Actually, some of us are concerned that when you hear it, you will leave your body and not come back." Often when I hear bhajans, I experience ecstatic bliss. Sometimes I feel as if only my body is in the room, while the rest of me is in some unknown, unseen, wonderful place. I was not at all worried, as leaving my body and not coming back seemed totally out of the question. I was, however, intrigued and eager to hear the song. Some time was to pass before I would have that opportunity, since Swamiji was in Bombay.

When in Calicut, I stayed with other ashram residents on the roof of the temple. There were several places on the roof where mounds of rough concrete rose awkwardly two to three inches above the surface. Several times when I passed a particular mound, my inner voice said, "Be careful, that concrete is dangerous." My response was, "I see it. I *am* being careful." I would then continue blithely on my way. One day, as I was walking to my sleeping mat, not paying a bit of conscious attention to what I was doing, I tripped over the mound of concrete and tore a big piece of flesh from the top of my toe.

The injury was very painful but that was the least of my concerns. Having an open foot wound in India seemed very dangerous. Most of the time I walked barefoot and the ground was filled with untold numbers and varieties of bacteria. My nursing background told me that the extreme heat and high humidity created a perfect breeding ground for bacteria. I cleaned the wound as best I could and went on with my life. I found I needed to stay very conscious of my surroundings because any

time I would lose concentration, I would hit my toe on something, sending waves of pain coursing through my body.

That same day, Swamiji arrived in Calicut. The evening program
ended with Mother and Swamiji leading *Jai Ma Ambe*, the song I had been
so eagerly awaiting. My friends were right, the song profoundly affected
me. Massive amounts of energy soared through my body and with it came
waves of deep grief. As I internally sobbed, "I want to go Home, I want to
go Home," another part of me noted that my experience was somewhat
muted due to the pain I was experiencing in my toe. I thought, "Well,
Mother, *that* was an interesting way to keep me in my body."

Mother and Swamiji singing bhajans

I was aware that the incident had already served three functions. It
reminded me of the importance of paying attention to the instructions
given by my inner voice. It showed me the universe would take care of
me, in that the pain kept me from going "too far" out during the song.
Also, the injury provided me with practice in mindfulness. I needed to
stay very conscious of my environment to avoid bumping my injured foot.
During the next several days I became aware of other opportunities for
learning.

A minister once taught me that you have to use the faith you have before you will be given more. I saw I was being given the opportunity to trust I would be taken care of and, at the same time, trust that whatever happens is for my own good. During the next several days, my toe healed rapidly. I would not have expected it to heal so quickly, even in the United States, where cooler temperatures and a cleaner environment would have made it easier for me to protect and take care of the injury. The speed at which I healed increased my faith in the power of the spiritual energy flowing through me.

Shortly before that pilgrimage to India, I attended a workshop led by Stephen Levine. Levine is considered by many to be a master teacher in the realm of living and dying consciously. He said that if we want to pursue a spiritual path, we have to be willing to feel fear.[1] I certainly had been given the opportunity to face my fear of infection and pain!

Because of the injury, I stayed focused on the programs at the ashram. A number of devotees decided to explore the city. The fact that my foot hurt when I walked made it easy to say "No" to diversions and stay focused on my spiritual process.

My lesson count was now up to seven! I wondered how much more I had learned at an unconscious level. I was also aware that my friends had the opportunity to learn from my experience. I was awed by how much "good" could come from a single event.

That incident was also a component of another series of lessons. So many things "went wrong" that same week, it became obvious I was being given the opportunity to learn even more. When I carefully reviewed each of the week's events, looking for themes, the lesson became evident.

Over and over during that period of time, my inner voice had "warned" me of potential problems. I repeatedly discounted those warnings. First, I hurt myself when I ignored the warning about the pile of concrete. Next, my daughter Chaitanya, a friend and I took a taxi to the Singapore Airlines office in downtown Calicut. We drove in circles for an hour, unable to find the office. Once there, we discovered we needed to go to the Indian Air office before we could make the necessary changes with Singapore Airlines. As we left the Singapore Airlines office my inner voice said, "Make sure you write down the address so you can get back here." I responded, "That is not necessary, the next taxi driver will

---

[1] Stephen Levine Workshop, Bellevue, Washington, December 3–4, 1994.

know the way." Later, when we left the Indian Air office, we spent another frustrating hour searching for the Singapore Airlines office.

While in Calicut, I needed to relay an important message to a person at the Amritapuri ashram. I arranged to send it with a friend who was returning to the ashram sooner than the rest of us. The night before my friend's departure, my inner voice said, "Write the note and give it to her NOW." I answered, "No, that is not necessary, she will not be leaving until tomorrow afternoon." When I awakened the next morning, I discovered my friend had abruptly changed her plans, taking off for the ashram at daybreak.

As we cleaned our living area, the morning after the program's end, I noticed a piece of paper on the floor beside my sleeping mat. My inner voice said, "That looks like a train ticket." I answered, "My ticket is in my wallet." When we arrived at the train station a few hours later, I discovered that our tickets were missing.

My series of misfortunes did not end there. Chaitanya was scheduled to leave India two days after our return from Calicut. A friend cautioned me to pack Chaitanya's most important items in her carry-on luggage. I inwardly responded, "Everything is already packed and I do not want to start over, that is unnecessary." After driving the three hours from the ashram to the airport, we discovered we had left Chaitanya's suitcase sitting in our room at the ashram. That suitcase contained everything she needed for the school report that was due upon her return to the United States. There was no way to retrieve the suitcase before her plane departed.

When I reflected on each of these events, I remembered a minister once saying that the voice of God is most often the first quiet voice we hear inside. God's message may also be relayed through another person, such as in the incident with my daughter's suitcase. The minister pointed out that once God gives instructions, another voice frequently emerges. This one offers a flood of discounting messages such as, "That's wrong." "It will never work." and "Do this instead." The minister said if we consistently ignore God's direction, the Divine voice will start to fade.

As I continued to ponder my behavior, I realized that after years of being so intensely focused on my spiritual path, I had developed a rather cocky attitude about my ability to hear and respond to my inner voice. I was shocked to see the reality of the situation. Over and over again, I had been warned of an impending problem and had discounted, ignored, and contradicted the warnings. I was awed by how much pain I could have saved myself had I listened to each instruction. I was thankful for the powerful display of this particular spiritual pitfall and vowed to be much more conscious and conscientious in the future.

A big transition in Chaitanya's spiritual process occurred during the Calicut program. At first, she participated only during bhajans. Then, she attended an occasional archana. Next, she began to sit on the stage watching Mother, sometimes until 3:00 a.m., long after I went to bed. One day she commented, "I am getting just as crazy as the rest of you!" I was reminded of Mother's 1993 comment to Chaitanya, "You may think you are not connected to me, but I have been connecting to you!"

During the Saturn puja, Chaitanya and I sat across from each other. When we sang "Om Namah Shivaya," I saw tears pouring down her cheeks. As she looked at me, I fantasized she was thinking, "What is happening to me?" I was fascinated, and rather shocked, by her rapidly moving process.

One day, after returning to the Amritapuri ashram, we were notified that Swamiji wanted to meet with the western devotees on the roof of the temple. The ashram is located in the middle of a small fishing village. The villagers' ways were very traditional and the influx of westerners was not entirely welcome. They saw us as uncivilized, immoral beings and we fairly regularly did things to reinforce that image. Some of our behaviors were causing a lot of trouble for the ashram. Even activities that seemed to us to be totally innocent, such as women chatting with Indian men in teashops, were scandalous as far as the villagers were concerned.

Swamiji wanted to talk to us about two serious incidents that had just occurred. First, villagers had rushed to Swamiji saying that a western man was in the village screaming in pain. Swamiji hastened to his side and asked what was wrong. The man said he felt called to pour out to God the pain that was in his heart. Swamiji in his calm, quiet manner instructed him that if he needed to pour out his pain in this way to please do it on the ashram grounds, not in the village. The second incident was even more serious. The previous night, villagers had found a western couple having sex on the beach. Swamiji asked us to be more conscious of how our behavior would affect the relationship between the ashram and its neighbors.

Several weeks later, I participated in the temple rededication programs in Trivandrum. The trip home from that program was a good example of what traveling with Mother can be like. We were instructed on the last night of the program to be ready to leave the next morning at

9:00 a.m. Instead, we were awakened around 5:00 a.m. and told to pack and get on the bus immediately! We scurried around, packing and dressing, and boarded the bus within a half-an-hour. Once loaded, we drove one block and then parked, for almost three hours! We then drove forty minutes south of Trivandrum, the opposite direction from the ashram, to meet Mother for a swim.

That swim was one of the major highlights of that trip to India. The sky was deep blue and clear, a steady stream of water gurgled over rocks. Everyone poured into the water following Amma. The coolness of the water was a welcome relief from the hot, humid air. Mother explored the river, climbing over slick rocks. Soon she discovered a small waterfall. She called us to her and, while balancing on a rock, received each one of us individually. She grasped our hands, drawing us towards her. She then dunked each of our heads in the waterfall! Many of us felt as if we had been baptized. Such wonderful memories are created at times like this.

Relaxing with Amma by the roadside

Some time later, we returned to the buses where breakfast awaited us. Next, we drove several hours north, stopping at Mother's orphanage in Paripally. We ate lunch and rested while Mother gave darshan to all of the children. After a number of hours, we climbed into the buses once again and completed the trip to Amritapuri. This journey, in normal circumstances, would have taken three hours. With Mother it had taken fourteen!

I returned from the Trivandrum program tired and sick. We had been in Calicut and Trivandrum for a week each and would soon leave on Mother's annual North India tour. It was Amritapuri that felt like home to me and I was sad I had spend so little time there that year. The sickness provided the opportunity for me to remedy that situation. I decided, as did several others, to spend a few more days at the ashram so I could start the North India trip healthy. After a few days rest, we took the train to Bangalore and rejoined Mother's group. I was grateful that my wish to spend more time at the ashram had been realized.

That year was the first and only time I have participated in Mother's North India tour. The tour is grueling. There are many reasons why people find the trip so difficult. There are long days of bus travel, sometimes more than twenty-four hours at a time. Seating is cramped on buses that were made for short Indian people. The already scarce leg-room is reduced further by supplies packed under the seats and in the aisles. At the program sites, there are huge crowds, a lack of privacy and long hours of work.

Mother skillfully uses these situations to teach flexibility and surrender. The day before we were to leave, the brahmacharis did a magnificent job of packing the buses, utilizing every spare space. It soon became obvious that *magnificent* was my judgment, not Mother's. When she came to inspect the buses that night, she threw everything out and made them start all over again. I was reminded of the story of a guru who tested a disciple's patience, obedience and surrender by having him repeatedly rebuild a house over a period of many years.

Our trip was continually delayed for one reason or another. We stopped frequently for flat tires. At other times, we were shuffled from bus to bus before being told that we had been on the correct bus in the first place. The general travel rule seemed to be, "Hurry up and wait!"

The biggest torture for me was that, due to childhood traumas, I find it impossible to release my bladder by the side of the road, or whenever people are waiting for me. There was one period on the trip during which I was unable to release urine for twenty-six hours. Needless to say, that was hell! "Why do I do this to myself?" I wondered.

That question was answered almost immediately. It was now evening. We stopped for a short swim and then watched as Mother, with the help of the brahmacharis and brahmacharinis, built a fire, prepared and served dinner and chai, and then led bhajans under the glorious Indian night sky. Mother talked and laughed as she interacted with those sitting around her. I knew there was no way I could have this type of informal experience with Mother except on a trip like this.

Mother pouring chai

Traveling to Bombay was one of the most significant parts of the trip for me. My heart hurt as I saw miles and miles of shantytown shacks built of corrugated tin. I visualized the horror of living in those huts at night, when the rats roamed freely. I also imagined the nightmare they would be year-round in daytime temperatures ranging between 90 and 120 degrees. My heart continued to hurt as I saw children growing up in the middle of busy railroad yards. Wherever there was twenty feet between the criss-crossed tracks, families erected tents. I grieved as I saw a woman, legs totally useless and crossed stiffly in front of her, inching her way down the sidewalk on her buttocks. She moved so slowly that one had to look very carefully to even see that she was moving.

India's poor

Those scenes and others moved me to tears. I wondered what *I* could do to make the situation different. I remembered the message of the 1992 movie, *The Power of One*. One person may not be able to change the entire system but he or she can certainly make a difference.

Swami Ramakrishnananda once told a story that is another powerful reminder of this lesson. Someone walked up to a man who was throwing beached sea organisms back into the ocean, and commented that since the shore was virtually covered with such creatures, there was no way he could ever hope to solve the problem, or even make a significant difference. The man responded, as he put yet another creature back into the water, "Well, it made a difference for that one."

India's poor

Another memorable event occurred during the Bombay program. For some time, Mother had completely ignored both Sreejit and me. I was not particularly bothered by her behavior towards me, but I was becoming increasingly angry at how she was treating my son. During that program, Mother called the westerner's for darshan, a rare event on the North India tour. She was quite pleasant with me but I was more interested to see how she would interact with Sreejit. When she virtually ignored him, I was outraged. I took a seat directly in front of her and let the anger explode within me. Internally I screamed, "You can mess with me but do not mess with my son. I know you can read my mind, so let me give you something to read! I think you are a mean, nasty, evil WITCH!" I relish this experience even today. After a childhood of pouting, I enjoyed the thought of having a mother that could read my mind as I poured

out my venom. I also enjoyed having the opportunity to release the feelings while another part of me fully believed that what she was doing was
for his highest good. She, of course, seemed fully unscathed by my "blast"
of negative energy.

My Reality is Challenged
Winter/Spring 1995

During the first few weeks after I returned from India, I was told three different times that I had said something I had no memory of having said. My fear in hearing this was heightened by the fact that in two of those incidents what I was reported to have said did not sound like something that would come out of me. One instance I could have accepted, but three! My scare further compounded when I discovered an item I had searched for, in a place I had repeatedly looked. What was going on? Did I have Alzheimer's disease? Did I have multiple personality disorder? I thought I was too young for Alzheimer's, and I did not believe I had a history that would lead to multiple personality disorder.

I decided to make an appointment with David Calof, an expert in dissociation processes such as multiple personality disorder. I knew he could differentiate between physical and mental/emotional problems. With some trepidation, I shared some of my spiritual experiences with him, such as the dancing, drumming, and mudras. I did not know what kind of spiritual processes, if any, he was involved in. I did not want to be seen as a spiritual flake, but I knew he needed this information to make a knowledgeable diagnosis.

After hearing my story, David said I need not worry. He told me the unconscious mind finds the way to get our attention when it is needed. It was obvious to him that my unconscious mind had discovered that if my memory was challenged, it would immediately have my attention. After hearing his response, and putting it into my own vocabulary, I concluded that whenever I had an experience that challenged my memory, I needed to see if there was a lesson present that I had not recognized or was discounting. If that was not the case, then I needed to watch for a lesson that was on its way.

The lesson that was on its way became evident shortly thereafter. By early spring, I began to realize that something was profoundly wrong in my professional community. Some time in April, I started piecing things together, and by the beginning of May, I knew without a doubt that one of my male co-therapists had been in a secret relationship with one of our ex-clients, one that started soon after the client left therapy. This was an ethical violation by any therapeutic standard but it particularly violated all of the tenets of our form of therapy. This was one of my biggest professional fears come true.

In addition to all of the professional implications, the ramifications for my personal life were significant. This therapist was one of my closest friends. The fact that he had been maintaining this secret for two years almost defied belief. I lost trust in one of my best friends and most admired colleagues. My whole reality was called into question. If I did not know about this, what else in my world was false?

The next few months were a nightmare. I tried to support the client as I struggled to deal with my own trauma. This therapist was one of the primary leaders of our therapeutic community, so it threw the whole community into chaos. Differences in opinions created splits that have yet to be healed. I felt as if my world was falling apart. I experienced not only all the feelings about the current trauma, but also those from the reopened abandonment wounds from my past.

I was afraid that I would lose my practice as a result of this crisis. Our process is built on integrity and on providing safety for clients. What if all my clients left? I thought about what I would do if my worst case scenario came true. The obvious answer was that I would move to India for a few years. It would not be the end of the world. Thinking in that way helped relieve some of the terror I was experiencing.

The next weeks and months were filled with introspection. In what ways had I contributed to this situation? Stephen Levine once commented that what we often consider to be unconditional love is actually a high tolerance for other people's behavior.[2] I looked for ways I let myself and others down by not confronting unhealthy behaviors.

I ended my professional relationship with that colleague. I continued leading groups with my other three co-therapists. We examined ways our therapy process may have contributed to this incident. As a result, we made a variety of changes in the way we conducted our groups and ourselves.

---

[2]Stephen Levine Workshop, Bellevue, Washington, December 3–4, 1994.

It Was the Best of Times,
It Was the Worst of Times
Summer Tour 1995

Luckily, Mother's United States tour was near. I so longed to be with her. When she arrived, I melted into her arms. Throughout the summer, every time I entered her presence, my tears poured. I was thankful to have her help in releasing the sadness within me.

Mother seemed to make the pain I was experiencing in my personal and professional life more bearable by granting one long-term desire after another. From the time she named me Karuna in 1990, I had longed to hear her call me by name. A continuous stream of people came to me, excited that Mother had called *them* by name, but never did she say mine. I took consolation in the fact that Swamini Amma called me Karuna a few times. I reasoned that if Swamini Amma knew my name, then Mother did as well. Obviously, I had chosen to ignore the fact that it was Mother who had named me in the first place.

Mother with Swamini Amma

At one point the previous summer, when I was standing in the San Ramon kitchen, Mother walked into the room. She graced us by individually feeding us ice cream. After she left, one of my friends said, "Karuna, she called you by name!" I could not believe it. Mother had finally said my name and I had missed it! Now, a year later, after five years of waiting, my time had finally come. As Mother held me, she whispered "Karuna" in my ear. I cried with joy. She continued to call me by name almost every time I was near her on that tour. I was relieved that the many years of longing were over.

For years, I had desired to have my two spiritual families together in the same place. I had fantasies of bringing Mother to Power House church but since that was out of the question, I considered ways to bring the church and its music to her. I knew I could ask the choir to sing at the Seattle city program. Conservative Christians, however, are often very negative about eastern religions, so I did not think Pastor Jenkins would allow the choir to come. I decided to "test the waters" by to asking him if I might ask his wife to sing for Mother. (In that setting, it is proper protocol to ask the pastor first.) I was a bit shocked when he consented. Mrs. Jenkins also agreed! I requested she sing a song entitled, *Mother Prayed for Me*. The devotees loved the song. Many devotees approached her afterwards, requesting that she come back the next year.

Mrs. Jenkins and I lingered for a while, watching Mother give darshan. She sat there with big eyes, like a child exploring a new world. When she saw the people sitting in meditation, she asked if they were praying. Our kind of prayer was so different from the loud praising form of prayer that happened at her church. She asked what people were giving Mother and what she was giving them. (Many devotees give Mother fruit or flowers. She gives them flower petals and a Hershey's kiss.) Mrs. Jenkins asked if Mother was praying for the people as she held them. She commented, "There is so much love here." As we left that day she said, "Next year, I will come back and we will see if we can get these people moving!" I laughed inwardly and outwardly. I was overjoyed that I had been able to bring my two worlds together in this way.

Prior to coming to the San Ramon program, I sought help in dealing with the emotional pain I was experiencing. During the session, the therapist requested that I check in daily with the three-year-old part of myself, asking what that child part wanted and needed. I tried this for the first time at San Ramon. My "three-year-old's" immediate response was

"I want an Amma doll!" I was aghast. Since their inception, I had been uncomfortable with adults carrying around Amma dolls. In therapy, my clients have the opportunity to do regressive work, that is, they may role play a child of any age. This is a way to heal old traumas or to fill in developmental gaps. The client contracts to do the therapeutic work during a specific period of time, usually fifteen to twenty minutes. Outside of this situation, regression is discouraged. I judged adults carrying around dolls to be a big case of regression without a contract.

My "child's" request seemed reasonable, however, so I bought the doll. I tucked her away in a respectful but quite remote spot. I then sat down in the temple, near the darshan line. I noticed I was sitting next to a person known for carrying a doll at all times. I felt smug, judgmental and superior. Soon thereafter, a friend passed me on her way through the darshan line. Before I knew what happened, that friend took her own doll and plopped it in my lap, saying, "Here, hold my doll for me." "MOTHER!" I internally screamed. "This is not funny!" I felt humiliated, yet at the same time part of me was able to laugh at the leela. I let the doll sit there and just shook my head. Mother is so skilled at putting us into the middle of our resistance.

Although my negativity towards adults carrying dolls remained, my attitude about the dolls themselves shifted markedly soon thereafter. I took my doll into the tree house with me and in the quiet and privacy of my personal space, held it to my heart each night. The grief I experienced was immense. It seemed as if the doll actually pulled the grief from my heart. Such a comfort it was, helping me survive that summer of pain.

Shortly before the Rhode Island retreat, I was asked if I would be willing, once again, to sew during the retreat. Using my best organizational skills, I devised ways to arrive early so I could complete the sewing by the beginning of the retreat. I forgot that trying to control anything around Mother is futile. My well-laid plans were foiled, time after time. I was not even able to *start* the project until late the second night of the three-day retreat. Again, I struggled to maintain the most positive attitude possible under the circumstances. I grieved all that I was missing. My co-worker and I labored most of the night. By the time we finished the job the following evening, the last Devi Bhava of the tour was well under way. I was so exhausted I could not even enjoy the music, much less enter any kind of meditative state. I walked outside, lay down on the

grass and started to cry. I strongly considered returning to my dorm room
and going to sleep but I knew I would be furious with myself later if I ran
away. I forced myself to go back into the hall and enter the darshan line.
I had not been feeling the sadness I normally feel when Mother leaves the

Devi Bhava

country. By now, I was so depleted and my defenses were so low that the repressed grief started pouring out. As she held me, I was able to deeply take in her love. Once again, I appreciated the power of being taken beyond one's tolerance. From that point comes the possibility of great growth. I remembered a sign I used to have hanging on my bathroom mirror, "Growth comes from the challenge not the consolation."

The Best and the Worst Continues
Summer/Fall 1995

In August of 1995, Sreejit, who had returned from India in the spring, was preparing to move to the San Ramon ashram. At the same time, my friend, Saroja, was arranging to move to the India ashram. That meant that the Seattle satsang was losing its two primary musicians. I had been struggling for years to lead bhajans. My singing had improved, but there was no way I could be considered a lead, as I had so much difficulty with timing. Soon after they left, however, I experienced a huge shift. During a Sunday satsang, I lead the song, *Murali Krishna*. I played and sang like never before. The energy in the room was electric. I was so filled with shakti that when I finished I had to go out into the back yard and spin to release the overload of energy that was within me.

Mother had certainly graced me. My skill level increased daily. Even though I still struggled with timing, the difference was marked. Soon I was able to play songs I had yearned to play for years. Mother had granted me my primary desire. Other musicians joined the satsang and once again we had a strong bhajan team. This was a powerful demonstration not only that Mother will provide what is needed, but also that none of us are indispensable.

I reflected back on the long, arduous journey that had led me to this point. I had purchased my harmonium weeks after I met Mother. I was easily able to figure out the melodies but I soon discovered I had a major timing problem. I played for awhile and then gave up. Months or years later, the urge to play resurfaced and I would try again. I could see improvement each time but still could not play in a competent way. My frustration was compounded by the fact that Sreejit could play so skillfully, with seemingly little effort.

My desire to lead bhajans in a way that promoted meditation, as opposed to annihilating it, intensified. It seemed like a perfectly reasonable and respectable desire. I could not understand why Mother was not granting it.

Now that my desire was finally realized, I was able to see all that had occurred on this particular journey. Unlike my son, I had years and years of negative programming to overcome. The mudras, exercises, drumming, and dancing as well as the many years of being near Mother had allowed me to release old energy and to open the part of myself that had natural rhythm. By not granting my desire automatically, Mother had allowed me the opportunity to differentiate between holding on and letting go, impatience and patience, competition and cooperation, judgment and acceptance, failure and success, shame and self assurance, despair and hope, and pride and humility.

For the first time, Chaitanya and I decided to attend Mother's birthday celebrations in San Ramon. That wonderful day was filled with bhajans and talks by devotees sharing their transformative experiences with Mother. My favorite part occurred in the evening when all of the musical equipment was moved to the porch outside the temple. Swami Ramakrishnananda then led bhajans while dinner was being served in the cobble-stoned courtyard. The bhajans lasted well into the night. Occasionally, I have what seem to be past-life flashbacks of singing bhajans around a campfire. This was the closest I had ever come to recreating that memory. I could not believe I had missed this event for years and resolved I would not miss it in the future. I enjoyed myself as much I do when I am in Mother's physical presence.

Later that fall, I received legal papers informing me that the client with whom my co-therapist had been in relationship had decided to sue not only him, but me as well. I could not believe it! Another enormous professional fear had become reality. Was I going to have to face every one of my fears? At one point, I half jokingly whined to a friend, "What about all the pujas I have done? This kind of thing is not *supposed* to happen!" I had once been told that when you participate in pujas you create a bank account of spiritual points to be used in the future. I had completed many pujas over the years, so I concluded that I had built up a stockpile of points. My friend responded that if I had not done the pujas, it might have been *me* that made the big mistakes. That line of thinking seemed quite reasonable.

I was very frightened. Swami Ramakrishnananda was still in the United States, but would be rejoining Mother soon. I asked him to tell Mother what was happening. A major portion of my fear disappeared about the time he shared the information with her. Once again, Mother helped me as I began what was apparently a necessary life experience.

Swami Ramakrishnananda

PART 3

Listen to the call of my heart... O Mother
Darkness has spread all around; the path is not visible to
me, O Mother!
How shall I search for You? How shall I see You?
O Mother listen to me!

This child of Yours is just a toddler.
How can he live alone, without his Mother?
Who will take care of him? Who will nourish him with love?
O Mother... Listen to me![1]

The Purification Fire Gets Hotter
India, Dec. 1995-Feb. 1996

I decided to travel to India in mid-December, so I could be at the ashram during the Christmas season. I greatly appreciated the opportunity to experience Christmas in a religious setting, far away from the commercialism of the west. For days, ashram residents and visitors practiced traditional Christmas carols. It felt rather bizarre to sing the carols in the hot, humid weather of Kerala. I found it interesting to sing with the Europeans. Some songs we had in common, but others were new. The Europeans thought our song, *The Little Drummer Boy*, was very weird.

---

[1] "Sunle Pukar," *Bhajanamritam Volume 3*, San Ramon: Mata Amritanandamayi Center, 1997, pg. 234.

They obviously had to stifle their laughter each time we practiced that song, particularly when we sang *Pa rum pum pum pum, rum pum pum pum, rum pum pum pum*. We spent Christmas Eve sitting in the temple with Mother watching devotees perform a wonderful play and beautiful dances. I resolved to make Christmas in India an ongoing part of my life.

One of the major highlights of that trip occurred near the beginning. I was sitting with the musicians, singing bhajans during daytime darshan. My friend, Saroja, was leading the bhajans. At one point, she leaned over and asked if I wanted to lead. In stark terror, I instantaneously responded, "NO!" Immediately thereafter, I started thinking about it. I really would like to lead. Did I have the nerve? Could I do a decent job? The next morning, I told her I wanted to lead after all. When my turn came, I took my place in front of the harmonium. I soon discovered I felt less fear than when I played during satsang in Seattle. It seemed as if Mother was pulling the fear right out of me. I was elated. I could barely believe that *I* was singing for Mother in her temple in India!

When I went through the darshan line the next day, Mother asked me to sing. The following day, she asked me to sing again. This had to be heaven! I felt so blessed.

The experience was not without challenges, however. One of the first times I led, I asked a man, whom I knew to be a musician, to play the tabla. Timing was still a problem for me and I needed strong percussion to hold on to the beat. I soon discovered that he could not keep a steady beat. In fact, most of the time, he was totally offbeat! I was able to hear someone behind me playing the tambourine, so I fixed my attention on that.

When I finished the song, someone leaned forward and asked me to get rid of the tabla player as they found his playing very distracting. I did not want to be rude, but I knew I could not continue to play with him either. I told him I had trouble with timing and that it would be easier for me if only the tambourine player played. I then asked the person with the tambourine to move directly behind me. As soon as I started the next song, I found myself with another challenge. The tambourine player sang loudly, totally off key!

I looked at Mother, both laughing and frustrated. "MOTHER, what are you doing to me?" I continued, playing the best I could. Later, when I talked to Saroja about the incident, she said she had had similar experiences when she first came to India. At that time she concluded Mother was telling her she needed to go inside to find what was needed.

Sreejit had been telling me that for years. Now, however, the task seemed possible.

Numerous people approached me later, offering a mountain of unsolicited advice. Among their suggestions were "sing more gently," "sing softer," and "sing from your heart." After trying to incorporate all of these requests, I finally gave up. I knew my work was to find and hold on to the beat. When the basics were firm, I could concentrate on other refinements.

I discovered that if I focused on Mother, I could play smoothly. Whenever my attention wandered to my next song, or to evaluating how I was doing, I would make mistakes. I found if I was having trouble, I could pull myself back by focusing on Mother's eyes. What a wonderful opportunity to practice single-minded concentration!

Focusing on Mother, however, was much more challenging than one might imagine. The distractions seemed endless. Once a group of drummers from the village started playing in front of the temple. I leaned over to someone and asked if I should stop. They responded, "No." Therefore, I continued to lead bhajans with dissonant drumming in close proximity. Usually crowds of people blocked my view of Mother. Chaos and chatter abounded. Rarely was there any kind of percussion available. Even if there was, the person playing may have been simply experimenting with the instrument. Someone playing off beat or playing intermittently was more of a problem than no percussion at all. I thought how easy it would be now to play in Seattle, with everyone completely focused on singing, the surroundings still and quiet, cymbals, sticks, drums and tambourines all playing on beat.

Mother has often said that healing from past traumas is like squeezing pus from a wound. The process will cause pain but it is necessary pain. That year Mother apparently decided I was to release more old grief.

Each January, tens of thousands of Swami Ayyappa[2] devotees take a forty day pilgrimage to Sabarimala. Many of the pilgrims stop by the ashram on their trek. For years, my eyes had filled with tears whenever I saw these men dressed in black shirts and black doties. As I mentioned earlier, when I sing particular bhajans I often feel like I am singing them near a campfire. I speculated that perhaps I had once been an Ayyappa devotee and had regularly taken the pilgrimage to Sabarimala. My sad-

---

[2]Ayyappa - son of Vishnu and Shiva.

ness was compounded by the fact that I could not take the pilgrimage now, even if I wanted to, as only men, children and very old women were allowed to participate.

While I had experienced sadness in the presence of the Ayyappa pilgrims for years, that year the grief exploded within me. Whenever I saw an Ayyappa group I would burst into tears. Once, when someone sang an Ayyappa song, I experienced despair so deep that I ended up in my room dry heaving.

Another event regularly triggered my grief. At that time, one day a week was reserved for Mother to give darshan to the residents. While visitors could receive Mother's darshan several times per week, this day was the only time residents could go for darshan unless there was some special need. I appreciated that Mother took care of the residents in this way. While nonresidents were welcome to watch, they were not supposed to join the darshan line unless they had just arrived or would soon be leaving. Regardless of this restriction, each week many nonresidents joined the line. Later in the week, I would watch as these same people received regular darshan as well. I was annoyed by their ongoing disregard for the rules.

For years, my heart ached as I watched Mother giving darshan on that day. My pain had always intrigued me, as I did not feel similar pain in other situations where going to darshan would be inappropriate, such as when the crowds were large or when we attended the rededication programs in other cities.

That year, I decided to avoid the pain by going to darshan *only* on residents' darshan day. I had been coming to India for so long, I felt like an ashram resident even though I did not live there all of the time. I rationalized that as long as I was willing to tolerate the once-a-week limitation, it was acceptable for me to consider myself a resident. As I rose to get in line for the first time, I overheard one of the western brahmacharinis telling the devotee sitting next to her that darshan on that day was *only* for residents. As no one said anything to the nonresidents who had already joined the line, I felt as if Mother had given me an indirect message.

I returned to my seat immediately, my heart filling with immense pain. This level of pain returned each residents' darshan day for the rest of that trip. I would watch until my heart hurt so much that I could not tolerate it any longer. I would then "run" to my room and cry myself to sleep.

One might wonder why I continued to participate in resident's darshan day when I experienced so much pain there. The major reason was that it was also great fun to watch Mother giving darshan to the residents. She was so spontaneous in her interactions with them. One of my favorite memories occurred the day Mother stopped the brahmacharinis in the middle of a song that was extolling her for her virtues. Mother interrupted them mid-sentence, saying she was not feeling like that kind of Mother at the moment. She then spontaneously created and sang a song about a mother who was angry because she had found a stone in the rice! Everyone burst into laughter.

I tried to make sense of my pain. I knew some of it was because my access to Mother was blocked. I assumed I was also experiencing leftover pain about my father not allowing me to come home. I was reminded of childhood memories of feeling I did not belong anywhere. We moved so often that I never felt part of any group. I always felt different, either I was too liberal, too conservative, too shy, or too awkward. As a child I became withdrawn and stayed on the outside of all groups.

At a more current level, I believed the pain resulted from feeling trapped between two worlds. I felt like an ashram resident, yet I was not. I was also not a new devotee. As a result, I could not have the privileges of either group.

At a deeper level, I felt trapped between the ashram world and the bigger world. Neither world seemed right for me. I remembered an astrologer once telling me my job in this lifetime was to find the middle ground between ashram living and living in the world. I recalled Jesus saying that even though we are in the world, we are not of the world.[3]

At a still deeper level, I believed I was tapping into past life memories of times when I did live in monasteries or ashrams. Denying my place as an ashram resident was denying my old reality.

As I write this and remember how much I hurt, I am in awe of the amount of pain that resides within each of us. While this particular pain is still with me, I am very thankful for how much it has lessened. Most of the discomfort I feel now is from wondering if I am giving up an opportunity to be with Mother because I am trying to be good, choosing to follow the rules when others do not.

There was yet another event that consistently triggered my grief. Throughout that trip, I was repeatedly asked to leave the darshan line. It

---

[3] St. John 17:16,18.

happened so many times that I reached the point where I was reluctant to even join the line for fear that I would be asked to leave.

Mother never *directly* asked me to leave. The direction more often came in the form of one brahmacharini or another saying something like, "Mother is tired, please do not come for darshan," "Mother says the westerners should wait" or "Mother says no darshan for westerners today." There were times when these instructions were given to only one or two westerner's, others being allowed to stay in the line. Each time I would run to my room and cry from the massive pain in my heart. After some weeks, I realized I was responding as I often did during my childhood, by spending large blocks of time pouting in my room. I began to force myself to sit with the singers as I dealt with the pain in my heart.

One day, I decided I would go through the large Indian darshan line rather than the smaller line for westerners. Maybe that strategy would work. Just as I reached the door that provides entrance to the inner temple where Mother sits, an Indian woman directed me to leave the line. Later, when I told someone what had happened, she said, "Why did you do what *she* told you to do? That woman is crazy. She has no authority to tell you anything." I realized what a metaphor that was for life. We have a goal and we let crazy people, or crazy ideas of our own, throw us off course. I realized the incident had other metaphorical implications as well. How often in this process do we get to the door and look inside yet not know what to do to get past the threshold to the other side. Once we have had a glimpse of the other side, there is no way we are going to leave, but we can not figure out how to get through.

Whenever I did reach the front of a darshan line, Mother generally ignored me. She can be so skilled in not giving attention when provoking or testing a devotee for one reason or another. Sometimes, she shows no sign of recognition. At other times, she gives a brief hug and then moves on to the next person without even giving you a glance! During my last darshan before the annual Calicut programs, she took the provocation a step further. I went through the darshan line wondering what would happen this time. Would I make it to Mother? How would she treat me? She seemed quite angry when talking to the person in front of me. That mood continued during my darshan. While I believed she was not angry with me, I was not sure. I was handling these seeming rejections pretty well, but I could feel myself wearing down.

That year, two memorable events occurred during Devi Bhava programs. One day, feeling disconnected and exhausted, I sat on the balcony watching Mother give darshan. I was so miserable, I could not even concentrate on the bhajans. I decided I might as well go for darshan and then go to sleep for a few hours. My plans abruptly changed, however, when, after hugging me, Mother instructed me to sit beside her. The instant I sat down, Kathy Zavada, a western devotee, began to sing. I drifted immediately into an altered state and, for the first time ever, felt grief about my mother's death. The meditative state lasted until Kathy finished her last song, forty-five minutes to an hour later.

During my next Devi Bhava darshan, Mother again told me to sit next to her. Once again Kathy began to sing. This time, I *saw* myself as a happy child, playing and cuddling with my mother. This was my first memory of a happy time with my mother. It was a touching moment and I could feel my heart soften.

For years, Mother had given me a tremendous amount of sorely needed maternal energy, but in terms of directly dealing with my childhood pain, most of my experiences had been centered on healing the wounds associated with my father. Was I moving into a new era? Would my focus now be on healing old mother wounds?

Soon thereafter, we left for Calicut. Upon arrival, I was shocked to discover that most of the western devotees had been assigned to stay in the newly built ashram school. Calicut had become one of the major highlights of my trips to India, primarily because I was able to immerse myself in the loud bhajans that played day and night. For years, we had stayed on the roof of the temple. From there we could hear the bhajans almost as well as if we were in the program hall. At the new school, the sound of the music was greatly muted. It was further distorted and muffled by the presence of a loud generator. I felt immense grief and loss.

It occurred to me that I could ask to move to the temple roof. That presented me with another dilemma. It was my fantasy that the roof had been reserved for the ashram residents who were doing most of the work at the program. I had led workshops for years and believed that it was important for staff to have time away from program participants. I did not want to "invade" their private space.

The grief I experienced over the next several days escalated so rapidly that I started to feel sick. As a fever took hold, I became frantic. I realized I needed to do something quickly. I found Jani, the renunciate in charge of housing, and in a very incoherent and rambling way tried to explain my predicament. I was crying so profusely I could hardly talk. Jani immediately offered to let me stay in a house located next to the ashram grounds. I would be able to hear the music from there. I was elated. When I followed her into the house, she went to a room on the second floor and quickly began to shut all of the windows in the already stifling room. "What in the world is she doing?" I thought. "This will be better," she said. I was perplexed. After a few moments, I realized she did not understand my problem. She was used to people complaining about the blaring music. Never before had anyone been upset because the music was not loud enough! When I clarified the problem, Jani informed me she had announced two days ago that anyone who wanted to move from the school to the temple could do so. I just shook my head. It was so like Mother to first lead me directly into the pain, and then in the end give me exactly what I had wanted in the first place.

With immense relief, I moved to the temple roof. I was limited in what I could do because I was so sick. At least, as I lay on my mat, I was able to receive the comfort of the music.

As usual, the challenges were balanced with joys. One of my special memories of that trip came when I was asked to hold a hot water bottle to Mother's back. During darshan at these rededication programs, Mother sits cross-legged on a stage. She hugs every person that comes to her and then hands each a packet of ash and a piece of candy. She may hug 7,000–10,000 people per day, sometimes at a rate of one person every three seconds. Darshan may last six or more hours at a time. While the person who receives the hug sees only Mother's smile and shining eyes, those of us who sit and watch can sometimes see her exhaustion and pain. I felt relieved and graced to be able to offer even a tiny bit of assistance.

There was a less enjoyable dimension to this "gift" as well. You might remember that Mother was angry at the time of my last darshan in Amritapuri. I had not had any interaction with her since then. As I sat holding the hot water bottle, I had to deal with fear that she would look around, see it was me and, in disgust, send me away. I told myself that this was an irrational fear. I also reminded myself that if, perchance, she did send me away, it would be for some higher good. I was able to stay grounded and in a place where I felt I could handle whatever happened. After some time, Mother indicated that she wanted me to remove hot water bottle. I left the stage, feeling relieved that my fantasy had not come true and encouraged that I had been able to stay grounded and in control of my mind as it tried to pull me off center.

The challenges of the Calicut trip were not over. On the last day of the program, I decided to again participate in the Saturn puja. This time, I ended up sitting in a place where I could not see Mother at all. I felt depressed and miserable. During one point of the puja, Amma leads a meditation. She instructed us to imagine dancing with our favorite deity. For me, that would be Mother. An unexpected reaction arose from within me. An indignant teenage voice blurted, "I do not want to dance with *you*, I'm mad at you. I am going to dance with SWAMIJI!" I was surprised, as I had no awareness of being angry with Mother.

At the retreat in Seattle, when Mother had instructed the swamis to dance, she apparently told Swamiji she did not want him to dance because he had grown so big. She reportedly had said that she did not want his body bouncing all over the stage![4]   Now, my rebellious side remarked, "I do not care if his body does bounce, I'm dancing with Swamiji, not *you*!" Swamiji and I then danced away in a western polka style dance. The images were wonderful and I had great fun. I smile even now as I recollect the memory.

The temporary lightening of my mood did not last. The night was long and the crowds were huge. There were probably 10,000 people crowded into the small space. I decided I would use my last bit of energy to get some juice. I pushed my way through the crowd until I made it to the juice bar. After I had placed my order and given the woman the few rupees I had left in my pocket, she informed me I had not paid for the fruit I had eaten that morning. She kept my money and refused to give me juice. I was shocked. I did not believe I had neglected to pay for the fruit. This was the last straw! I pushed my way to the temple, went upstairs and cried myself to sleep.

Why is it necessary for us to be pushed to the point where we can tolerate no more? Amma has said we are to learn to be like an eye, able to easily adjust to any situation. Her constant testing gives us many opportunities to learn how to stay in a place of equanimity. We have an opportunity to observe our vasanas as well as to discover that we are stronger than we might think. If the tests result in despair so great that we can do nothing other than cry out to God for solace and help, so much the better. Mother often says that crying to God for five minutes is worth an hour of meditation.

I decided to take the train home from Calicut. I mentioned earlier that Mother could turn a three-hour trip into a fourteen-hour one. I knew the trip from Calicut would involve hours of waiting and would probably become a twenty-four-hour event. The morning of our departure, I learned that Mother had chastised a boy for deciding to take the train home, rather than enduring the challenge of the bus trip. I wondered if this was a message for me as well. I examined my reasons for choosing the train and decided that I had reached the limit of my tolerance. It was okay for me to know my limits and take care of myself. I did not think Mother would disagree. I loved arriving home many hours before the main group, allowing time for showers, laundry, bhajans and rest. I was pleased I had taken care of myself in this way.

---

[4]One never knows whether stories like this one are truth or rumor!

A few weeks later, I participated in the five-day Trivandrum rededication program. For years, during these programs, a few western devotees consistently sat near Mother during darshan, never moving to give others the same opportunity. A new system had been devised that ensured rotation of seats. There were now stage monitors who kept track of the length of time each devotee had been sitting near Mother. After fifteen to thirty minutes, depending on how many people were wanting to be close, the stage monitor would tell the devotee that it was time to give the seat to someone else. I frequently worked as a stage monitor during that program. It was wonderful to see the excited disbelief on the faces of new people when told they could sit near Mother. It was also nice to be able to give those "old timers" who never sat close to Mother, the opportunity to do so.

The stage monitors worked long shifts and rarely if ever sat down. Although it looked like easy work, I found it very tiring. There were people who objected to the new system. I found it very draining to deal with their negative attitudes and behaviors.

Two incidents that occurred when I was working on stage left me with treasured memories. At one point, someone offered to relieve me so I could sit with Mother. I sat down but could not even see her as my vision was totally blocked by the people in front of me. That situation lasted about ten minutes. Then, in the space of about a minute, one person after another stood up and left the stage, allowing me to move closer and closer to Mother. The instant I arrived in the seat beside Mother, Swamiji began to sing *Manugal Mutum* one of the Swami Ayyappa songs. I had heard that song a few times at the San Ramon ashram in 1989, but never since. At that time, it had touched me deeply and I had longed to hear it again. My tears began to pour. That was the last of Swamiji's songs. Soon after he stopped singing and left the stage, I decided to go to my room. When I passed Swamiji in the hallway, he gave me a huge smile. I believed he knew what a gift the song had been for me.

A day or two later, another person offered to give me a break. The instant I sat down, Swami Pranavamritananda started singing *He Govinda, He Gopala*, the other song most likely to hit that core place of grief and bliss within me. Once again, my tears poured and my heart filled with wonder and gratitude. When I opened my eyes at the end of the song, I noticed that the person who had offered to relieve me was gone. As I jumped up and returned to my position, I was enormously thankful for once again having been given the gift of a song.

That trip to India had been exhausting and trying. The challenges and tests seemed endless. One day after returning to Amritapuri, I was sitting with friends in the western canteen. A woman who had just met Mother joined us. She was full of bliss. She commented that she could not imagine how we could handle so much bliss, day after day. Some of us glanced at each other with knowing looks, smiling inside. We all remembered the glimpses of that joy-filled world Mother showed us when we were new. Now, we felt barely able to keep our heads above water. The process of Mother exposing and working on our vasanas, much as the ocean wears away and smoothes out the roughness of stones, was frequently painful and draining. Luckily, as we learn to reconnect with our true nature, Mother continues to give us glimpses of the joy that is there for us. These shining moments provide the motivation we need to keep us stepping ever forward.

At some point during that period, I walked past one of the ashram photographers, apparently looking quite despondent. She said, "I have something that will make you feel better." She took me to her room and pulled out a picture of me holding the hot water bottle to Mother's back in Calicut. I had always wanted a picture of Mother and me together, and there it was. Such a wonderful gift!

Karuna assisting Mother during the Calicut program

As a result of all of the painful events on this trip, I had the opportunity to examine the ways Mother teaches us the benefits of surrender. She is a master of provocation, testing and pushing her devotees either directly or indirectly. In this way, we have plenty of chance to see our negative tendencies and plenty of practice in staying calm and centered. Mother is also an expert in doing things that make absolutely no sense to our minds. This provides us the opportunity to see both our level of faith and our level of surrender.

Even though I still experience doubt from time to time, I find the more my faith grows, the easier it is to move through the doubt. The development of faith is an ongoing process. When we first meet Mother, she plants the seeds for faith to develop by showing us that she knows us inside and out, through her eyes, through her actions, and through her words. As our experiences multiply, our faith grows and our ability to surrender increases.

I have learned many tools for helping me move through doubt. For example, I have found that it can be immensely beneficial to talk with one of the swamis when I am plagued by doubt. Even though I might not agree with what they have to say, I find it useful to include their information in my thinking. I also find it valuable to discuss my doubts with a person who knows more than I do and whom I know loves Mother. If I talk with people who are full of their own doubts, I am much less likely to make peace with the situation.

As I mentioned earlier, my therapy community has a saying, "When in doubt, get closer." The natural response when we are uncomfortable or upset with someone is to move as far away as possible. If we can, instead, force ourselves to move closer we may be able to work through the difficulty faster. I find this even more true with Mother than in the world at large. If I stay close, I can allow her love to wash over me. At times, that is all that is needed to remove my doubts.

Rand Hicks, the director of the Integral Yoga Center in Pensacola, Florida, once commented that it is absurd for us to judge a particular action of a realized soul because we have no way to see the whole picture. The saint has the ability to see the past, present and future. What makes perfect sense to the saint will often seem senseless to us.[5]

---

[5]Rand Hicks, *The Yoga of Seva*, Workshop, Issaquah, Washington, August 26–27, 1995.

When in doubt, I think about the changes I have seen in my children, friends, other devotees, and myself. I also note the changes in the senior swamis. During the years I have been with Mother, there have been times when it seemed like the swamis evolved daily. The peace and the light emanating from them often grows palpably from contact to contact. When my doubts flare, I remind myself that these transformations would not be occurring, if Mother were not indeed a great soul.

I also look at Mother's endless stream of charitable projects. Her projects multiply at a phenomenal speed. Mother herself is a supreme example of selfless service. When my doubts are up, I look for any evidence of personal gain from what she does, but I never find any. The only personal gain I can imagine is the joy that comes from watching her children grow.

Not only do doubts arise because of our own experiences, they are also triggered or aggravated by the attitudes of those around us. The western world is very intolerant of the guru-disciple spiritual path. When other people's doubts are fueling my own, I remember something Mother said one of the first times I heard her talk. Her instructions at that time were, "Take what fits and throw away the rest." That gave me permission to use my discrimination and free will as opposed to expecting her to do my thinking for me.

When I am beating myself up for having doubts or for not progressing faster, I remember several of Mother's lessons. Many times, she has said our past should be like a canceled check, that is, we should learn from our mistakes and move on. When in this state, I remind myself it is useless to obsess about what I have or have not done in the past and think about what changes, if any, I need to make now.

I also remind myself that Mother does not have a timetable for me. I can take the express bus Home or I can take the bus that makes a lot of stops. She will love me and be there for me whichever bus I take. She will accompany me until I learn all I need to learn on this journey Home.

During the rest of that year's trip, I continued to lead bhajans whenever the opportunity arose. I particularly looked forward to leading the last day before I was to leave India. When I woke up that morning, however, I discovered that since Mother was soon to depart on the North India tour, the crowd was the biggest I had ever seen. The temple was already jammed with people.

I took one look at the crowd and said, "No way, I'm not playing." I then proceeded to hide in my room. At some point during the morning one of the brahmacharis came to my room and said, "Mother wants you to come sing, NOW!" I did not know if Mother asked for me directly, or if she had simply said that the westerners should sing. It did not matter, I was the one he had found. I panicked. Not only did the size of the crowd intimidate me, but to make matters worse, the sound system had been hooked up in such a way that the songs were being broadcast all over the ashram grounds. When I told a friend I could not do it, she reassured me that I could. Combing my memory for the easiest songs I knew, I took a deep breath, walked downstairs and sat in front of the harmonium. I focused my attention on Mother and began to play, pretending the microphones did not even exist. In this way I was able to lead the bhajans without incident. I was delighted that I was able to move through the fear. I not only survived the challenge but also enjoyed the experience of success.

Large crowd in Amritapuri temple

There was one more opportunity for me to receive darshan before my departure. Since it was to be my last darshan, I felt sure I would not be sent away. I entered the line, looking forward to a pleasant interaction with Mother. Almost immediately, I was directed to come back later. I felt only a momentary pang of pain. An hour later, I rejoined the line. I once again was instructed to leave. "But, this is my *last* darshan," I said. "Come back later," the line monitor responded firmly. This time as I left the line, I felt a bit panicky. I noticed that only one other westerner had followed the line monitor's instructions. Were the others ignoring her, or had they never been given the instruction? Even though my heart hurt, I marveled at how consistent this form of provocation had been throughout my trip.

I rejoined the singers and worked with my pain. I tried to tell myself to let the music be enough. I knew, however, that I was just rationalizing. I did not want to face being sent away again. Towards the end of the darshan period, I returned to the line, wondering what would happen this time. I was delighted and relieved to at long last spend a touching moment in Mother's arms.

Finally, it was time to leave. This had been by far my most difficult visit. While I felt some sadness about leaving, mostly I was jubilant. I had made it through to the end and had not run away!

Finishing Unfinished Business
Winter/Spring 1996

As soon as I returned from India, I had to face the reality of the law suit. If only the client and I could sit together and talk, perhaps all of the misunderstandings could be resolved and healing could begin. The legal process, however, prohibited any contact between the parties involved. That form of problem resolution seemed unhealthy and unproductive. I felt powerless.

During the winter months, I felt an inner direction to take a mediation course. I did not have as many psychotherapy clients as usual, so thought I might be receiving some direction for the future. Perhaps some day I would work as a mediator. I found the course fascinating. I was not sure how I would apply the new knowledge, but liked having new skills. The course also served as a refresher, reminding me of communication techniques I had learned years before.

During late winter, I was notified that the client wanted to settle the case through mediation! When the mediation occurred in May, I participated feeling knowledgeable, confident and trusting of the process. The day was long, but by the end, the issues had been resolved to everybody's satisfaction. Cases such as this often drag on for three or more years. We had reached resolution in less than seven months!

Patience, Enthusiasm, and Innocent Faith
Summer tour 1996

I first learned the song, *Venkataramana*, from an old tape of Avadutendra Swami's music. There was another song on that tape I loved to hear as well. I asked one of the Indian devotees in our satsang to transcribe the song so I could learn it. After listening to the tape, he informed me that the song was too difficult for me to learn. I tried unsuccessfully to convince him otherwise. A few days later, when I played the song for another devotee, she said she wanted to learn it. I told her I had not been able to convince our friend to transcribe the song. She was sure she could persuade him, but she was wrong.

His saying "No" to the two of us really triggered our rebellious and competitive natures. We decided to have some fun. Another Indian devotee was returning to Seattle soon, so I asked him to teach us the song. We spent many hours a day over the next few weeks learning the chant, which by then we had discovered to be the *Hanuman Chalisa*. When we were ready, we sang it at satsang. The devotee who had refused to teach us, looked confused as we began to sing, and then smiled broadly. It was great fun for all involved.

Other satsang members wanted to learn the *Hanuman Chalisa* as well. We spent weeks practicing it. On the first night of the summer tour, we sang the song for Mother. We were a bit surprised when she showed no reaction. Soon, many of us started to laugh internally, choosing to consider her behavior as provocation. We had no doubt she had heard us and knew how much effort we had put forth.

Another highlight of that summer tour occurred at the Seattle city program. I had decided to ask Pastor Jenkins if the Power House church choir could sing at the program. Somewhat to my surprise, he immediately consented. On the day they were to perform, I stood outside the program hall waiting for the choir to arrive. As the appointed time came and went, I wondered what had happened. Were they lost? All of a sudden, I noticed a large caravan of cars coming towards the program hall. I had thought, in all likelihood, four or five people from the choir would sing. When I saw the procession of cars, however, I realized most of the choir had come!

They sang song after song. The choir members were having such a good time, they asked to sing even more songs than I had requested. As I was very focused on the choir, I did not notice what was happening around me. I could hear people clapping, so I knew the choir was being well received, but I had no idea how thoroughly people were appreciating the music. During the last song, I turned around and saw that people were dancing all over the auditorium. I learned later that the swamis were in the balcony thoroughly enjoying themselves. Mrs. Jenkins goal of "getting these people moving" had certainly been realized. Truly the church had come to Mother.

A few devotees were displeased that the choir members left without receiving Mother's darshan. Did they not realize what a miracle it was that these two groups were together in the same room? I felt so blessed and grateful.

Another important moment for me occurred during the Seattle program when our satsang was singing for Mother. My eyes were closed as I sang. At one point, I opened my eyes and looked at Mother. There in her arms was the client who had sued me. I was startled and shocked. I knew it was no accident that I opened my eyes at just that moment. I experienced a variety of feelings. Part of me was really happy to see her receiving Mother's love. At the same time all of the fear and sadness I had repressed during the six months of the lawsuit came pouring out with the power of a bulldozer. Luckily, at that moment, we stopped singing. I was able to go into a back room and, with support, feel the residual feelings. All of the events surrounding the lawsuit had been such a traumatic process for me. Hopefully, it was over forever and healing could now take place for all concerned.

Mother has said to be successful a person must have patience, enthusiasm, and innocent faith. We should be like toddlers, who fall down and get right back up again rather than being like teenagers who have enthusiasm without patience, or like many of the elderly, who have patience without enthusiasm.

Mother gave me an opportunity to work on these qualities, and others, through the process of writing and publishing Book 1 of *Getting to Joy*. I wrote the book during the summer of 1993. The content virtually poured out of me and, as a result, I completed the book in an amazingly short period of time. Then the leelas began!

I believed it important to get Mother's authorization to publish the book, so I sent a copy to Swami Paramatmananda in San Ramon. He read it and told me to send it on to Swamiji. I gave a copy to Swamiji in January of 1994. He said he would read and approve the manuscript before I left India. When I checked with him at the end of my trip, he said he had not had time to review it. He was so busy that I could not imagine how he would ever have time to read it.

When I checked with him in San Ramon in June of 1994, he still had not reviewed the book. In January of 1995, I checked with him again. This time he indicated he had read enough to approve publication, providing he was able to get Mother's consent. He had not talked with Amma by the time I left India, so, once again, I returned home with no answer.

I naively developed what I considered to be a foolproof way to get a final answer. In June of 1995, I would go through the darshan line when Mother and Swamiji were together. If he had yet not obtained authorization, I would suggest he ask Mother at that time. I carried out my plan and it seemed to succeed in that she said "Yes, you may publish the book." After a moment, however, she added, "But, wait until we get back to India." What did that mean? I looked at Swamiji questioningly. He sheepishly said, "She wants me to read it more thoroughly." He said I would have an answer no later than October.

During the same Seattle program, Mother asked me to relay a message to another devotee. She said that it can be very difficult for a person who has no prior spiritual experience to meet a saint as they do not understand the process that is triggered within them simply by being in the saint's presence. She asked me to tell this devotee to read books about people who had experienced spiritual transformation. Some part of me knew she meant stories about "regular" people, not saints. While this message was being sent to someone else, I believed she was also telling me that my book would serve a useful function.

October came and went with no word from Swamiji. In November, Mother traveled to New York City to give a speech at the United Nations 50th Anniversary celebration. One of my friends was going to New York, so I asked her to check with Swamiji. He told my friend that he had not yet looked at the book.

In January of 1996, I decided to try again. I went to Swamiji's office and asked if he had finished reviewing the book. He said, "If Mother said you can publish it, you can publish it." I reminded him that he believed Mother wanted him to look at it again. Foolish me! He responded that he would talk to her. As my departure date neared, I wondered what I should do. I took my dilemma to Swamini Amma. She told me not to worry, *she* would get me an answer. I heard nothing more from her about the matter. Once again, I left India without an answer.

I had believed for some time that all of these delays had little to do with Swamiji and his schedule. This had all of the makings of one of Mother's leelas. At each step, I had to look at the situation and determine if I was too attached. I did not feel particularly invested in publishing the book, as simply writing it had been such a valuable process for me. However, so many people had found the book helpful, I had an ongoing sense that it was meant to be published.

Continuing with this process was a major lesson in patience. When I have an idea, I am used to manifesting it immediately. Putting something on hold goes against my nature. Surrendering in that way was a huge challenge.

In 1995, I decided I would do no more editorial work on the book until I knew it would be published. In the fall of 1995, I attended a workshop led by Rand Hicks, the editor for books published by the Sri Aurobindo ashram. After the workshop, I asked Rand if he would be willing to edit my book, when and if I received authorization to publish. He agreed to the seva.

As the summer tour of 1996 approached, I was undecided about whether I would ask about the book again. I would make the decision during the tour. A few days before I left for the San Ramon programs, someone vandalized my yard. My roommate advised me to inform Mother. I did not feel particularly concerned, but decided to follow her suggestion. Mother's response was, "Do not worry." As I turned to leave, Swamiji stopped me, asking, "Have you published your book yet?" I breathed deeply, had a few sarcastic thoughts, and then said "No," reminding him that he had wanted to talk to Mother about it. He talked to her on the spot, and she gave final consent to publish the book. As I walked away, I was laughing inside. "Wouldn't you know it, she gives me the answer when I didn't even ask the question!"

While this long delay had certainly been a test in persistence, patience, enthusiasm, and faith, I quickly discovered the delay had other advantages as well. During the three-year wait, I had written numerous articles. As a result, my writing skills had improved markedly. I also now had distance from the original writing. As I re-edited the book, I was able to understand feedback people had given me earlier, and could make changes that had not made sense to me then. Also, because of the wait, Rand would edit the book.

I was aware of another possible reason for the delay. During the first years after I had written the book, I felt hesitant about publishing it. Since provocation is one of Mother's primary strategies for exposing our ego, I knew Mother was bound to do things that would upset people. I assumed that some of these people would not only judge her, but me as well. My faith at that time was not strong enough to offset my fear of large-scale judgment. During the three-year wait, however, my faith in Mother had grown significantly. I felt much more capable of dealing with whatever came my way as a result of publishing the book.

People often ask how I decide when to ask Mother for direction. Sometimes, as in the case of seeking authorization for publishing my book, I have an inner knowing that I should ask. Usually, when I have a question, I check inside and see what answer comes from my "higher self." If the answer is clear, I usually do not ask. If I do not get an answer or if the answer that comes sounds suspiciously like my "everyday self," then I am more likely to seek her advice. I also watch for the answer to come in unexpected ways. Occasionally, people will walk up to me and out of no where give me the answer to a question! I am most likely to ask if I have no idea what action is in my best interest. I do not ask Mother for her input, however, unless I intend to follow her instruction.

More Time with Mother!
Summer/Fall 1996

In October, Chaitanya and I went to San Ramon to celebrate Mother's birthday. Towards the end of that weekend, I received a call from a Seattle devotee notifying me there was an article in a local newspaper about the incident between my co-therapist and our client. My friend went on to say that the newspaper identified me as the other therapist in the client's group. Later, when I saw the newspaper, I discovered the story reported distorted and incorrect information about me. Would this nightmare ever end? I was thankful that the story had been printed at a time when I felt filled with Mother's love. Even though Mother's body had not been at the ashram during the birthday celebrations, her presence was palpable.

The next few weeks were difficult for me. I assumed that my neighbors had read the newspaper and I worried about what they were thinking. I was concerned about the effect the article would have on my life. Would potential clients be wary? While my satsang friends were very understanding, very few of the colleagues in my therapy community initiated any kind of support. I felt painfully estranged from them. Later, I realized I must have experienced a small taste of what it must be like for Mother to endure the endless political and religious criticism from people in India who do not approve of her actions. (Some of Mother's programs are controversial, such as her decision to allow women priestesses to conduct pujas.)

For the first time, Mother returned to the United States in the autumn to offer a series of public programs and a retreat. While many devotees travel all over the country during Mother's summer tour, this was the first time so many of us had come together in one place. It was quite a reunion!

My primary goal for that visit with Mother was to lead bhajans. Since I was to leave for India a month after the retreat, I decided I would not attend the first public program. I would complete my weekly therapy groups in Seattle and then travel to San Ramon in time to participate in one evening program and the retreat. Within five minutes of entering the temple, I was informed that Mother wanted the Seattle satsang to sing. My primary goal had been met the moment I arrived. What else was to come?

Over the years, I had noticed that some devotees do not go for darshan unless Mother calls them individually. At the end of a darshan program, she might beckon them to come forward. As the crowds were very large and I had been with Mother for a long time, I decided I would not go for darshan unless she called me.

On the second day of the retreat, Mother asked one of the Seattle devotees, "Where is Karuna? Is she not coming to the retreat?" While part of me knew this was a game, since I had led a bhajan the first night and I had been seated near her several times since then, another part of me was incensed. How could I wait for her to call me, if she did not even know I was there? I took this provocation as a not too subtle way of telling me it was fine to come for darshan. With some indignation, I entered the darshan line at the next possible opportunity. When she held me she whispered, "Karuna, Karuna, Karuna" into my ear, once for each darshan that I had missed! Such a Mother we have!

Eight weeks before I was to begin my yearly pilgrimage to India, I felt an inner direction to start saying my mantra, a lot! While there have been other periods in my spiritual journey that I have focused on my mantra, japa has never been a consistent part of my sadhana. I began to say my mantra 1,000 to 10,000 times per day, sometimes more. I also began to chant the *Lalita Sahasranama*, the Thousand Names of the Divine Mother, about five times a week.

A few days before my departure, Pastor Jenkins sent a junior minister to me during a gospel concert. The junior minister asked if I would be attending church on Sunday, adding that Pastor Jenkins wanted me to read a poem during that service. Never before had Pastor Jenkins asked me to do anything of the sort! After the concert, with some trepidation, I approached the pastor asking, "I understand you have a poem you want me to read at the Sunday service." "No," he said, "I want *you* to pick one." What poem could I read that would be both meaningful and acceptable? When I fretted to my daughter about my dilemma, she reminded me of the poem a devotee had read during a talk at the November retreat. "Perfect," I thought. The poem, believed to have been written by a hospitalized patient, seemed universal in its wisdom. I felt confident that it would be received as well by the congregation as it had been by the devotees at the retreat.

AMONG MEN MOST RICHLY BLESSED

I asked God for strength that I might achieve
I was made weak that I might learn humbly to obey.

I asked for health that I might do great things
I was given infirmity that I might do better things.

I asked for riches that I might be happy
I was given poverty that I might be wise.

I asked for power that I might have the praise of men
I was given weakness that I might feel the need of God.

I asked for all things that I might enjoy life
I was given only life that I might enjoy all things.

I got nothing I asked for but everything I had hoped for.

Almost despite myself my unspoken prayers were answered.

I am among men most richly blessed.

Anonymous

When I read the poem that Sunday morning, the congregation was vocal in their appreciation, enthusiastically calling out their praise, "Amen," "Yes," and "Thank you Jesus!"

PART 4

O Mother, Dweller in the heart, Embodiment of affection.
I could utter nothing but Thy sacred Names.
O Mother of the World, be gracious enough to enable me to
tell Thy story.
I want neither worldly enjoyment nor pleasure. I want only
pure devotion.[1]

My Faith Grows
India December 1996- February 1997

Occasionally before my annual visit to Mother's ashram in India, I have felt the need to update my will. This was one of those years. Within days of my departure, two clients told me independently that they sensed I was in danger. The morning I left, I felt compelled to write Madhuri a note saying that if I died on this trip, I would like Mrs. Jenkins to sing at the memorial service, should one be held. What was going on?

The journey started out just like any other. There were five Seattle devotees on the airplane, including my daughter. We traveled to Singapore without incident. After an eighteen-hour layover in Singapore, we boarded the airplane for the final leg of our trip. I remember thinking, "Just a few more hours and we will be sitting beside Mother during Devi Bhava. We are in the home stretch. We have it made!"

---

[1] "Hridaya Nivasini", *Bhajanamritam, Volume 1*, San Ramon: Mata Amritanandamayi Center, 1992, pg. 252.

Not so! Halfway between Singapore and India, our plane started shaking. Simultaneously, all of the oxygen masks fell from their compartments. As we struggled to put on our masks, the plane started falling. Later, we were told that it had first dropped 15,000 feet, then another 10,000. The entire fall took about a minute. As the plane began to descend, my daughter and I glanced at each other and then we each focused inward. My mantra started flowing freely within me. With the mantra came a great sense of peace.

Many thoughts flowed through my mind. I felt immensely thankful that I had been directed to focus on my mantra prior to the trip. I believed that it was this preparation that now made the mantra so accessible. I noted that the premonitions of danger had been correct. I realized that should I die now, I could leave the earth without regret. I had no sense of unfinished business. I felt curious about what would happen when, and if, we hit water. Would we live? Would we die? Would we struggle? Would we experience pain? Those thoughts were present, but there was matter-of-fact energy associated with them. Mostly, I felt relaxed and peaceful. All that was important was my mantra.

The reaction of other passengers was far different from that generally portrayed by the media. A woman screamed for about two seconds as the plane began to fall. After that, there was complete silence aboard the plane until the pilot spoke, about fifteen minutes later. When he did speak, he informed us that there had been a decompression problem. He said everything was now under control. He had turned the plane around and was heading for Malaysia.

Once we arrived in the skies above Malaysia, the pilot informed us that he had decided to continue on to Singapore. He said, "They will be able to handle the situation better there." What did that mean? Were we going to crash upon landing? The two-hour journey following the fall seemed endless. During that time, we had no idea whether we were going to live or die. The pilot had said everything was going to be fine, but why should we believe him? What was he going to say? "We are going to crash shortly. Prepare to die." Even through all of this, I was, for the most part, free from fear. All that was important was my mantra.

At some point during the first hour, I became aware of a strange odor. I decided to take off my oxygen mask to try to identify the heavy, pungent smell. I concluded it was burning electrical wire. The implications of that did not hit me until much later when a newspaper reported that a fire had caused our plane's decompression problem. Other news reports said that it was a miracle that the plane had been able to land safely in Singapore.

There were some moments of levity during the incident. One man stood up with his video camera, happily recording passenger's reactions for posterity. Perhaps the funniest moment occurred when the pilot said something along the lines of, "Don't worry. Please stay onboard." I suppose we were experiencing the result of language differences. Chaitanya and I looked at each other and laughed. Chaitanya still laughs when she remembers that one of her first reactions to the plane falling was to look at me and say, "Has this ever happened to you before?"

When we arrived in Singapore, the airline provided us with meals and lodging. Finding a substitute flight to India was no easy matter this close to Christmas. We discovered there had been two devotees from Los Angeles on the plane, in addition to the five from Seattle. We met together in our hotel room, singing bhajans accompanied by a small keyboard and percussion instruments created from spoons, glasses and anything else that could make sound. We felt close to Mother and to our home satsang group who was meeting at the same time. On our third day in Singapore, my daughter and I discovered a Kali temple. That night all of us walked to the temple and participated in a puja. I imagined most of us were praying for swift and safe passage to India. The next day, we were once again on a plane headed for Mother!

One of the first things I noticed after arriving at the ashram was a sign on a bulletin board, which read, "Life is not a right, it is a gift from God." I had a stronger sense of that sentiment than ever before!

A devotee told me that earlier in the week, one of the brahmacharis had informed Mother that our plane had crashed. Mother had responded, "The plane did *not* crash, my children were on board." Later, another devotee told me Mother had been aware our plane was in trouble from the time the plane began shaking.

The next day, when I went for darshan, Mother described the entire plane incident to those seated near her. Later that same day, I silently wondered about how much danger we had actually been in. During my next darshan, she once again told the crowd what had happened to the plane and then whispered in my ear, "Karuna, BIG problem." That was all I needed to end any lingering doubt that she had actually been present.

I do not know, and will likely never know, whether or not Mother saved our lives that day, but I was clear that she had been with us through the ordeal. I had no doubt that her presence was the primary reason I had felt such a sense of peace.

In the weeks and months that followed, I became aware of how much this experience had affected me. My faith in Mother had significantly increased. She had known I was in trouble and had been there for me. I carried a stronger sense of confidence that she would be there for me when I needed her in the future. I also noted how events that would have been very upsetting in the past, now barely phased me. I was much more capable of "going with the flow" and letting life unfold, trusting that whatever happened would be in my best interest.

For about a year, I had played around with learning some Malayalam and some Sanskrit. I particularly enjoyed learning to write the Malayalam letters. I had no expectation that I would ever be able to speak these languages but wanted to be able to understand the bhajans when I sang them. I also fantasized that I would someday write Mother a note using Malayalam script. That fantasy entered my mind once again, so with my limited knowledge and some vocabulary help from my friend Bipin, I wrote Mother a poem, in Sanskrit.

The English translation of my poem:

I bow to Amriteshwari
Who lives in my heart
Who protects Her devotees in air, on sea and land
Whose mantras bring peace of mind
Who takes away the mood of fear
Please grant me selfless devotion.

Once translated, I transcribed the poem into Malayalam script. When I was ready, I entered the darshan line, keeping Chaitanya behind me so she could observe what happened. I had no idea if I had translated my poem correctly and my script was very much that of a beginner. Mother took the note and placed me on her lap. Chaitanya said she looked at the note very quizzically, then picked me up, gave me a big smile and said "Malayalam!" I felt like a first grader who had taken an assignment home for her mother to see. I was elated.

One day, out of curiosity, I decided to find out what my astrological chart had to say about the day our plane fell. I was shocked to discover that three malevolent factors were in effect at that time. The one predominant positive feature was blocked. I was impressed. I decided to ask what my chart had to say about spring of 1995, the time when I first learned of the relationship between my co-therapist and our past client. The astrologer said I was having problems with a business partner! My faith in the accuracy of Vedic astrology increased once again.

Every year when I arrive in India, I discover that much has changed, particularly in terms of the facilities. When I first visited in 1990, the ashram was on a small piece of land surrounded by water. In the years that followed, the water was filled in with sand. Buildings were constructed on the resulting landfill. In 1990, there were three toilets to service the entire ashram. Each morning found lines of restless people pounding on the doors demanding that those inside hurry up. By 1997, there were plenty of toilet and bath facilities. In the early years, we had to pump water for flushing toilets or taking showers. We ran out of water almost daily. There were hours and even days when no water was available for either toilet or shower. By 1997, there was almost always enough water to meet the needs of the ashram. In 1990, a group of thirty westerners was considered large. In 1997, there were times when 300 westerners

Living conditions of India's poor

New living accommodations built by Amma's charitable foundation

were present. Tailors, a fabric shop, a post office, a hospital and a cafe were now available on the property. More huts had been added, and two apartment complexes, seven and twelve stories high, were under construction. What would Mother dream up next?

Her service projects had grown at an even faster rate. Schools, colleges, vocational programs, orphanages, and clinics were among the programs she sponsored. She had recently pledged to build twenty-five thousand houses for the poor. A tertiary care hospital was under construction in Cochin.

The ashram schedule also changed from time to time. For many years, residents had complained that they did not have enough opportunity to meditate because Mother placed so much emphasis on seva. Mother had recently designated Tuesday as a meditation day. The meditation started at 6:00 a.m., after the morning archana. She would join the residents on the temple roof around 9:30 a.m. Occasionally, she would instruct everyone to stand up and meditate while slowly turning around. From time to time, she tossed small pebbles at devotees who were falling asleep, directing them to meditate standing up. Around 11:45 a.m., Mother would ask everyone to lie down for a few minutes. This was a particularly funny experience, as the rooftop was so crowded, lying down was next to impossible. Afterwards, Mother led the entire group in walking three times around the temple. Then we all climbed back up to the temple roof where she served us lunch. After lunch, devotees spent time studying scriptures while Mother greeted newly arrived visitors. Meditation began again mid-afternoon, lasting until 6:00 p.m.

As I still had neither the ability nor the inclination to meditate in a quiet, sitting position, I found this type of day mentally and physically grueling. I was generally able to force myself to participate at least until after lunch. I loved the opportunity to be with Mother.

When I come to India, I frequently have a queasy stomach and a little diarrhea for a day or two. The previous year, I discovered I could prevent those symptoms by eating only food that had been prepared at the ashram. While I had had some bouts with illness over the years, the only time I had ever been significantly sick during a trip to India was in 1993.

This year, however, illness became a major theme. I experienced six separate episodes of flu during the seven weeks I was in the country. I had no doubt that I was undergoing a purification process. I would be very sick for a day or two. Afterwards, I would feel fine and have a tremendous amount of energy. Days later, I would once again be bedridden.

There seemed to be a purpose for the sickness beyond its purification value. Some months before, I had begun to create a workbook for westerners who wanted to learn to read and write Malayalam script. I planned to type the book while I was in India since I did not have Malayalam fonts on my home computer.

I was sick the day that everyone left for the annual trip to Calicut. I felt much better the following day, but knew it would be wise to take a day or two of recovery time before taking the train to Calicut. I decided to use the extra time to begin typing the workbook. Over the next week, every time I tried to leave for Calicut, I relapsed. Actually, I do not know if "relapse" is the appropriate word, since my symptoms were always different.

Finally, I gave up the idea of going to Calicut and focused on the workbook. I finished the first draft only hours before Mother and the devotees returned. It appeared that Mother wanted me to complete the workbook more than she wanted me in Calicut. Perhaps, I was being tested to see how I would respond to missing the trip. You might remember that it was in Calicut, the previous year, that I had been frantic and grief-stricken because I was housed so far away from the music. Strangely enough, this year I never experienced any grief at missing the trip. My attitude throughout had simply been, "Whatever!"

When Mother returns from a trip, particularly a long one, she often wanders through the ashram. She may give darshan to the residents who were left behind. Someone once asked why she does not rest and take care of herself when she returns home. She responded that not only do the devotees miss her when she travels, but so do the plants, insects and even the inanimate objects. They need to feel her presence and celebrate her return as much as we do. When I heard this story I realized, once again, that there is so much I do not know about Mother and this world in which we live.

I mentioned earlier that one of the changes I noticed throughout the trip was that my mood remained steady and peaceful in situations that would have evoked tumultuous feelings in the past. There was one notable exception.

Midway through my visit, one of our roommates returned to the United States, leaving an empty bed. Our new roommate presented us with quite a challenge. This woman showed complete disregard for any ashram rule. In addition, she did not seem to have any concern about how her behavior affected others. When she came into our room, she turned on the light and loudly rustled around regardless of whether it was midnight or 3:00 a.m. I became so enraged by her behavior, I found it next to impossible to have any compassion for her. After futile attempts to resolve the problem, I realized I was going to have to simply let go. That of course was easier to say than to do.

My general evenness in mood extended also to bhajans. As I have related throughout this book, Mother's music had consistently evoked strong feelings of grief or bliss within me. That trip was different. While I still loved the music, I was much more likely to feel peaceful and content. At times, I missed the intensity of my earlier reactions.

Were my tears a thing of the past? Was the grief over? Swamiji once mentioned that he had cried daily during his first seven years with Mother. Afterwards, he experienced a profound shift in his process. While he still cried from time to time, it was not an everyday occurrence. Was my pattern going to be similar?

I was quite surprised to discover that I did not feel sad even when it was time for me to leave India. Prior to that year, I had always experienced at least a day or two of grief as my departure drew near. This time, I had a strong sense of, "I'm here, I'm there. What's the difference?"

I had quite an amusing experience my last night at the ashram. Mother started to sing one of my favorite songs, *Venkataramana*. Normally, hearing that song on my last night would have been enough to start my tears pouring. This time, however, as I was enjoying the song, a vision of my bathtub at home came into my mind. The words, "Bliss comes in many forms," accompanied the picture. I started laughing inside. I have no attachment to my bathtub and putting the music in India and the bathtub at home into the same realm of importance was absurd. Throughout the rest of the song my awareness was pulled between the music and the bathtub. I still laugh when I recall that experience.

Back in the World
Winter/Spring 1997

A number of times after I returned to the United States, I found myself telling friends and clients what an easy trip it had been for me. As I heard myself, I had to laugh. Let's see, I almost died in the plane on the way over, I missed my favorite program in Calicut, and I had six cases of flu in seven weeks. This had been an *easy* trip? I saw once again how my moods had evened out and my ability to take life events in stride had increased.

I had written Pastor Jenkins about our plane experience. When I returned home, he asked me to give my testimony before the entire congregation. As I prepared my testimony, I decided to focus not only on the grace that spared my life but also on the grace that prepared me for the experience. I believed it was grace that directed me to focus on my mantra for eight weeks preceding my trip. Reading the poem in church had reminded me that God works in unexpected and sometimes undesired ways. That reminder was grace. Grace had made my mantra the primary focus of my internal experience during the plane's fall. Through God's grace I had been able to feel peaceful through what could have been a terrifying event.

Although I did not mention it in my testimony, I knew it was grace that provided me with an experience that increased my faith in my teacher and in Spirit. Grace also allowed me, a devotee of an Indian guru, to give this testimony in a fundamentalist Christian church. I was impressed that my relationship with these people was solid enough that I could give a testimony using words like "ashram" and "mantra" without anyone blinking an eye. Once again, sounds of *"Amen," "Praise the Lord" and "Thank you Jesus"* filled the church.

For several years, I had participated in a monthly class led by Diana Bigelow. Although I call it a voice class, it was certainly not so in the traditional sense. During the class, each member of the group allowed whatever sound was inside of them in the moment to be vocalized. The aim was to be completely in the moment by giving up control of the process. The songs that emerged came from deep inside of us. It was as if we were learning to sing our soul's song.

My "song" was often accompanied by body postures and mudras. Tremendous amounts of energy frequently moved through me during the process. I knew the class played an important part in my spiritual journey.

When I returned from India in February, it occurred to me that I might be able to compose a song by combining some of the altered state processes. Perhaps if I held my hands above the harmonium, as I did with the drums, they would start playing on their own. As I sat in front of my harmonium, I thought about what words I would want to put to music. I decided to use some of the Sanskrit words from the poem I had written to Mother after the plane fell. I chose, *Om Amriteshwariyai Namah* and *Nikama Bhakti Dehime.* As I focused on the words, I allowed myself to enter the space where my hands and my voice operate on their own. In a very short period of time, a song using my chosen words emerged. Not long thereafter, after having visited a Krishna temple, a tune to the words *Om Hare Krishna* popped into my head. I realized that a new era in my process had begun.

Over the previous four or five years, I had attended the graduation ceremonies of many friends and clients who had attended *Leap of Faith*, a training offered by a group known as Warrior Spirit. Jeff Alexander, founder of Warrior Spirit, uses instruction in self-defense as a method of encouraging participants to open up to the tremendous spiritual and physical power contained within them. From the time I attended my first graduation ceremony, I knew that it was important for me to take the training. Even the thought of defending myself during the simulated attacks, however, filled me with terror. I knew I would attend some day, but I put it off year after year.

Now, I noticed a sense of readiness to participate in the training. I registered soon after returning from India. By May, I was eager and ready to begin.

Leap of Faith was a major life experience for me. At the self-defense level, I discovered I had the ability to act in the moment with power and assurance. I discovered that my body, which I had judged to be weak and ineffective, was able to perform with amazing strength and endurance when necessary.

I was struck by how little fear I felt during the weekend. I saw each confrontation as a challenge and an opportunity. Over and over again, I experienced old traumas coming to the surface of my mind. During one of the fights, a teenage memory of being pinned to the wall by a garage mechanic surfaced. My inner voice said, "Oh, I've been here before, and guess what guy, there is going to be a different ending!" Immediately my body exploded into action and I freed myself from the restraint of the here and now attacker.

Leap of Faith gave me much more than self-defense skills. I experienced the vitality and joy that comes with being totally in the moment. I experienced power and peace bubbling up from a place of silence within me. I experienced the love that occurs whenever humans share profoundly moving moments together. In many ways, I felt as if I had spent a weekend with Mother.

I noticed changes within myself for months afterwards. I was aware of a more solid sense of personal power. I saw myself quickly move into action in situations which in the past would have evoked hesitation, avoidance and fear. I gave self-critical thoughts less weight. I felt the surge of creative energy that generally occurs only after I spend time with Mother. I still feel immense gratitude for all that I received from that training.

Practice in Flexibility and Letting Go
Summer tour 1997

For years, the program hall at the Seattle retreat had been crowded. Even though there was always "enough" room, we decided to explore the possibility of providing more comfort by renting a large tent. We wondered if using a tent in the rainy Northwest was a viable option, particularly since we sit on the ground and programs go late into the night. The rental company assured us this would not be a problem. They would put the tent up three days ahead of time to ensure that the ground was dry. They inspected the property and said it was an excellent site for erecting a tent.

We arranged for Steve, a Seattle devotee, to be present when the tent was set up. The company canceled the original set-up date, saying that the previous users had not returned some of the needed tent parts. In hindsight, that was a strange statement, since the company employees themselves were the ones who had taken down the tent. At the time, however, it did not alert us to the problems ahead. Steve drove to the site the next morning. The workers did not arrive until late in the afternoon. They had mistakenly gone to a site on Whidbey Island instead of to our park, which was located on the Olympic Peninsula. These sites were in completely different parts of the state, hours away from one another! Steve had given the company detailed driving instructions. What was going on?

The leelas did not stop there. When the workers finally arrived, they discovered that they still did not have all of the necessary equipment. As a result, they returned to Seattle three different times, each at best a three-hour journey. Was this ineptitude at work, or Mother?

When we arrived at the retreat center at noon the day of the retreat, the tent was still not up. Many devotees helped with the work. The tent was not ready for us to decorate until two hours before the program began. We scrambled to complete necessary preparations before

Mother arrived. Even though the setup was chaotic, when the program started that night, we all thoroughly enjoyed the extra space.

That night, the worst rainstorm in thirty years descended upon us. When we arrived at the tent the next morning, we discovered the floor of the tent was sopping wet, almost to the middle. It was completely unusable. As we moved everything back to the original hall, a devotee commented, "This is just how Mother likes things. We are working together, being flexible, saving money and crowded!" Since the company had broken so many agreements, we would challenge the bill. They had not erected the tent on time, failed to provide a tarp under the tent, and given us equipment that was badly damaged. We had to fix a number of tables in order to use them and the tent provided for shoes had fifty holes in the roof! We spent the rest of the retreat in the old program hall where, once again, we experienced an intimate, abundant time with Mother.

Prior to that retreat, I had considered whether I should consult my astrological chart before picking the date for my next trip to India. I was aware that I had no desire to do so. If anything, I felt a strong aversion to the action. Once again, I examined my avoidance of astrology. I remembered that, for me, a great deal of enjoyment comes from watching life unfold, not knowing what is going to happen next. Astrological predictions would interfere with this. I also believed that if my chart predicted times to be hard, then I would be much more likely to focus on the negative. This would increase the likelihood of my creating a self-fulfilling prophecy.

I told Mother of my aversion and asked if my attitude was foolish. She kept me waiting beside her for a long time. During that time, an Indian family came for darshan. Apparently on the previous day, Mother had asked to see the astrological chart of one of the daughters. In my presence, Mother reviewed the chart and gave the family direction. I had never seen her do anything like this before. I was awed by the synchronicity of what was happening. As soon as the family left, Mother answered me. "Just come," she said. "Mother is with you." I found this to be a powerful reminder that we all have individual paths. What is right for one is not right for all.

During a class at one of the retreats, Swamiji commented that the guru will wear many faces. She might appear happy, angry, sad, concerned or confused, depending on what the devotee needed to see. He said our goal should not be to see the guru's outward smile, but rather to desire that the guru will smile inwardly when thinking of us. That seemed an important lesson to remember.

Another comment by Swamiji embedded itself into my memory bank. He said that it is Mother's job to make us disciples, not ours. That is not to say we are puppets or helpless victims and that she does everything. It does mean, however, that she will guide us to the lessons we need to learn. We can learn them now or later, with resistance or with surrender. The choice is up to us.

The first volume of *Getting to Joy* was published shortly before the 1997 summer tour. Throughout the entire tour, people came up to me expressing thanks for having written the book. Many said it helped them make sense of their experiences. I was pleased to hear that devotees were finding the book helpful as they walked their own paths towards joy.

There was a point in Santa Fe, when a devotee asked me what it was like to be beyond anger. I was shocked. I could not imagine what I had said in the book that would make her think I was beyond anger. The timing of the comment was quite noteworthy because I had been almost continually angry for the last several days. I would stay in that state of mind for the next few weeks. I reacted to almost anything my children said to me with anger or grief. I felt as if I were going crazy. Towards the end, I realized most of my reaction was misplaced anger and grief stemming from ways my mother treated me as a child. At the time, my feelings were so intense that I had a strong desire to run away. I would have booked an airline ticket home, if I did not know that I would have regretted it forever.

I cannot say that Mother was at all helpful in getting me out of this negative place. When I went for darshan, she would tweak my cheeks and laugh at me. Needless to say, I was quite irritated with her as well. My mind and my emotions overwhelmed me. I could relate to the line in the song *Manasa Vacha* that says:

> O Mother, give me a little peace of mind lest I become a lunatic. I am tired Mother, it is unbearable. I do not want such a life. I can not stand your tests O Mother, I can not endure it.[2]

---

[2] "Manasa Vacha," *Bhajanamritam, Volume 1*, San Ramon: Mata Amritanandamayi Center, 1992, pg 21.

My mood began to lift in Boston when I was asked to coach a new line monitor. That action jolted me back into the present moment and gave my mind something to focus on other than my suffering.

I have since discovered a bhajan that I find helpful in breaking depression if it has not become too debilitating. One of the ways to move out of suffering is to exaggerate it. The song, *Ambike Jagadishvari*, when sung in Malayalam sounds like a lullaby. When I hear it, I can imagine Mother holding me as a small infant. The translation, however, read with a bit of indignation and humor, can be very helpful when working to shift my energy.

> *O Ambika! Sustainer of the Universe! the Supreme Ruler! Compassionate One! Won't you kindly deign to hear this desperate cry?*
>
> *Why Mother, why, why do You mercilessly drag this child of yours through endless sorrows? How unfair of You, Mother, that having thrown this blind babe into this dark world, You stand apart and enjoy the game! Why did You push this innocent, artless, helpless child into this jungle, full of cruel beasts?*
>
> *That You made me the scapegoat for fulfilling your mysterious magical play, may be my callous fate. Are You not renowned as "love personified" and "supremely compassionate"? Then, why do You persecute me like this?*
>
> *Now I can only cry, "Ambike, Jagadishwari, Parameshwari, Karunamayi." Destitute that I am, I had to be born as Thy child. O Mother of the Universe, to come to the rescue or to commit infanticide, is entirely up to Thy whim.*[3]

I coached new line monitors during the remainder of the summer tour. I loved that seva. I was more assured than ever that part of my purpose in being in the world was to teach what I learn, whether it be

---

[3] "Ambike Jagadishwari," *Bhajanamritam, Volume 3*, San Ramon: Mata Amritanandamayi Center, 1997, pg 14–15.

through line monitoring, writing books, conducting workshops or guiding my psychotherapy clients.

That summer, I became aware of how much I have changed in the way I spend time with Mother. In the early years I watched her for hours, days and weeks. I could not bear to take my eyes off of her face. Now, I can hardly force myself to sit with her, unless someone is singing bhajans. I am much more interested in working on craft projects for the bookstore. I need to remind myself to sit with her when I am in pain. I am thankful that from time to time, she directs me to sit close-by.

During the last retreat of the summer tour, I strongly felt the urge to dance. Occasionally at programs in the United States, a few devotees dance in the back of the room during bhajans. I had not danced as yet because I did not want to embarrass Sreejit or Chaitanya. At that point, I decided I did not care. Perhaps, they would not even see me! I went to the back of the room and danced to my heart's content. I found out later that someone had actually gone to Sreejit and informed him I was dancing! He did not seem to care. I also learned that Chaitanya had turned around from her seat in the front of the room and seen me. When I told her that I had been saving her from embarrassment, she responded "Mom, you have embarrassed me so many times, go ahead and let it all hang out!" I laughed then and laugh now as I recall the incident.

Always when near Mother, I am filled with respect and awe for her endless patience and compassion. My heart fills with love. My prayer is that contained in the bhajan, *Oru Tulli Sneham*, "O (Mother) I want neither heaven nor liberation, only pure devotion to Thee."[4] As I reflect on this statement, I remember that Mother says it is easy for us to love her. What she wants is for us to love each other. To learn how to do that is our work.

Towards the end of the tour, I once again felt directed to write my story. This time, I was to focus on the 1993-1997 period. As I constructed a time line of the important experiences during those years, I noted how the professional and legal problems that occurred in 1995 had essentially slammed me back into this worldly realm. Gone were the unpredictable altered states I experienced prior to that event. I essentially never drummed any more. While I could still access the spontaneous yoga and exercises, I almost never made the effort. Now, the only altered states I experienced

---

4 "Oru Tulli Sneham," *Bhajanamritam*, *Volume 1*, San Ramon: Mata Amritanandamayi Center, 1992, pg 72–73.

were those that occurred when I danced in church, the occasional mudras that formed during bhajans and the experiences I had during Diana's voice class.

Choosing a form of ongoing sadhana had long been a dilemma. At times, I was overwhelmed by how many forms of devotional practice had emerged in my process, for example tongues, mudras, exercise, yoga, dance, and drumming. And of course there were the practices that are a regular part of a spiritual path with Mother, such as silent meditation, bhajans, chanting of 108 names of Mother, and chanting of 1000 names of the Divine Mother. I knew also that chanting the *Guru Gita* and the *Hanuman Chalisa* were powerful practices. Frequently, I was so overwhelmed by the number of choices, that I ended up doing nothing. Most often, all I wanted to do was to work on craft projects for the bookstore. While I knew that the handiwork was seva, and that seva was a form of sadhana, I wondered if it was enough.

When I stood back and looked at my years with Mother, I could see that one form of sadhana had flowed into another. Did that mean now was the time for my sadhana to be seva, or was I being undisciplined and lazy?

During and prior to that tour, I had recurrent dreams of missing darshan with Mother because I was doing too much seva. While I had never missed a physical darshan with Mother because of seva, the dream seemed to be telling me that my life was out of balance, that seva was an important component of my sadhana, but so were the altered state experiences. It was during the altered states that I felt Spirit's presence most strongly. I noticed I felt a pull to begin to dance and drum again. I resolved to provide myself with opportunities for those forms of sadhana when I returned to Seattle.

Mother Provides What is Needed
Spring/Fall 1997

When I thought about all of the events that were to occur between the end of the summer tour and the time I would leave for India, I became concerned. There were fewer clients in my groups than ever before. I knew I would go to India, but how in the world was I going to fund trips to San Ramon for Chaitanya and myself to attend Mother's birthday celebration in October and the retreat in November?

One day, my roommate commented that the windows were really dirty and needed to be washed. Since my house is three stories high and on uneven ground, I always hire someone to wash the windows. At that point, neither one of us could afford to hire anyone. That awareness compounded my financial fear. I internally said, "Mother, if you want Chaitanya and me to go to your birthday celebrations and to the retreat, you will have to help. I don't see how I can do it and still go to India." Almost immediately, I received a phone call informing me that Vasishtha, a devotee who had been living in Santa Fe, was returning to Seattle. He needed a place to stay for a few months, while he earned enough money to move to India. I saw this as the answer to my prayer. When he came to town, I offered him a place to stay. Not only did his rent produce exactly the amount of money needed to take Chaitanya and me to the San Ramon ashram twice, but since he was a window washer, I was also able to negotiate window cleaning as part of the rental agreement! I loved the vivid reminder that Mother will provide us with what we need!

I pondered how to honor my commitment to spend more time drumming and dancing. For several years, I had noticed an ad in a local newspaper, *The New Times*, for a group called Dances of Universal Peace. For one reason or another, I had never attended their programs. Once again, the ad caught my eye. This time, I participated! Everyone who attended had the opportunity to learn to sing and dance to the music of many different spiritual traditions. The evening was a delight. It was definitely the altered state experience I craved. I resolved to attend as often as possible.

In November, Mother conducted another mini-world tour. That year, I attended all of the San Ramon programs. Perhaps the most significant part of my experience was that I realized another long-term goal. For some time, I had desired to write a song in Malayalam, Mother's native tongue. By then, I had written several Sanskrit songs but Malayalam is a much more difficult language. The task seemed daunting. Could I do it?

As I sat in Mother's presence in San Ramon, the desire re-entered my mind. I pondered it awhile and then thought, "Well, if I were going to write a song, what would I want it to say?" I thought it would be wonderful to write Mother a song that was a prayer. The words *Mother, may my hands always be in service* came to mind. I took the line to Meera, a Seattle Indian devotee and asked if she would translate it into Malayalam. She handed me the translation soon thereafter. It read, *Amma ende karangal ennum ninne sevikate.* I looked at it incredulously and thought, "I can't do it, it is impossible!" Mother was beginning to lead a meditation. I decided to say the line over and over to myself to see if a tune emerged as I allowed an altered state to come. I was quite shocked to discover that it did. I sang the line to myself repeatedly during the rest of the meditation, hoping I would not lose it. As soon as the meditation was over, I ran to a harmonium and picked out the notes of the melody. After I wrote it down, I went back to my seat and pondered what else I would want to say to Mother in my song. All of a sudden, it seemed like the venture might be possible. I was excited by the idea of being able to directly share with Mother the devotional feelings that were growing inside of me.

I quickly finished the text of the song.[5] After Meera translated it, I was able to complete the tune using the same process of disengaging my mind from my hands and allowing the freed hands to do the work. I looked forward to singing the song to Mother when I arrived in India. Little did I know what was in store for me before I would have that opportunity!

My next trip to India was rapidly approaching. Shortly before I was to leave, I received notice that it was time for my annual physical exam. As I was feeling perfectly fit, I decided I would wait until I returned from India. Uncharacteristically, the clinic sent me a number of reminder notices. When I received the third or fourth one, I thought, "Okay, okay, I will go, if I can get an appointment with this short notice." I believed a minor miracle occurred when I called the clinic and was able to immediately schedule the appointment.

Much to my surprise, during the pelvic exam, the doctor discovered a mass in my uterus. An ultrasound revealed that the mass was a fibroid, which was of no concern. In the course of doing that exam, however, a tumor on my ovary was discovered. The tumor was of much greater concern. I was sent to a specialist, who concluded that surgery was called for. It was unlikely that the surgery would be scheduled until the beginning of the year, as it was so close to Christmas.

If I had to wait until January for the surgery, I did not see any reason why I could not go to India for a short visit. The specialist strongly opposed that plan, so I decided to try to ask Mother. This was no easy matter, as she was conducting programs in Madras at the time. Bipin, one of the Seattle devotees, reminded me that his wife, Geetha, was in Madras with Mother. If Bipin could reach Geetha's uncle who lived in Ma-

---

[5] I have used the English translation as the closing for this book.

dras, perhaps the uncle could get a message to Geetha and Geetha could talk to Mother!

The plan had an endless number of possible complications. Bipin would have to find the uncle at home, the uncle would have to find Geetha, Geetha would have to see if she could find a way to talk to Mother. Since Mother is so busy during the rededication programs, making contact was in no way assured.

When Bipin and I finished talking, he called Madras. He expected the uncle would be at work, so was pleasantly surprised when the uncle picked up the phone. Bipin said he needed to get a message to Geetha. The uncle immediately responded, "Just a minute, I will give her the phone. She is standing right here!" Events can seem so synchronistic when our actions are in harmony with God's will.

Geetha was able to get direction from Mother. Mother's advice was to stay in Seattle and have the surgery! I was comforted to know that Mother knew of my physical condition and was thankful to have her direct guidance.

I could not understand why it was acceptable to wait until the New Year if the surgery was so important. I called the doctor to ask that question. Before I could get the words out of my mouth, she informed me she had been able to schedule the surgery for the week before Christmas!

While I felt sad to miss my trip, mostly I grieved not being able to sing my song for Mother. One day, it occurred to me that I could tape the song and send it to Mother with one of the other Seattle devotees who would soon be making the trip. Members of our satsang spent hours learning, rehearsing and taping the song. Soon the tape was on its way to India. I felt so happy to have found a different way to meet my goal.

As time for the surgery drew near, I felt a desire to ask for the prayers of members at Power House church. The thought frightened me, however, because I was concerned if I did so, some members might show up at my house. While many knew I was involved with Ammachi, I did not think they really understood I was a devotee of a guru. I thought they would be shocked and upset at seeing pictures of Mother on almost every wall of my house. I did not want to deal with the negative energy that might result.

The desire grew. One day, I realized I could present my dilemma to Pastor Jenkins, who knew a whole lot more about my path with Ammachi than did the church members. When I presented the situation, he responded that I should, of course, inform the members of my health problems. I was surprised. I said, "Do you understand that I am a devotee of an Indian guru and my house is like a temple?" He responded, "I don't have any problem with that and I don't think they will either. What they will see is a sick sister. If there is a problem, we will deal with it." I was shocked. Once again, my stereotypical beliefs about this fundamentalist church were being torn down.

The day of surgery arrived. I was admitted, given the standard pre-op procedures and then held in a waiting room. A surgery staff member was supposed to pick me up at 2:00 p.m. but by 3:00 p.m. no one had arrived. I sent my daughter to find out what was happening. She was told that I would not be picked up for at least another forty-five minutes.

I then asked Chaitanya to update the satsang friends who were waiting in the lobby. One of them sneaked into the holding area where they were keeping me and put a copy of the new *Amritanandam*, a magazine published by Mother's San Ramon ashram. It was opened to an article I had submitted earlier in the year. I did not know the article had even been accepted for publication. My eyes were immediately drawn to the illustration Swami Paramatmananda had created, a picture of Mother's hand holding up our plane. He also had developed a subtitle, "Amma solves a BIG problem." Almost immediately the surgical attendant came for me, long before the forty-five minutes were up. I went into the surgery with the picture and the subtitle in my mind. I felt that Mother had once again intervened, sending me a reminder of her presence. I felt very seen, known and taken care of.

When I woke up after the surgery, I was told that the tumor was benign. The surgery had been more extensive than originally planned, because the tumor had burst between the time it was discovered and the time of the surgery. The contents had formed adhesions on the uterine wall. I was extremely grateful that I had been pestered into making the original doctor's appointment. I was also thankful that Mother had directed me to stay in Seattle. Having surgery or a bursting tumor in India would have been terrifying.

With the help of Chaitanya, Sreejit and my friends, my recovery was rapid. After a week or two I was back to my normal schedule, although my energy level was significantly reduced.

The day after Christmas, while eating brunch with friends, I half-jokingly said that next year I thought I would *ask* Mother if I should

Mother holding my plane!

come to India. Normally I just go, I don't ask. However, since my plane had fallen during the previous trip and this year's trip had been canceled due to the tumor, I wondered if it would be in my best interest to start asking. After I made that statement, one of my non-devotee friends snapped, "Why don't you just check in with YOURSELF." Greatly taken aback, I responded with some ineffective statement and then kept my mouth shut.

A few days later, I read an article in *The New Times*, in which Sobonfu Somé stated:

> *People in the West tend to live unbalanced lives….so they search for a guru of some form to take care of their spiritual needs.*

> *The idea of a guru doing everything and all we have to do is show up and tell the guru, "this is what I need, fix everything and I can get out of here," does not work. The guru takes the individual's involvement away and once the individual's involvement is not there, nothing can really happen.*[6]

After dealing with my initial desire to defend, justify, rationalize, explain and judge, I began to examine Somé's attitude more carefully.

In my nine years of being a devotee of a guru, I have discovered that discipleship is anything other than mindless pursuit. I have learned that I need to become and stay exceedingly conscious and attuned to what is happening both within and around me, to strive to be impeccable in my actions, and to stay in integrity. I have to discriminate between when to ask my teacher for help and when to find the answer within. I certainly have not "given away my power" but rather have been learning about surrender.

I know some people do use gurus in the way that Somé described. I once talked with Swami Ramakrishnanada about my concern that some devotees follow Mother's instructions in ways I consider to be mindless. He said that immature devotees often act out of blind, mindless faith. The faith and surrender displayed by mature devotees, however, comes from having watched, tested and experienced the guru for years. It is in no way mindless.

I can see that other tools, such as astrology, may be used either in an immature or mature fashion. It seemed to me that when individuals make most or all of their decisions based solely on astrological readings, they create self-fulfilling prophesies, give away their personal power, and stay stuck in self defeating behaviors. As a result, they limit their personal

---

[6]"Two Wise Women on Rituals and Relationships," This article originally appeared in the January 1998 issue of *The New Times* published in Seattle, Washington, Reprinted with permission.

growth. Other people, however, use astrology as a guide to life, rather than a tool that has every answer. Any tool used in an obsessive and mindless manner is likely to undermine the purposes for which it was created. That is not the fault of the tool or of the system, but rather problems created by misuse of the tool.

My years with Mother have been filled with an almost unbelievable level of challenge and growth. My personal spiritual journey has amazed me. I believe that asking Mother to be my guide and teacher resulted in speeding up the rate in which the universal "lessons" come. She has provided me with the support I need as I move through each challenge. I am thankful that I have her to guide me as I make my way through unknown territory. I am also thankful, and quite certain, that she does not "do it for me." As far as I am concerned, meeting and going through each challenge is what creates the joy of living. I would not want anyone to do it for me. That does not mean, however, that I have to learn all I needed to learn without help.

There are so many ways to connect with Spirit. I wish we could honor, rather than criticize, each other's chosen spiritual paths. With that attitude, we would be better able to support one another as we learn the lessons we are here to learn. I resolved to work on my own attitude towards other's chosen paths.

As the year came to a close, I was struck by how well I had handled losing my opportunity to go to India. I experienced virtually no sadness, once I found a way to share my song with Mother. This was such an amazing change from my first trip to India. At that time, I cried from the time I entered the country until six months after my return to the United States. I so wanted to live in India, yet I knew the timing was not right. Now, I had missed my trip altogether and was content. My growth was obvious. I marveled at the methods Mother uses to show us the work we have accomplished.

AFTERWARD

M y recovery from the surgery proceeded so rapidly that I began to wonder if it would be possible for me to go to India after all. Since I did not know why my trip had been blocked in the first place, I decided I would not go unless I could get Mother's support.

Chaitanya had postponed her trip to India so that she could help me during the postoperative time. Once I had sufficiently recovered, she made the journey. I thought it would be fun to surprise her by arriving unannounced at the ashram.

I wrote a devotee at the ashram requesting that she ask Mother if I could come to India. When I received no response by the time Mother left for Calicut, I decided the devotee had not received my letter or the answer had been an indirect "No."

A few days later, I received a phone call from Chaitanya saying that Mother had approached her on the way to Calicut, asking how I was doing and if I was coming to India. Chaitanya responded, "If Mother says it is okay." (Interesting that would be her response when she did not know that I was even considering the trip.) Mother told Chaitanya it was fine for me to come.

Soon, I was on my way to India. I could not have tolerated walking the distance from one part of the ashram to another, climbing the many flights of stairs, or sitting on the concrete floors, during the first weeks of my recovery. At that point, however, I was able to handle the challenges of ashram living as long as I used discretion and took it easy. I normally dislike the heat, but that year my body craved it, the hotter the better. It was as if I was in a sauna, expelling all of the toxins from the anesthesia.

Most noteworthy was the difference I noticed in my attitude. The first few years I grieved because I could only stay for three weeks. This time I was elated, "*I get to go to India for three whole weeks!*"

One of the most significant things that happened during my visit was that Chaitanya asked Mother if she could move to the India ashram on a permanent basis. Mother said, "Yes." I remembered back to 1993, when Mother laughed as Chaitanya told her she did not feel drawn to her spiritually.

As I write this, Chaitanya is days away from moving to India. Sreejit is still a resident of the San Ramon ashram. I am preparing for my tenth trip to India. I am so grateful for the ways Mother has loved, guided and taken care of my family. I love my journey and eagerly await discovering what is around the next turn.

It is my wish that I spend the rest of my life learning, growing, serving and following where Mother leads. My heart's desire is that when I die, Mother will meet me on the other side, look me in the eye with the look only she can give, and utter the words Jesus spoke in Matthew 25:21, "Well done, good and faithful servant."

September 1998

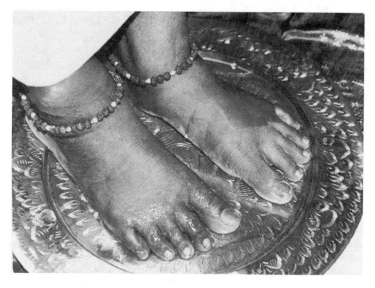

Mother, may my hands always be in service,
May my mind be filled with mantra.
May my voice forever sing your praise,
May my feet dance in joy.

May my love shine ever brighter,
May my faith continue to grow.
May I become each day more like you,
It is only for this that I pray.

GLOSSARY

Amma: Mother.

Ammachi: Respected Mother.

Amritapuri: Location of Mother's main ashram in India.

Arati: Waving burning camphor in front of a holy person as a way of giving them salutations and honor. The camphor, which leaves no residue, indicates the total annihilation of ego.

Archana: Repetition of the names of a deity; in this case the 1000 Names of the Divine Mother.

Ashram: Residence and teaching center of a saint .

Bhagavatam: The book about the incarnations of Lord Vishnu, especially Krishna.

Bhakti: Devotion.

Bhakti Yoga: Path of devotion.

Bhajan: Devotional song.

Brahmachari: Male celibate student under the training of a Guru.

Brahmacharini: Female celibate student under the training of a Guru.

Brahman: The Absolute, The Whole.

Chai: Tea.

COGIC: Church of God in Christ.

Darshan: Audience of a holy person or deity.

Devi: Divine Mother.

Devotee: One who is strongly dedicated to someone or something.

Divine Incarnation: God taking a human birth to re-establish the ways of righteousness, religion, duty, responsibility, virtue, justice, goodness and truth.

Gopis: Cowherd girls known for their devotion to Lord Krishna

Guru: Dispeller of darkness; spiritual master or guide.

Hatha Yoga: Path of physical and mental exercise.

Householder: One who seeks God while fulfilling the responsibilities of the world.

Japa: Repetition of a mantra.

Jnana Yoga: Path of knowledge and wisdom.

Karma Yoga: Path of selfless service.

Krishna: Divine incarnation; principal incarnation of Lord Vishnu.

Kundalini: Spiritual energy depicted as the serpent power coiled at the root of the spine. This energy rises to the head by spiritual practices, leading one to Liberation.

Kundalini Yoga: Path of meditation, breathing and purification.

Leela: God's play.

Mantra: Sacred formula, the repetition of which can awaken spiritual energies and bring the desired results.

Mata Amritanandamayi: Mother of Immortal Bliss.

Mudras: Hand signs indicating spiritual truths.

Mukti: Liberation.

Murari: Another name of Krishna.

Murti: An image or icon of God used during workshop.

Puja: Worship rite.

Radha: Consort of Krishna.

Raja Yoga: Path of restraint, observance, exercise, breath control, withdrawal, concentration, meditation and samahdi.

Sadhana: Spiritual practice

Sadhu: Renunciate.

Samadhi: State of absorption in the Self.

Satsang: A spiritual discourse by a sage or scholar; a spiritual gathering.

Seva: Service given without thought of reward or personal gain.

Shakti: Spiritual energy.

Shanti: Peace

Tabla: Indian drum set

Vasana: Latent tendencies, both positive and negative.

BIBLIOGRAPHY

Abelar, Taisha. *Sorcerer's Crossing*, Middlesex: Penguin Books, 1992.

Amritasvarupananda, Swami. *Awaken Children V*, San Ramon, Ca: Mata Amritanandamayi Center, 1993.

Bhajanamritam: Devotional Songs, San Ramon, Ca. Mata Amritanandamayi Center:
> Volume 1
> 1994 Supplement
> 1996 Supplement
> Volume 3

Campbell, Joseph. *Oriental Mythology: The Masks of God*, New York, New York: Penguin Books, 1962.

Castaneda, Carlos. *Power of Silence*, New York: Washington Square Press, 1987.

Chaitanya, Br. Amritatma, *Mata Amritanandamayi: Life and Experience of Devotees*, Vallickavu: Mata Amritanandamayi Mission Trust, 1988.

Frager, Robert and Fadiman, James. *Personality and Personal Growth*. New York: Harper and Row, 1984.

The Holy Bible. King James Version, 1611.

Kornfield, Jack. *A Path with Heart*. New York: Bantam Books, 1993.

Mata Amritanandamayi, *Amritanandam*, Volume 36/37, November/December 1989 and Second Quarter 1994, San Ramon, Ca. Mata Amritanandamayi Center.

Morgan, Margo. *Mutant Message Downunder*, Lees Summit: MM Co., 1991.

Muller, Wayne. *Legacy of the Heart: the Spiritual Advantages of a Painful Childhood*, New York: Simon and Schuster, 1992.

Palkhivala, Aadil. *Yoga Centers Newsletter*. Bellevue: Yoga Centers, Volume 3 (1), January-August, 1992.

Paramatmananda, Swami, "For My Children: talks by Br. Nealu based on Mother's *FOR MY CHILDREN*," *Amritanandam*, First Quarter, 1994.

Redfield, James. *Celestine Prophecy*, Hoover: Satori Publishing, 1993.

Roth, Gabrielle. *Maps to Ecstasy: teachings of an urban shaman*, Mill Valley: Nataraj Publishing, 1989.

Roth, Gabrielle and the Mirrors, *Initiation*, Red Bank, The Moving Center, 1988.

Sams, Jamie and Carson, David. *Medicine Cards*. Santa Fe: Bear Co. 1988.

Songs to Ammachi. Madison: Blackburnian Records, 1989.

Subramuniyaswami, Satguru Sivaya. *Dancing with Shiva*, India, USA: Himalayan Academy, 1993.

Teach Me the Language. *Santa Fe Bhajan Tape #1*. Santa Fe: AMMA Center of New Mexico, 1995.

Two Wise Women on Rituals and Relationships. *The New Times*. Seattle, Washington, January 1998.

Zavada, Kathy. *Mother's Song*. Mount Shasta: Precious Music, 1996.